CU00923536

EXPLORING
ACTS

VOLUME ONE
ACTS 1-12

EXPLORING ACTS

VOLUME ONE
ACTS 1-12

by

JOHN PHILLIPS

MOODY PRESS

CHICAGO

© 1986 by
THE MOODY BIBLE INSTITUTE
OF CHICAGO

Library of Congress Cataloging in Publication Data

Phillips, John, 1927–
    Exploring Acts.

    Contents: v. 1. Acts 1–12.
    I. Bible. N.T. Acts—Commentaries. I. Title.
BS2625.3.P44   1986   226'6077   86-23491
ISBN 0-8024-2435-X

2 3 4 5 6 7 Printing/VP/Year 91 90 89 88 87

Printed in the United States of America

GENERAL OUTLINE

Volume One

Note: Each of the segments in this general outline is expanded at the appropriate place in the commentary. See the page indicated.

Foreword

The book of Acts is the inspired history book of the church and should be treated as such. It is a book of transition: it begins by showing us how the church came into existence on the day of Pentecost in Jerusalem; at the end we see the final official rejection of Christianity by the Jews of the Diaspora in Rome, the church firmly established in that great Gentile city, and the great apostle to the Gentiles still reaching out boldly with the gospel. It covers the period between the gospels and the epistles, and we would be greatly impoverished without it.

The story of the book revolves around the personalities and ministries of three men—Simon, Stephen, and Saul. Simon Peter was the apostle to the Jews, and Saul of Tarsus—the apostle Paul—was the renowned apostle to the Gentiles. Stephen provides the link between the two.

Peter and Paul are a study in contrasts. Peter was a Palestinian Jew; Paul was a Hellenist Jew. Peter was what the world would call an ignorant and unlearned man, a fisherman by trade; Paul was a scholar, a genius, a trained rabbi, an educated Pharisee, a Greek cosmopolitan, a Roman citizen. Peter was a personal disciple of the Lord Jesus in the days of His flesh; Paul met Christ as the Lord from heaven on the Damascus road, when marching forward to persecute the church, and was an apostle "born out of due time" (1 Cor. 15:8). One cannot study Acts in depth without becoming aware that Luke is always balancing Paul with Peter. For instance, of the eighteen addresses in the book of Acts, Stephen, James Gamaliel, and Tertullus each have one. The remaining fourteen are equally divided between Peter and Paul, both of whom speak seven times. The same direct parallelism can be discerned between the miracles of Peter and Paul.

The story of the church in the book of Acts is one of almost constant expansion. Take the ministry of Paul, for instance. In just a little more than ten years Paul pioneered four Roman provinces (Galatia, Macedonia, Achaia, and Asia) and left behind him thriving churches in the key cities of each of them. Before A.D. 47 there were no churches in these provinces, but by A.D. 57 Paul could speak of his work in those areas as having been completed and could announce plans to evangelize Spain and the far west.

This commentary on the book of Acts is designed to give to the reader a comprehensive and usable outline of the book. It endeavors to bring to life the interesting people who crowd the pages of Acts. It endeavors to examine carefully in the light of their context often misunderstood references to the baptism of the Spirit, miracles, healings, and other such phenomena of the book. Above all, it keeps in mind the transitional nature of the book of Acts and the well-founded dictum that we go to the epistles, not to the book of Acts, for our doctrine.

So come, then, and let us explore the book of Acts together. It should prove to be an exciting experience. One of the ladies who helped with the typing of the manuscript said, "It reads like a story. I can hardly wait to get the next installment!" My prayer is that this commentary will not only introduce you to a great book of the New Testament but that the study of that book will lead to greater personal devotion to the Lord Jesus, better understanding of the church and its mission, and greater zeal for the cause of Christ.

Part One:

Introduction (1:1-26)

I. WALKING WITH THE SAVIOR (1:1-11)

    A. The Person (1:1-2)
    B. The Proofs (1:3)
    C. The Promise (1:4-5)
    D. The Priorities (1:6-7)
    E. The Program (1:8)
    F. The Parting (1:9)
    G. The Prospect (1:10-11)

II. WAITING FOR THE SPIRIT (1:12-26)

    A. The Faithful Exercise of the Apostles (1:12-15)
        1. Their Assembly (1:12-13)
        2. Their Assurance (1:14-15)
    B. The Formal Expulsion of the Apostles (1:16-26)
        1. The Sin of Judas Reviewed (1:16-20)
            a. The Prophecy of His Sin (1:16-18)
                (1) The Serious Treachery That Marred His Life (1:16-17)
                (2) The Sordid Tragedy That Marked His Death (1:18)
            b. The Publicity of His Sin (1:19)
            c. The Punishment of His Sin (1:20)
        2. The Substitute for Judas Revealed (1:21-26)
            a. Their Quest (1:21-23)
                (1) A Sifting Process (1:21-22)
                (2) A Serious Problem (1:23)
            b. Their Quandary (1:24-26)
                (1) They Voiced Their Perplexity (1:24-25)
                (2) They Voted Their Preference (1:26)

Part One:

Introduction (1:1–26)

I. WALKING WITH THE SAVIOR (1:1–10)

A. THE PERSON (1:1–2)

The former treatise have I made, O Theophilus, of all that Jesus began both to do and teach,

Until the day in which he was taken up, after that he through the Holy Ghost had given commandments unto the apostles whom he had chosen.

The human life of Christ on earth and His subsequent translation to heaven was just the beginning. But what a beginning! It was the beginning of One who had no beginning. Jesus was the eternal, self-existing, uncreated second Person of the Godhead, who existed before time existed—the One described by the Holy Spirit as "the everlasting Father" (i.e. "the Father of eternity"; Isa. 9:6). His human life was the beginning of a new mode of living, one He will never relinquish through all the eternal ages yet to be. For now He has something He never had before, a battle-scarred and glorified human body, in which He is now seated on His Father's throne on high. His incarnation was the beginning of a new kind of living.

It was also the beginning of a new kind of doing. "He went about doing good" (Acts 10:38) was Peter's pungent summary of that life. Other good people have lived, but none like Jesus. Adam was good when God first made him. He was made in the image and likeness of God. He was intelligent, upright, and good, the crown of creation, lord of the earth, one with whom God delighted to commune in the cool of the day. But Adam's goodness was the goodness of innocence; it was goodness untried. How long it lasted we do not know, but it came to a sad end at the Fall.

Jesus was the second man. When He came it was the beginning of a new kind of doing as well as a new kind of living. As He stepped out of eternity into time He said: "Lo, I come (in the volume of the book it is written of me,)

to do Thy will, O God" (Heb. 10:7). And so He did. As a babe in the cradle, as
a boy around that Nazareth home and in the synagogue school, as a teen, as a
man; working at the bench or tramping the highways of His native land as the
Servant of Jehovah, it was a new kind of doing. We see Him before the
Sanhedrin, before Pilate, before Herod, on the cross, in the tomb, ascended
on high—and we see a new kind of doing. Whether cleansing the leper,
healing the sick, freeing the demon-possessed, giving sight to the blind,
enabling the lame to leap, raising the dead, feeding the hungry, stilling the
storm—it was a new kind of doing.

It was the beginning of a new kind of teaching. Those who heard Him
said, "Never man spake like this man" (John 7:46). He taught "as one having
authority, and not as the scribes" (Matt. 8:29). They marveled, "Whence hath
this man wisdom?" (13:54). He Himself affirmed, "A greater than Solomon is
here" (12:42). It was a new kind of teaching. Where in all the world is to be
found anything to compare with the Sermon on the Mount? Who ever told
stories like Jesus—the Prodigal Son, the Good Samaritan, the Rich Fool, the
Unmerciful Servant, the Unjust Steward, the Sower and the Seed? Who ever
had such a grasp of the future? His teaching was marvelous, saturated with
Scripture, pungent, understandable, practical, loving, true, convicting. It was
delivered with compassion and courage and with a total grasp of all the
factors of space, time, and eternity. And all was given in complete harmony
with His Father and the Holy Spirit.

A beginning: The things "that Jesus began both to do and teach." But
not an ending: That living, doing, and teaching is still going on—which is
what the book of Acts is all about.

He did not leave for Home, either, until "*after* that he through the Holy
Ghost had given commandments unto the apostles." Matthew, Luke, and
John highlight those commandments. We have them in the Sermon on the
Mount, in the upper room discourse, in many a pungent parable and precept.
Luke, the author of the book of Acts, recalls some of the commandments in
his gospel. Let us summarize his account as a means of introducing "the rest
of the story," as Luke records it in his gospel.

    1. THE SOURCE OF THE MESSAGE (Luke 24:44–46)
       a. Illumination (vv. 44–45)
          "These are the words which I spake unto you, while I was yet
         with you, that all things must be fulfilled, which were written in
         the law of Moses, and in the prophets, and in the psalms [the three
         great divisions of the Hebrew Bible], concerning me. Then opened
         he *their* understanding, that *they* might understand the scriptures."
          They were to handle the Bible with the same kind of insight and
         authority as He.

b. Illustration (v. 46)

"And said unto them, Thus it is written, and thus it behoved Christ to suffer, and to rise from the dead the third day."

So He had confidently taught them. Now they understood that His assurance came from the Scriptures, the significance of which He had grasped with an understanding above all others.

2. THE SUBSTANCE OF THE MESSAGE (v. 47)

"That repentance and remission of sins should be preached."

That was the substance of the new message. Manward—repentance; Godward—remission. It could now be preached because Christ *had* suffered and *had* risen from the dead.

3. THE SIGNIFICANCE OF THE MESSAGE (v. 47)

". . . should be preached *in His name*."

That was the significant thing. From now on everything was to be linked with that Name. His was the name that would inspire the apostles and infuriate their foes. His was the name that would ring through Jerusalem and challenge the very might of Caesar in Rome.

4. THE SCOPE OF THE MESSAGE (v. 47*b*–48)

". . . among all nations, beginning at Jerusalem. And ye are witnesses of these things."

There were twelve witnesses. Even Judas, dead and damned, was a witness—to the serious consequences of not enthroning Christ.

5. THE SUCCESS OF THE MESSAGE (v. 49)

"And behold, I send the promise of my Father upon you: but tarry ye in the city of Jerusalem, until ye be endued with power from on high."

And what power! The book of Acts is one long illustration of the power that came with the Holy Spirit at Pentecost.

This teaching was entrusted to "the apostles whom he had chosen." In his gospel, Luke has already told us of the timing and solemnity of the choosing of the twelve. Peter, James, and John were already committed disciples (Luke 5:10–11) and so was Matthew (5:27–29). In fact, Jesus had many disciples. His Galilean ministry was outwardly a great success, but already official opposition was surfacing because of His Sabbath activities. Then, after all-night prayer, Jesus deliberately chose twelve from the ranks of His disciples, "twelve whom also he named apostles" (Luke 6:13). In the synoptic gospels, the word *apostolos* (in the singular and plural) occurs just nine times; in Acts and the epistles it occurs sixty-nine times. In the historical books it always refers to the twelve (except in Acts 14:4,14). The word also occurs once in John 13:16, where it is used of one sent on a special errand (see also 2 Cor. 8:23 and Phil. 2:25).

The word *apostle* is applied to a select few besides the original twelve who were commissioned by the Lord. The eleven chose Matthias to take the place of Judas and appointed him to be an apostle (Acts 1:26). Paul and Barnabas are called apostles (Acts 14:4,14). Andronicus and Junia, kinsmen of Paul, saved before he was and addressed by him as "fellowprisoners" (the word literally means "war captives"), are hailed by him in Romans 16:7 as being "of note *among* the apostles" (the inference being they were included in their number). In writing to his Thessalonian friends, Paul associated Silvanus (Silas, also a prophet, Acts 15:32) and Timothy with himself as apostles (1 Thess. 1:1; 2:6).

It was, however, to the original very limited and carefully selected group that the Lord gave His new marching orders.

B. THE PROOFS (1:3)

To whom also he shewed himself alive after this passion by many infallible proofs, being seen of them forty days, and speaking of the things pertaining to the kingdom of God.

Before the apostles could undertake the humanly impossible task of convincing a Christ-rejecting world of the truth of the gospel, they needed a forty-day period of post-resurrection contact with the Lord. Soon He was going Home, but before He finally went, He gave them "many infallible proofs" of His resurrection.

We can see from the gospels that they took some convincing! Astonishingly enough, although the disciples very quickly forgot what Jesus told them about His resurrection, His enemies remembered it, warned Pilate about it, and had the tomb sealed to prevent it. The disciples, however, took a great deal of convincing, even after it happened.

Jesus was dead and had been buried. One and all, they concluded it was over. On the eve of the High Sabbath the women prepared the spices and balm (Luke 23:56) to complete the Lord's entombment. (A double Sabbath could only occur during the week of the three great feasts. The first day of those feasts is a Sabbath "high day" and was the "first," or great, Sabbath no matter upon what day of the week it fell [Lev. 23:7,24,35]; the ordinary weekly Sabbath then became the second Sabbath [Luke 6:1].) At the close of the weekly Sabbath the women came to the tomb ("the first day of the week"—Matt. 28:1; Mark 16:1–2; Luke 24:1; John 20:1), wondering who they could get to remove the great stone that sealed it. They were very brave but quite unbelieving about the promised resurrection. They found the stone removed (Matt. 28:2–4) and were confronted by an angel who told them the Lord was alive from the dead (Mark 16:4–5; Luke 24:2; John 20:1). As they were leaving the tomb they met the Lord Himself, who calmed their fear and gave them a message for His disciples. They approached Him, held Him by the feet, and worshiped Him (Matt. 28:9–10). Then, in obedience to His command, they went and told the disciples and Peter (Mark 16:9–11; Luke 24:10,11; John 20:2) that Jesus was alive from the dead.

In the meantime, the guard had fled into Jerusalem to report what had happened at the tomb itself (Matt. 28:11–15).

It was now the turn of Peter and John to visit the empty sepulcher. John believed, but apparently Peter still doubted. After examining the evidence of the grave clothes, they went home (Luke 20:12; John 20:3–10). Next, Mary Magdalene went to the grave and had her rapturous encounter with the risen Lord (John 20:11–18). The women, to their credit be it said, were much more easily convinced than the men. Later that same day, two disillusioned disciples, having discounted as worthless the stories of the resurrection that were now beginning to circulate in Jerusalem, met the Lord on the road to Emmaus (Luke 24:13–22).

At some point in that sequence the Lord appeared to Peter privately (Luke 24:33), an event that did something to dispel the pervading unbelief. The two Emmaus disciples, now convinced that Jesus was alive, hurried back to Jerusalem to add their testimony, but their witness was not believed either (Mark 16:9). Then the Lord made His first appearance to the eleven (Luke 24:36–44; John 20:19–23) and gave them His commission. Thomas was absent and resolutely refused to believe the united testimony of all the others. A week later (on the day following the second Sabbath of the seven in the reckoning to Pentecost) the Lord appeared to the eleven again, dealt with Thomas's unbelief (Mark 16:14; John 20:24–29), and again commissioned them to preach the gospel.

The eleven next went off to Galilee to keep an appointment with the Lord (Matt. 28:9–10; 16–18). There He appeared to them on a mountain, and they worshiped Him, though as Matthew says "some doubted [i.e., hesitated]" (28:17). The Lord again challenged them with His Great Commission.

Later He appeared to seven of the disciples, who, led by Peter, had gone back to fishing (John 21:1–23).

So for forty days the Lord came and went, overcoming the unbelief and hesitation of His disciples by "many infallible proofs" so that, in the end, they were absolutely convinced of the reality of His resurrection. No doubt was left in their minds.

Further, He spoke to them of "the things pertaining to the kingdom of God."

When God created Adam, He crowned him king: "Let them have dominion," He said (Gen. 1:26). Adam, however, surrendered his sovereignty to Satan, and at once sin reigned; then death reigned; and over all, Satan reigned. When Adam's children were born they were born into the wrong kingdom, subject to the wrong sovereign. They were born in sin and were subject to Satan.

It was necessary for God to assert His own sovereignty, so He came into the Garden, pronounced judgment on the serpent and on the sinners, declared war between the seed of the woman and the seed of the serpent, and provided the means to put away the sinner's guilt so that fallen men might once again obtain citizenship in the kingdom of God.

Entrance into the kingdom of God is by the new birth as Jesus reminded Nicodemus: "Except a man be born again he cannot see the kingdom of God" (John 3:3). The "kingdom of heaven" is included in the kingdom of God, so the two have many things in common. The kingdom of God, however, is spiritual and continues forever, whereas the kingdom of heaven is temporal and temporary.

During the forty-day period following His resurrection, the Lord Jesus spoke to His disciples of "things pertaining to the kingdom of God." Some years before, in the Sermon on the Mount, He had directed His disciples away from a lifelong quest for material things with the words "Seek ye first the kingdom of God, and his righteousness; and all these things shall be added unto you" (Matt. 6:33). During the talks with His disciples after His resurrection, He doubtless reminded them of the many Scriptures that spoke of the kingdom, including His own considerable teaching on the subject.

Because the Jews had rejected their King, the visible kingdom was now in abeyance. The "mystery" period (Matt. 13) had begun. The church age was about to begin too, and it would be contemporaneous with "the mysteries of the kingdom" (Matt. 13:11). The promised kingdom age was not cancelled entirely, only postponed. The literal kingdom, foretold by the prophets, would be set up on earth at a future date, and He would reign as King of kings. Satan, too, would be finally defeated (at the end of the millennial age), and the kingdom would be delivered up to God (1 Cor. 15:22–28). In the meantime the disciples must preach to all nations the gospel of God's grace and offer all men a place in Christ's kingdom through the new birth.

C. THE PROMISE (1:4–5)

And being assembled together with them, [Jesus] commanded them that they should not depart from Jerusalem, but wait for the promise of the Father, which, saith he, ye have heard of me. For John truly baptized with water; but ye shall be baptized with the Holy Ghost not many days hence.

Waiting! That is often the hardest thing to do. The excitement of the post-resurrection visits must have filled the Lord's disciples with excitement and fired them with enthusiasm. They must have felt that, with marching orders from a Man who had conquered death, there was nothing they would not dare, no crowd they could not sway, no country they could not conquer, no confrontation where they could not succeed.

But such enthusiasm would not last. It was noble perhaps, it was sincere, but it had no staying power, and certainly it had no saving power. It was born of the flesh. They needed more than that—they needed the Holy Spirit. Their task was an impossible task. Even with the Great Commission in their hands they would need more than willingness if the world was to be won. In the shelter of the upper room they could have no idea of the impossibility of the task, of the stubborn unbelief of men, of the entrenched, vested interests of government, commerce, and religion that would oppose them, or of the cruel persecution that awaited them. The exotic atmosphere of Christ's presence with them around the table in their quiet meeting place was good, but they needed more. They needed "the promise of the Father." It was John who best remembered and almost alone recorded, in his gospel, the Lord's previous long conversations with them in that same upper room about "the promise of the Father." He had said, "I will pray the Father, and He shall give you another Comforter" (John 14:16). They would need that Comforter, the Holy Spirit.

1. They would need the Holy Spirit to *enlighten* them:
   a. *As to their memories.* The New Testament was to be written. The many things Jesus had taught them would have to be recalled and written down under the same divine inspiration that had produced the Old Testament. They would need the Holy Spirit for that.
   b. *As to their message.* They were not to preach words of man's wisdom but words supplied by the Holy Spirit. The Old Testament would have to be seen in a new light and preached with a new relevance. The significance of Christ's death, burial, and resurrection would have to be understood and proclaimed. They would need the Holy Spirit for that.
   c. *As to their movements.* When to go! Where to go! Who should go! Who should evangelize Europe, Asia, Africa? They would need the Holy Spirit for that.
2. They needed the Holy Spirit to *energize* them.
   a. *To preach with power.* No man, however enlightened, zealous, and willing, has what it takes to convict, convert, and consecrate. They could no more convert a soul than they could create a star. They needed a power outside themselves to make the Lord Jesus real to lost

men and women, blinded by Satan, enslaved by sin. They would need
the Holy Spirit for that.

b. *To live the life.* They did not have what it takes to live the Christ life. As
He had given His life *for* them, so now He must give His life *to* them.
They would need the Holy Spirit for that.

3. They needed the Holy Spirit to *encourage* them.

They were full of enthusiasm now, but what about when they were alone,
when they were in prison, when they were scourged and threatened with
a cruel death? They would need the Holy Spirit for that.

We need the excitement and enthusiasm of an evangelistic crusade or a
Christian rally—inspired singing, the crowds, the stirring message, the ur-
gent invitation. But then it is necessary to go back home and wait, to get into
the presence of God for the next step. Where now, Lord? What is the next
move? Am I to stay where I am or go to Bible school or take some other
action? What gifts do I have? Should I consider the mission field? We need
the Holy Spirit for questions like that.

So the disciples were told to wait. In due time they would be baptized
with the Holy Spirit. There are only seven *direct* references to the baptism of
the Holy Spirit in the New Testament. Those seven references tell us all there
is to know about the subject. The vast amount of misinformation being
propagated on the subject today has no foundation in New Testament fact. We
need to pause here for a moment to see what the Scripture says.

The first five references are *prophetical.* Four of them simply record the
words of John the Baptist (Matt. 3:11; Mark 1:8; Luke 3:16; John 1:33) when
he announced to Israel that whereas he baptized with water, One was coming
who would baptize with the Holy Spirit (a reference to the present dispensation) and with fire (a reference to the second coming of Christ). The other
prophetic reference is the one we have here in Acts 1:5. The Lord Jesus links
His own statement to the previous statement of John the Baptist, but adds
that the baptism of the Spirit would take place "not many days hence." In
actual fact it took place ten days later on the day of Pentecost in the upper
room.

The sixth reference, in Acts 11:16, is clearly *historical.* It is found in
Peter's report to the Jerusalem church of what had recently happened in the
house of Cornelius: "They were baptized with the Holy Ghost, the same as we
were at the beginning," he said. This second baptism was necessary to bring
Gentiles into the church and as a sign to the Jews that there was now no
difference between Jew and Gentile. Both became one in Christ, equal members of His Body, united in the church.

The final reference to the baptism of the Spirit, in 1 Corinthians 12:13, is *doctrinal*. It explains what the baptism of the Spirit is and what it does: "For by one Spirit are we all baptized into one body." The baptism of the Spirit is that operation of the Holy Spirit which takes an individual believer in the Lord Jesus and makes that person a member of Christ's mystical Body, the church. Paul says that *all* believers are baptized by the Spirit. It is the way God makes us members of the Body of which Christ is the Head. The verb *baptized* is in the past tense. The baptizing took place in the upper room and it is a past experience so far as the church is concerned. Believers in Christ come into the good of that baptism automatically, and they become functioning members of the mystical Body of Christ.

It is wrong to ask God to do for you that which He has already done. The vast amount of false teaching about the baptism of the Spirit results from a failure to recognize the scriptural meaning of that baptism. These seven Scriptures constitute all that the Holy Spirit has to say about the subject. Nowhere does the Bible say that speaking with tongues and the so-called "charismatic" gifts are proof of the baptism of the Holy Spirit. It is not a "second blessing." It is inherent in all that happens at the time of our conversion. It is not given to a favored few but to *all* believers. It is not a mark of a new, special kind of holiness. The Corinthian Christians, all of whom Paul says were baptized with the Holy Spirit, were mostly carnal and worldly, quarrelsome and conceited.

So then, the Lord promised His disciples that they would shortly be baptized with the Spirit. The birthday of the church was just ahead.

D. THE PRIORITIES (1:6–7)

When they therefore were come together, they asked of him, saying, Lord, wilt thou at this time restore again the kingdom to Israel? And he said unto them, It is not for you to know the times or the seasons, which the Father hath put in his own power.

Jesus had gripped their hearts—especially when He had talked to them about the kingdom of God. Now they wanted to know when that kingdom was to be restored to Israel. He had been talking about a spiritual kingdom; they were still thinking of a secular kingdom. There was nothing wrong with their question except that it was out of context and it betrayed their lack of spiritual comprehension. The kingdom *is* to be restored to Israel, but the question as to *when* is a divinely kept secret. They should have known that it was not to be "at this time" from some of the Lord's former parables, particularly those of the kingdom (Matt. 13). A new age, the church age, had to intervene before the kingdom could be restored to Israel. Israel was still unrepentant, still Christ-rejecting—and about to reject the ministry of the Spirit as it had rejected the ministry of the Savior. So their question, although natural, was not spiritual. He had been with them for forty days now, teaching them about the kingdom, and they were still confused. That was just another proof of how much they needed the Holy Spirit.

We must make allowance for them. They had been nurtured since infancy to expect that the Messiah would set up a literal, millennial kingdom on earth. They were right as to the *truth* of that, but they were wrong as to the *time* of it. The establishment of the millennial kingdom awaits His coming again. They had grasped Old Testament truth but not New Testament truth—but at least they believed there was a national and glorious future for Israel. Millions of Christian people today, with the full light of New Testament revelation before them, are far more confused about kingdom truth than were those disciples, and with far less excuse.

The Lord Jesus did not rebuke them for asking a valid question. He simply told them that the time was God's secret. It was going to be a long time. The Jewish national clock had stopped and would not start again for hundreds of years. The church age was about to dawn. There would be a brief period of overlap, with Israel still in the land in unbelief and the church reaching out in evangelism to the world; then the things about which He had previously told them would take place (Luke 19:41–44; 21:5–24). Jerusalem would be destroyed; the Jews would be scattered; the curse the nation had invoked on its own head ("His blood be on us and on our children" [Matt. 27:25]) would fall. Meanwhile the King Himself was going on a long journey, and He was entrusting His affairs in the world to them. They must stop looking for a material kingdom and start working for a mystical one. The things He had told them about the *kingdom of heaven* were now going to happen. They must concentrate on things pertaining to the *kingdom of God*. Millions of people would never see that kingdom unless they were born again (John 3:3). That was the important thing now. He redirected their attention to the great task of world evangelism.

E. THE PROGRAM (1:8)

But ye shall receive power, after that the Holy Ghost is come upon you: and ye shall be witnesses unto me both in Jerusalem and in all Judea, and in Samaria, and unto the uttermost part of the earth.

The very last words Jesus spoke before He left for heaven were these: "The uttermost part of the earth." That was the Great Commission. They were to tell the story to the untold millions still untold. They were not called to be lawyers, not called to argue the case before the minds of men. That was the work of the Holy Spirit. They were called to be witnesses. A witness simply tells what he has seen and heard. He tells what happened. It is the Holy Spirit who does the pleading and who calls for the verdict. True, He uses men in the process, but it is words supplied by the Holy Spirit that make the difference (Mark 3:11). Supremely the Holy Spirit uses the Bible.

Here, too, we have the Lord's master plan for world evangelism. They were to begin in Jerusalem—*their own community*. They were to begin with neighbors, family, friends, people all about them. That is where all witness properly begins.

They were to reach out next to Judea. They were to evangelize *their own country*. They were to be concerned with those who spoke the same language, had the same customs, lived in the same environment and under the same government. This would be their first trial in reaching beyond their immediate neighborhood. This next venture would give them experience in following the Holy Spirit's lead, in meeting strangers, in getting used to traveling, adjusting to new situations. Home missions are just as important as foreign missions. If we are not exercised about reaching our own country, how can we be exercised about reaching someone else's country?

The way Saul and Barnabas became foreign missionaries shows this principle at work. The church's first two foreign missionaries were people already actively engaged in evangelism where they lived.

Then the disciples were to go to Samaria. They were to reach out beyond the confines of their own country and begin evangelizing *their own continent*. Samaria was their neighbor country. It represented the foreign culture with which they were most familiar because it was the one closest to them. They knew all about Samaritans. Indeed, they had deep-seated racial and religious prejudices against Samaritans. As it turned out, none of the twelve was willing to make the first move. The Holy Spirit had to send Philip, a deacon. It was not until revival broke out in Samaria that the apostles themselves showed any willingness to go there.

Finally, they were to evangelize "the uttermost part of the earth." They were to reach to the regions beyond. "Go ye therefore, and teach *all nations*" (Matt. 28:19, emphasis added)—from pole to pole, from sea to sea. A new page was about to be turned in the first chapter of a book that is not finished yet.

Verse 8 is really an index to the book of Acts. The Holy Spirit followed this master plan. How quickly our world could be evangelized, even at this late date in the church's history, if every church would take this plan seriously and begin with its own immediate community, reach out to its own country, become involved in missionary activity to the farthest reaches of its own continent, and then send out its ambassadors to all nations. The world would be invaded by armies of believers from all nations reaching out to all peoples in all parts of the world.

"Ye shall be witnesses unto *me*," the Lord said. We are not sent out to spread American culture or to found colonies or to convert people to an ideology or a theological proposition. We are to introduce people to the Lord Jesus Christ. We are to be witnesses unto *Him*. The Holy Spirit does the rest.

F. THE PARTING (1:9)

And when he had spoken these things, while they beheld, he was taken up; and a cloud received him out of their sight.

What an unforgettable moment! His resurrection was a monumental moment, but whereas He arose in secret, He ascended openly, visibly, before the astonished eyes of a host of His disciples. His resurrection was a triumph of the highest order, signaling the conquest of the grave forever and for all His own. However, others had been raised from the dead. His own resurrection was accompanied by a whole crop of resurrections, a wave sheaf of resurrections, the firstfruits of the coming harvest (Matt. 27:52–53). Resurrection, rare as it was, remarkable as it was, was a known phenomenon. But that a man in a human body should defy the law of gravity and slowly but surely ascend upwards to the sky, that was a crowning wonder of a life full of wonders. In fact, the Holy Spirit considers the ascension of Christ so important that He mentions it in Acts and the gospels no less than twenty times and uses thirteen different words and expressions to describe it, each one reflecting a different shade of meaning.

Thus Jesus went home, angel escort and all, up through the clouds, up beyond the stars, back to the glory land whence He came. But now He was different; now He had a human body, a battle-scarred, resurrected, glorified human body. In that body He arrived at the gates of glory, which swung open before Him. In He went, into the glory land, along the golden streets, watched by the adoring angel throng, up to the throne of the Father, there to sit down at the right hand of the Majesty on high. A Man in a human body is now seated on God's throne, because, as God the Son, second Person of the Trinity, as co-equal and co-eternal with the Father, He has every right to be there.

The spiritual significance of that ascension must not be overlooked. It means we now have an Advocate with the Father, Jesus Christ the righteous. We have a Mediator in heaven, a great High Priest, touched with the feelings of our infirmities, able to minister on our behalf as that perfect Daysman for whom Job longed.

As the old hymn puts it:

> Lifted up was He to die,
> "It is finished," was His cry,
> Now in heaven exalted high;
> Hallelujah! what a Saviour!
>   (Philip P. Bliss, "Hallelujah, What a Saviour")

G. THE PROSPECT (1:10–11)

And while they looked steadfastly toward heaven as he went up, behold, two men stood by them in white apparel; which also said, Ye men of Galilee, why stand ye gazing up into heaven? this same Jesus, which is taken up from you into heaven, shall so come in like manner as ye have seen him go into heaven.

The attention of the disciples was riveted on the sky. They did not miss a move or a motion of that astonishing ascent so long as their beloved Lord remained visible. It was the end of an era. That which had begun in a cradle now ended in a cloud. God in Christ had come down to earth; now He had gone back to heaven. For thirty-three and one half years this planet had been visited from outer space. The Son of the living God had been born, had grown up, had ministered, traveled, and taught, had been killed and buried, had conquered death, and now He had gone home. Never before and never again, in all the history of the universe, would its like be seen.

So these awestruck people stood there on the brow of Olivet looking steadfastly to the sky, so occupied with Jesus as to be oblivious to the newcomers—two men who suddenly stood by them in white apparel. There seems little doubt they were angels. Angels had announced His birth, angels had watched His temptation, angels had strengthened Him in Gethsemane, angels had heralded His resurrection, and now angels had come to escort Him to the skies. Two of those shining ones tarried for a moment to give one last message to the earthly friends of heaven's Beloved. Silently they materialized on Olivet. Silently they joined that awestruck, upward-straining throng. Quietly they too gazed upwards with the rest as "they looked steadfastly toward heaven as he went up." For one brief moment the visitors from outer space had Earth's view of it all. Then the cloud cover closed in, and they spoke: "Ye men of Galilee, why stand ye gazing up into heaven?"

Human unbelief, our slowness and dullness to grasp eternal realities, always seems to amaze the angelic visitors to our planet. Often, from a sense of deep ignorance, in utter perplexity we ask the question, Why? Now the shining ones ask it. Why? Jesus had told His friends all about His return. He had given them a job to do in the meantime, so why did they stand staring skywards? Why treat this ascension as though it were the marvel of the ages? Why not simply remember His teaching and take it all as a matter of course?

"This same Jesus, which is taken up from you into heaven, shall so come in like manner as ye have seen him go into heaven." The words rang out in triumph. As those awestruck believers took them in, the visitors were gone— but the message remained. The first coming was over; the second coming was now the goal. The first coming had fulfilled scores of Old Testament prophecies to the very letter, but other prophecies remained. Those, too, would be fulfilled in the same pragmatic, prosaic way. This same Jesus was coming again: coming to the sky in the rapture, coming to Olivet's brow at the return. But in the meantime a new chapter had begun, and in the writing of that chapter they were to play the prominent part. The material body of Christ was now in heaven. Soon the mystical Body would be formed on earth.

II. WAITING FOR THE SPIRIT (1:12– 16)

A. THE FAITHFUL EXERCISE OF THE APOSTLES (1:12–15)

1. THEIR ASSEMBLY (1:12–13)

Then returned they unto Jerusalem from the mount called Olivet, which is from Jerusalem a sabbath day's journey. And when they were come in, they went up into an upper room, where abode both Peter, and James, and John, and Andrew, Philip, and Thomas, Bartholomew, and Matthew, James theson of Alphaeus, and Simon Zelotes, and Judas the [son] of James.

God had sanctified the Sabbath to Israel, setting it apart as a day of rest. The rabbis had turned what should have been a national blessing into a national burden. Not content with the bare but sufficient statement of the law and the Mosaic examples of its applications (no gathering manna on the Sabbath, no gathering sticks on the Sabbath), they had hedged it around with hundreds of additional rules. The Lord Jesus refused to keep those rules, so they accused Him of profaning the Sabbath and rejected Him.

The reference here to "a sabbath day's journey" (about 2000 yards) is interesting. It reminds us how thoroughly Jewish the first disciples were and how completely Jewish the infant church would initially be. The reference is also the tolling of the bell over Judaism and what it had become. Soon all such Sabbath questions would be swept away, and the church would choose a new day for worship—the first day of the week, the day of resurrection.

So back they went "a sabbath day's journey" to Jerusalem. It was a step of obedience. The Lord had recently commanded them that they must "not depart from Jerusalem, but wait" (1:4).

The upper room seems to have become the home of the eleven apostles, at least for as long as they tarried in Jerusalem.

The Holy Spirit now lists their names. As always, Peter headed the list. The last name, Judas the son of James, reminded everyone there was a gap in their company. There used to be another Judas, but that Judas was dead and damned, and his seat was empty and his name execrated. The very name *Judas* was well on its way to deathless infamy. Perhaps the name "Judas the son of James" was put last on the list, not because he was the least, but to point to that gap and also to remind us that the Lord had another Judas who *did* remain faithful. For the rest of his life Judas son of James would have his own special cross to carry. He bore the same name as Judas the traitor. In deference to the weight of that particular cross, the evangelists, writing the gospels, when they had occasion to mention *this* Judas would add *"not Iscariot."*

2. THEIR ASSURANCE (1:14–15)

These all continued with one accord in prayer and supplication, with the women, and Mary the mother of Jesus, and with his brethren. And in those days Peter stood up in the midst of the disciples, and said, (the number of names together were about a hundred and twenty).

This is the company which in ten days' time would explode the biggest spiritual bombshell ever detonated on earth and change the course of history forever. It might help us if we see what kind of a company it is God used to turn the world upside down.

It was a *persevering* company. "These all continued." They did not know how long they would have to wait, but wait they would for as long as it took the Lord to fulfill His promise and send the Holy Spirit. Nothing could deter them now; nothing could discourage them now. Jesus was alive! Jesus was above! He had promised power. He had told them to wait. They were in His will right now to do nothing but tarry. Did they know their Bible well enough to know that what they waited for would come on the day of Pentecost? It was all written in their Scriptures. In any case, they were a persevering company. The fact that nothing was happening did not disappoint them. No souls were being saved, no outreach of any kind was being made, as of yet they were incapable of effective witness, so they did what they were told. They waited, day after day.

It was a *purposeful* company. "These all continued with one accord." They were one. They would look at each other with shining eyes, in total harmony of purpose. There was not a dissenting voice, not a murmur of complaint. Peter was no longer asking what John should do; Thomas was no longer pouring cold water on things; John was no longer running ahead of Peter; Philip was no longer asking for signs. They were of one accord, unitedly, purposefully waiting for God's next move.

It was a *praying* company. "These all continued . . . in prayer and supplication." This prayer meeting lasted just ten days, but they would have waited for ten months or ten years. What did they pray about? One thing that evidently concerned them was the gap in their ranks caused by the suicide of Judas. No doubt they prayed for the coming of the Holy Spirit, prayed that they might be receptive to Him, not grieve or quench Him. What would we pray for under such conditions? For whom did they offer supplication? Their unsaved relatives? The leaders of their people? For poor, blind Israel, which had rejected the Savior?

Finally, it was a *precious* company. There was no company of individuals in the universe more precious to the Lord Jesus than this small company of believers crowded into that upper room. "These all . . . with the women and Mary the mother of Jesus, and with his brethren." That little company included the disciples themselves, the godly women who loved the Lord, and His now convinced brothers. What women were these, we wonder? Mary Magdalene surely, and the other Marys, including Mary of Bethany. Probably Martha was there. A man named Joseph Barsabbas surnamed Justus was there. A man called Matthias was there. Was Lazarus there? What about Nicodemus and Zaccheus and Bartimaeus?

Mary, the mother of the Lord, was there, quietly taking her place as just another one of them. Roman Catholic pretensions about the virgin Mary have no basis whatever in Scripture. This is the last we see of Mary. She is humbly praying with the others. She takes no lead; Peter does that. The others do not pray to her. Certainly there is no claim by her to be "the Mother of God." The others have no notion of praying to her to intercede for them with her Son. She was simply another earnest believer.

Her other sons are there. "His brethren," Luke calls them. Now finally and fully assured that Jesus was all He claimed to be, Jude and James and the others are all about to become charter members of the church—members, too, of the mystical Body of Christ.

What a precious company it was, and is. It is a much bigger company now. It includes in its ranks all those who have been saved since Pentecost—a multitude no man can number, a glorious church, many of its members safe already on the other side, others still down here carrying on the work that was begun in the upper room so long ago.

There were about one hundred twenty of them then. This is the only intimation we have of the actual size of the band of disciples. The Lord had chosen twelve. The ones now gathered to remember Him and to wait for the coming of the Holy Spirit were ten times that many.

It did not take long for Peter to take the lead. His disgrace has been quite forgotten now, as it had long since been forgiven. He was a natural leader—impulsive but utterly devoted to the Lord Jesus; forceful, knowledgeable about Jesus, one of the very first of His disciples, rough and ready but warmhearted and sincere, a rough diamond.

Peter took the floor. Something had been bothering him. Jesus had chosen twelve disciples, but one was missing. The empty space left by the treachery and suicide of Judas bothered him like a missing tooth, so suddenly he stood up and addressed himself to the others and to the issue.

B. THE FORMAL EXPULSION OF THE APOSTATE (1:16– 26)

1. *THE SIN OF JUDAS REVIEWED (1:16–20)*
   a. THE PROPHECY OF HIS SIN (1:16–18)
      (1) THE SERIOUS TREACHERY THAT MARRED HIS LIFE (1:16–17)

Men and brethren, this Scripture must needs have been fulfilled, which the Holy Ghost by the mouth of David spoke before concerning Judas, which was guide to them that took Jesus. For he was numbered with us, and had obtained part in this ministry.

Peter had been reading his Bible, or perhaps he had asked the Lord a question about Judas before His departure to glory. Or perhaps the disciples had been discussing the question of Judas, and one of them had remembered this text. Or perchance the verse just popped into Peter's mind like a lightning flash, enlightening him and causing him to act.

In any case, Peter decided something had to be done about the missing member in the apostolic ranks. And, Peter-like, it had to be done right away so that there would be twelve of them again. Perhaps, he may have thought, that was why the delay was so long. So in a terse sentence Peter quoted Scripture to describe the treachery of Judas. He had led the mob to the Master and then singled Him out with a dastardly kiss. That was his act of treachery. "He was numbered with us, and had obtained part of this ministry," he added, giving further weight to the charge.

He had been their friend. He had carried the bag, ministered to the poor, preached the gospel, healed the sick, cast out demons, seen the countless miracles of Jesus, listened to His wonderful words of life, broken bread at the Lord's table. And he had been "part of this ministry." His name might have been written in sparkling gems in the foundation stones of the Celestial City. He might, perhaps, have had the ministry later entrusted to Paul. He had thrown it all away for thirty wretched silver coins.

(2) THE SORDID TRAGEDY THAT MARKED HIS DEATH (1:18)

Now this man purchased a field with the reward of iniquity; and falling headlong, he burst asunder in the midst, and all his bowels gushed out.

Judas had purchased that field some time before. The actual money he received for betraying Christ he flung back at the feet of the chief priests (Matt. 27:3–10) as too hot to hold. He never spent a penny of it. The priests had no such conscience. They used it to buy a potter's field in which to bury strangers, thus fulfilling Zechariah 11:12 and also some spoken word of Jeremiah. The Greek words used to describe those two purchases are quite different. The high priests purchased a field (*agros*); Judas purchased a farm (*chōrion*). The priests bought on the open market (*agorazō*); Judas acquired his property by private purchase (*ktaomai*). The field purchased by the priests is called "the field of blood" because it was bought with the blood money given for the betrayal of Jesus; the farm bought by Judas is called "the property of blood" because it was there the wretched man committed suicide. Peter, speaking here of "the reward of iniquity," was not referring to the thirty pieces of silver (he knew Judas never spent a penny of *that* money) but to the thieving Judas had been doing all along (John 12:6).

With regard to the suicide itself, Matthew says that Judas departed from the presence of the priests "and went and hanged himself" (Matt. 27:5). So far as the priests were concerned that was all they knew about Judas. He had committed suicide. Evidently Peter gives a fuller description of the suicide. Judas did hang himself, but the rope snapped, and the man fell headlong and was dashed to pieces in the gruesome way Peter describes. Such was the traitor's end: he went "to his own place" (Acts 1:25). He was hurled headlong into a lost eternity.

b. THE PUBLICITY OF HIS SIN (1:19)

And it was known unto all the dwellers at Jerusalem; insomuch as that field is called, in their proper tongue, Aceldama, that is to say, The field of blood.

The suicide of Judas was common knowledge in the capital. Everyone talked about it at the time. Superstitious notions grew up around his name. The idea developed that he would come back as the Antichrist. Indeed, some scriptural grounds are advanced for that idea because the Antichrist will be called "the son of perdition" (2 Thess. 2:3), and the only other person so named in the Bible is Judas Iscariot (John 17:12). (Kenneth Wuest takes the use of the definite article as conclusive proof. G. Campbell Morgan goes further, taking a statement of Jesus concerning Judas ["one of you is a devil," John 6:70] quite literally and contending that Judas was not a true human being but a demon in human form.) It is easy to see how stories would attach to the name of Judas. His death was a sordid one, and swift and suiting. The name *Judas* has become a synonym for treachery. Slaughter-houses even to this day keep a special sheep whose job it is to lead the others to the butcher. Sheep instinctively follow a leader, a fact that makes the executioner's job much simpler. The other sheep follow this "Judas sheep" to their death. It is allowed to live—to lead the next batch to their doom.

c. THE PUNISHMENT OF HIS SIN (1:20)

For it is written in the book of Psalms, Let his habitation be desolate, and let no man dwell therein: and, His bishopric let another take.

Peter now quoted Psalm 69:25 as the Scripture upon which he proposed the disciples should act. Psalm 69 is one of the great prophetic psalms. Its first part is clearly *messianic*, taking us directly to Calvary. Its second part is *maledictory*, and embodies one of those resounding imprecations not uncommon to the Psalms. The third part is *millennial*, and anticipates the second coming of Christ. It was to that Psalm that Peter now appealed and to the imprecatory section, which he bluntly applied to Judas: "Let his habitation be desolate." The word *desolate* embodies the wish that the place Judas bought might become a desert. We can well imagine it quickly acquired a bad name.

Peter supplemented his quote from Psalm 69 with a quote from Psalm 109:8 (another imprecatory psalm) to lay the foundation for the action he was about to propose: "And his bishopric (*episcopē*, the office of an overseer) let another take." There are two words for "another" in the New Testament. There is *allos*, meaning another of the same kind, and *heteros*, the word used here, which means another of a different kind, usually denoting generic distinction.

2. THE SUBSTITUTE FOR JUDAS REVEALED (1:21– 26)

a. THEIR QUEST (1:21–23)

(1) A SIFTING PROCESS (1:21–22)

Wherefore of these men which have companied with us all the time that the Lord Jesus went in and out among us, beginning from the baptism of John, unto that same day that he was taken up from us, must one be ordained to be a witness with us of his resurrection.

Considerable difference of opinion centers on this action. Some think the apostles were wrong, that they should have waited until after Pentecost for the Spirit's mind on this matter, that because the man they now chose as substitute for Judas is never heard of again he could not have been the Holy Spirit's choice, and that God had already chosen Paul to fill out the ranks of the apostolate. Others are equally sure that they did the right thing, that casting lots was a valid Old Testament procedure, and that this was the last act of the old dispensation. Certainly the disciples felt strongly that the missing seat should be filled before the baptism of the Holy Spirit.

Peter underlined three pivotal points in the public ministry of the Lord: His baptism, His resurrection, and His ascension. It was at His *baptism* that the Lord Jesus publicly identified Himself with the race He had come to save. It was through His baptism that John the Baptist realized exactly who Jesus was (John 1:31–34), and it was through the testimony of John, and his subsequent pointing out of Jesus as the Messiah, that Andrew came to Christ, and through Andrew, Peter (John 1:35–42). It was through His *resurrection* that the disciples had their doubts and difficulties dissolved so that henceforth they would follow Him through fire and flood to the ends of the earth and to a martyr's death. The resurrection became the key to all their preaching. It was by means of His *ascension* that the Lord Jesus could take His place on the throne of God on high, there to minister as great High Priest for all His own.

Peter believed that whoever took the place of Judas should be a man who had intimate personal knowledge of the Lord from beginning to end. Evidently there were a number who qualified, which indicates that the number of faithful and consistent followers of Jesus throughout the years of His public ministry was more than the twelve.

(2) A SERIOUS PROBLEM (1:23)

And they appointed two, Joseph called Barsabas, who was surnamed Justus, and Matthias.

The sifting process proceeded according to the criteria laid down by Peter, until just two people were left, both of whom were equally qualified to fill the vacant spot. But now the apostles had reached a serious impasse— which of the two men should be the apostate's replacement?

We know nothing of these men beyond their names. Indeed, it is astonishing how little we do know about most of the apostles. Peter we know; James we know; Matthew, Thomas, Philip, Andrew all have a comment or two in the gospels, enough to enable us to get at least a sketchy idea of their general character. But even with the better-known apostles there are hardly any details. We do not know, for the most part, if these men were married, and if so how many children they had; where they made their homes; what their interests and talents were; or, in some cases, how they came to be disciples in the first place. The Holy Spirit is equally silent as to where the majority of these men went, how they served, when they died. We know a great deal more, for instance, about Paul than we do about nearly all these men.

b. THEIR QUANDARY (1:24–26)

(1) THEY VOICED THEIR PERPLEXITY (1:24–25)

And they prayed, and said, Thou, Lord, which knowest the hearts of all men, show which of these two thou hast chosen, that he may take part of this ministry and apostleship, from which Judas by transgression fell, that he might go to his own place.

All too often we make our own plans, pursue them to the best of our knowledge and ability, run into a quandary, and then ask God to bless what we have done and show us how to get out of the corner into which we have painted ourselves. Is that what Peter and the others had done here? Maybe so, but, on the other hand, the whole band of disciples had been continuing "with one accord in prayer and supplication" (1:14) for days, so perhaps the whole thing was of God after all.

However, they had now come to the crux of the matter. Only God knew the hearts. Outwardly, both these men had the qualifications, but only God knew which one had the inner spirit and strength to assume the awesome responsibility of apostleship. So "they prayed." Not just Peter. They all prayed—another mark of their unity—and they told the Lord the problem.

No higher office has ever been held on earth than that of an apostle of the Lord Jesus. An apostle had unique power with God and man. In the first place, he had the unique privilege of having kept close company with Jesus during the days of His earthly ministry. To the apostles was given the task of writing the greater part of the New Testament and, until such times as the writing should be finished, to be the custodians of New Testament truth. It was to be the work of an apostle to lay the foundation of the church and guide it upon its proper path. The history of the world for the past two thousand years has been keenly influenced by the ministry and apostleship of those humble ordinary men, chosen of God for the greatest work of all time.

These men were troubled by the dark shadow of Judas. He had gone "to his own place," but his ghost haunted them yet. These were their last recorded words ere Pentecost: "Judas by transgression fell, that he might go to his own place." And Jesus had chosen Judas. Were they suddenly afraid that they might choose just such another—a man who was outwardly impeccable but inwardly unsuited for the task and trust of apostleship?

(2) THEY VOTED THEIR PREFERENCE (1:26)

And they gave forth their lots; and the lot fell upon Matthias; and he was numbered with the eleven apostles.

Which is just what Judas had been—numbered with the others (v. 17). So they had their way. The number twelve was complete. Nothing was left to be done except turn the world upside down for Christ.

But this they could not do. They were powerless to witness. They could gather in fellowship, they could pray, they could act in unity, they could make decisions regarding the corporate life of the assembly, they could have assurance among themselves that their actions were right, they could talk to each other about Jesus, pool their expenses, share their stories, memories, and impressions. But they were powerless to witness. A hostile world lay beyond the walls of their upper room. They were powerless to impact that world for Christ. For that they needed the Holy Spirit, and for Him they had to wait.

Part Two:

The Founding Emphasis: Simon (2:1—5:42)

I. TESTIMONY (2:1–47)

  A. The Rushing Mighty Wind of the Spirit (2:1–4)
    1. That Which Was Scriptural and Essential (2:1)
    2. That Which Was Sensational and Ephemeral (2:2–3)
      a. The Awesome Sound (Wind) (2:2)
      b. The Awesome Sight (Fire) (2:3)
    3. That Which Was Spiritual and Evidential (2:4)
      a. An Infilling Presence: A Ministry of the Spirit That Was Strictly Temperamental (2:4a)
      b. An Outflowing Power: A Manifestation of the Spirit That Was Strictly Temporary (2:4b)
  B. The Resulting Mighty Witness of the Saints (2:5–47)
    1. The Promised Sign of Pentecost (2:5–13)
      a. The Advertisement (2:5–6a)
      b. The Amazement (2:6b–11); the Crowd Recognizes that:
        (1) The Disciples Were Local Provincials (2:6b–7)
        (2) The Dialects Were Linguistically Pure (2:8–11a)
        (3) The Discourses Were Largely Praise (2:11b)
      c. The Assessment (2:12–13)
        (1) Doubt (2:12)
        (2) Decision (2:13)
    2. The Powerful Sermon of Peter (2:14–40)
      a. The Word of Explanation (2:14–21)
        (1) Peter Rejected Their Supposition (2:14–15)
        (2) Peter Recited Their Scriptures (2:16–21)
          (a) The Fulfillment of Prophecy (2:16)

34

    (b) The Facts of Prophecy (2:17–21), Having to Do with:
       i. The Spirit of God: A Present Advent (2:17–18)
       ii. The Severity of God: A Postponed Apocalypse (2:19–20)
       iii. The Salvation of God: A Permanent Assurance (2:21)
  b. The Word of Exposition (2:22–40)
    (1) Condemnation (2:22–24)
      (a) Jesus Was a Recognizable Messiah (2:22)
      (b) Jesus Was a Rejected Messiah (2:23)
       i. God's Sovereign Government Explained (2:23 *a*)
       ii. Man's Solemn Guilt Explained (2:23*b*)
      (c) Jesus Was a Resurrected Messiah (2:24)
    (2) Confirmation (2:25–36)
      (a) What David Accurately Foresaw (2:25–28)
       i. The Timeless Deity of Christ (2:25–25*a*)
       ii. The Triumphant Death of Christ (2:26*b*–28)
         a. David's Faith (2:26*b*)
         b. David's Facts (2:27)
         c. David's Feelings (2:28)
      (b) What David Actually Foretold (2:29–36)
       i. The Incorrect Interpretation of David's Words (2:29)
       ii. The Incontrovertable Interpretation of David's Words (2:30–36)
         a. The Force of His Prophecy (2:30–31)
           1. The Messiah Would Be David's Son (2:30*a*)
           2. The Messiah Would Be David's Sovereign (2:30*b*–31)
         b. The Fulfillment of His Prophecy (2:32–36)
           1. The Present Witnesses (2:32)
           2. The Promised Wonder (2:33)
           3. The Prophetic Word (2:34–35)
           4. The Pungent Warning (2:36)
    (3) Consolation (2:37–40)
      (a) The Agony of Conviction Experienced (2:37)
      (b) The Answer of Conversion Explained (2:38–40)
       i. A Conscious Repudiation of the Guilt of the Hebrew Nation (2:38*a*, *b*)
         a. Separation—By Personal Acknowledgement of Jesus (2:38*a*)
         b. Salvation—By Personal Acceptance of Jesus (2:38*b*)

    c. The Return of Christ (3:19–26)
      (1) Peter Woos Them to Repentance (3:19–21)
        (a) The Times of Refreshing (3:19)
        (b) The Times of Restitution (3:20–21)
      (2) Peter Warns Them of Retribution (3:22–24)
        (a) The Appeal to Moses as Prophet (3:22–23)
        (b) The Appeal to Many Other Prophets (3:24)
      (3) Peter Wakens Them to Responsibility (3:25–26)
        (a) As Jews (3:25)
        (b) Regarding Jesus (3:26)
4. The Master (4:1–22)
  a. The Glory of His Name (4:1–12)
    (1) The Anger of His Foes (4:1–7)
      (a) It Was Focused (4:1–2)
      (b) It Was Futile (4:3–4)
      (c) It Was Formidable (4:5–7)
        i. The Quorum (4:5–6)
        ii. The Question (4:7)
    (2) The Answer of His Friends (4:8–12)
      (a) Its Power (4:8–10)
      (b) Its Point (4:11–12)
        i. Their Guilt (4:11 *a*)
        ii. Christ's Glory (4:11*b*)
        iii. God's Grace (4:12)
  b. The Greatness of His Fame (4:13–22)
    (1) The Dilemma of the Rulers (4:13–16)
      (a) What They Saw (4:13–14)
        i. The Man Who Had Been with Jesus (4:13)
        ii. The Man Who Had Been Brought to Jesus (4:14)
      (b) What They Said (4:15–16)
    (2) The Decision of the Rulers (4:17–22)
      (a) It Was Despotic (4:17–18)
        i. Their Opposition to the Salvation of God (4:17*a*)
        ii. Their Opposition to the Son of God (4:17*b*–18)
      (b) It Was Defied (4:19–22)
        i. Promptly So (4:19–20)
        ii. Properly So (4:21–22)
B. The Threatening Opposition Scorned (4:23–27)
  1. The Fellowship (4:23–30)
    a. Fellowship in Suffering (4:23)

B. The Spectacular Attendance of the Church (5:11–16)
   1. Its Absolute Purity (5:11–13)
   2. Its Abundant Progress (5:14)
   3. Its Apostolic Power (5:15–16)
C. The Sudden Attack upon the Church (5:17–42)
   1. An Ineffective Detention (5:17–26)
      a. The Apostles Are Fettered (5:17–18)
         (1) Why They Were Imprisoned (5:17)
         (2) Where They Were Imprisoned (5:18)
      b. The Apostles Are Freed (5:19–21a)
         (1) Deliberately—by a Miracle (5:19)
         (2) Designedly—for a Ministry (5:20–21a)
      c. The Apostles Are Found (5:21b–25)
         (1) The Assembling of the Sanhedrin (5:21b)
         (2) The Astonishment of the Sanhedrin (5:22–25)
            (a) Their Dismay (5:22–23)
            (b) Their Doubts (5:24)
            (c) Their Dilemma (5:25)
      d. The Apostles Are Fetched (5:26)
   2. The Ineffective Discussion (5:27–39)
      a. The Criminal Charge (5:27–28)
      b. The Counter Challenge (5:29–32)
         (1) The Question of Loyalty (5:29)
         (2) The Question of Liability (5:30–32)
            (a) The Truth About the Cross (5:30)
            (b) The Truth About the Christ (5:31–32)
      c. The Clear Choice (5:33–39)
         (1) Murder (5:33)
         (2) Moderation (5:34–39)
            (a) Gamaliel's Reputation (5:34)
            (b) Gamaliel's Reasoning (5:35–37)
               i. Be Wary (5:35)
               ii. Be Wise (5:36–37)
            (c) Gamaliel's Restraint (5:38–39)
               i. What He Considered a Probability (5:38)
               ii. What He Considered a Possibility (5:39)
   3. The Ineffective Dissuasion (5:40–42)
      a. Punishment (5:40)
      b. Praise (5:41)
      c. Proclamation (5:42)

Part Two:

The Founding Emphasis: Simon (2:1—5:42)

I. TESTIMONY (2:1–47)

    A. THE RUSHING MIGHTY WIND OF THE SPIRIT (2:1–4)

        1. THAT WHICH WAS SCRIPTURAL AND ESSENTIAL (2:1)
And when the day of Pentecost was fully come, they were all with one accord in one place.

The day of Pentecost had come fifteen hundred times before. Now it was fully come. It had come and gone, come and gone, ever since Moses instituted the feast. Now it had come to stay.

On the day of Pentecost, in Old Testament times, the Jews took individual grains of corn, ground them into flour, added oil and leaven, and made two loaves of bread. The loaves were then offered to the Lord along with the sacrifice of seven lambs without blemish, one young bullock, and two rams for a burnt offering—ten sacrifices in all, to symbolize the perfection and completeness of Calvary.

All symbolized what took place fifty days after the resurrection of Christ. Pentecost always fell on the first day of the week, symbolizing, even in Old Testament typology, the end of the Sabbath and the consecration of a new day for a new dispensation.

All this was highly significant. The oil typified the work of the Holy Spirit on the day of Pentecost. For instance, the inclusion of leaven in the loaves was unusual, for leaven was rigorously excluded from other meal offerings because it is a type of sin. The ordinary meal offerings symbolized Christ, who is wholly free from sin. Leaven was included in the loaves of Pentecost, however, because those loaves typified the church, and the church has never been free from sin.

The *burnt offering* aspect of Calvary was accompanied by the sacrifice of one kid of the goats for a *sin offering* and two yearling lambs for a *peace offering* (symbolizing the ground upon which the believer has perfect peace with God).

At the feast of firstfruits, individual stalks of grain, loosely bound together, were used to symbolize the resurrection of Christ and His own and their triumph over death. On the day of Pentecost those individual stalks and grains were replaced by a loaf, one homogenous body, to symbolize what would happen when the day of Pentecost would be "fully come." On *that* day, one hundred twenty individual believers, loosely bound together by the bonds of Christ, ascended the stairs to the upper room "with one accord." One Body of believers came down. Individuals went up; a church came down—one mystical Body. The fact that two loaves were used in the Old Testament ritual is equally significant. There was to be a second Pentecost, so to speak, some years later, in the house of Cornelius, which would bring Gentiles into that one Body on an equal basis with the Jews. Thereafter, in God's sight, there would be neither Jew nor Gentile, so far as the church was concerned, but one Body.

Thus that which was scriptural and essential was about to take place— the unique coming of the Holy Spirit as promised by the Savior and as predicted in the Scripture. Along with that which was scriptural and essential we have:

2. *THAT WHICH WAS SPECTACULAR AND EPHEMERAL (2:2–3)*

    a. THE AWESOME SOUND (WIND) (2:2)

And suddenly there came a sound from heaven as of a rushing mighty wind, and it filled all the house where they were sitting.

It was not wind but a sound like wind, something resembling a rushing hurricane. This sound was not of earth, but of heaven, and it was symbolic. It announced the presence of the Holy Spirit. The wind is another of those divinely chosen biblical symbols of the Spirit of God. He comes from heaven; He fills the world; He moves at will. He cannot be cornered or contained by any special interest group. His comings and goings are according to fixed laws, but He is sovereignly trammeled by none. He can be commanded by nobody. He is at the service of man, but He will do what *He* wants, not what we want, and He is omnipresent and omnipotent. All that is perfectly symbolized by the sound from heaven like a mighty rushing wind. In speaking to Nicodemus of the new birth, Jesus said: "The wind bloweth where it listeth, and thou hearest the sound thereof, but canst not tell whence it cometh, and whither it goeth: so is every one that is born of the Spirit" (John 3:8).

This aspect of Pentecost was ephemeral: it came and it went, never to return. It was a once-for-all phenomenon. It was something they heard, however, and it arrested their attention as it filled the house. Nothing was heard of this wind outside; it caught only the ears of those in the upper room. The age about to begin, however, was indeed to catch people by the ear. It was to be an age of faith—faith that "cometh by hearing" (Rom. 10:17). Also, they heard the sound, but there was no other sensation. They *heard* this wind, but they did not *feel* it. There was no emphasis on feeling at all, for it is *faith*, not feeling, that is the hallmark of this age.

b. THE AWESOME SIGHT (FIRE) (2:3)

And there appeared unto them cloven tongues like as of fire, and it sat upon each of them.

First the sound, then the sight: that was God's order. We would like to reverse it. We would like to see first; God puts the hearing first.

The fire was another symbol of the Spirit. Fire begins with a small flame but it *spreads*: it can devour a forest or consume a city. It *burns*: there is a judgment element associated with fire. The lost will spend eternity in a lake of fire. It *purges*: in 1066 London was in the grip of the Black Death; in 1067 came the great fire that purged the city of its scourge. It *illuminates*: for countless centuries fire was man's only source of artificial light. It enabled men to work and walk in an otherwise dark world. It *warms*: it enables men to penetrate hostile regions where snow and ice reign. It *smolders*: men can resist and quench ordinary fire, but Holy Spirit fire they can never put out. It will burn on quietly in the heart of some believer and will begin to spread again. All this and more is suggested by the fire of Pentecost, a fitting symbol of both the Holy Spirit and the church age. But it was not literal fire, for there was nothing to feel. Nor was this sign repeated, nor did the outside world see it.

"There appeared unto them cloven tongues like as of fire, and it sat upon each of them." This was the baptism of the Spirit, and they all partook of it. This mysterious baptism in symbolic flame embraced them all equally. Peter did not get a special baptism. The humblest, unknown, unnamed believer in that company had just as much of this baptism, anointing, and filling as the foremost among the disciples. God is no respecter of persons. This baptism was not a special work of grace given to some and not to others. The cloven tongue sat upon each one individually, equally, indiscriminately.

The phenomenon of the upper room was spectacular, but it was passing. It came, it went, and it never came again. We have, then, symbolic wind and symbolic fire to usher in a new age and a change in dispensation. The fact that "the day of Pentecost was fully come" heralded the death of the old ritual Jewish Pentecost and the birth of the church of God.

3. THAT WHICH WAS SPIRITUAL AND EVIDENTIAL (2:4)

a. AN INFILLING PRESENCE—A MINISTRY OF THE SPIRIT THAT WAS STRICTLY TEMPERAMENTAL (2:4a)

And they were all filled with the Holy Ghost . . .

Seven ministries of the Holy Spirit affect the believer in this age, including the *baptism*, the *gift*, the *indwelling*, the *seal*, and the *earnest*. Those are all sovereign acts of God bestowed on the believer at the time of his salvation. They are unconditional, sovereignly under God's control, and impartially administered to every believer in the Lord Jesus. They never need to be repeated, they are never withdrawn, and they guarantee the believer's eternal security and his glorious standing in Christ.

Filling is different. It *is* conditional. When Paul speaks of it in Ephesians 5:18 he uses the present continuous tense—literally, "Be ye being filled" —and he uses as an illustration being filled with wine—a fluctuating state. The filling is temperamental insomuch as it largely depends on the individual believer: he can be filled one moment and, because of some disobedience, empty the next. The purpose of the filling is to change our temperament and make us like Jesus in His nature, person, and personality so that in thought, word, and deed we might show Him to a lost world. The filling is always available to us, but our realization of it depends upon our cooperation with the Holy Spirit. On the day of Pentecost all those present were filled with the Spirit. The filling is available to every believer. There is no exception, and there can be no excuse for not being filled.

The remaining operation of the Holy Spirit in the life of the believer is the *anointing* for service. In the Old Testament, prophets, priests, and kings were anointed for their respective ministries. Not all men were anointed for the same task. The Lord Jesus was always filled with the Spirit, but He was not anointed until He began His ministry (Matt. 3:16; Luke 4:16–19). The usual word for *anointing* in the New Testament is "unction," and it is related to the believer's special ability to use the Word of God with power.

b. AN OUTFLOWING POWER—A MANIFESTATION OF THE SPIRIT THAT WAS STRICTLY TEMPORARY (2:4b)

. . . and began to speak with other tongues, as the Spirit gave them utterance.

There is no more misunderstood manifestation of the Holy Spirit today than this. The gift of tongues in the early church was evidential in character. Its purpose was to attest to the Jewish people the simple but solemn fact that Judaism was obsolete and that Christianity had taken its place. The importance of tongues is related to the fact that for two thousand years, if God had anything to say He said it in *Hebrew*; from now on He was going to reveal

Himself in *Greek*. For two thousand years, too, the Jews were a specially chosen and privileged people. From now on God was going to bring Gentiles into the place of religious privilege and would reach out to every kindred, people, and tongue.

Tongues was therefore an evidential gift, a sign to the Jews, the nation that that had been the depository of divine truth for centuries and that had now crowned all its other apostasies with the crime of Calvary. Having rejected the Savior, the Jews were to be given another chance—to accept the Spirit. That also being rejected, they could expect nothing but judgment. The book of Acts is the record, among other things, of the way in which the Jews, first of the homeland, then of the dispersion, turned in fury from the gospel. Tongues was intended to be a judgment sign upon the Jewish nation. Paul makes that clear in 1 Corinthians 14:21–22, where he quotes from Isaiah 28:11–12.

Tongues are mentioned on only three occasions in the book of Acts and nowhere else in the New Testament except in 1 Corinthians, where Paul has to deal with its flagrant abuse. Wherever tongues are mentioned, Jews are present, and unbelieving Jews are in the background.

Not all people had the gift of tongues. It was strictly a temporary and transitional gift. Moreover, Paul said it would come to an automatic end (1 Cor. 13:8). This temporary sign gift seems to have terminated with the destruction of Jerusalem—the judgment of which it was a warning sign. It was the least important of the gifts. It was abused and had to be put under severe restraint. Women, for instance, were told to keep silence in the church. No manifestation of tongues could exceed three occurrences at any one service, and a valid interpreter had to be present. A test was later added to guard against Satanic deception (1 John 4:1–3). Tongues as practiced today is unscriptural, of dubious origin, deceptive, and worthless as a sign.

B. THE RESULTING MIGHTY WITNESS OF THE SAINTS (2:5–47)

1. THE PROMISED SIGN OF PENTECOST (2:5–13)

a. THE ADVERTISEMENT (2:5–6a)

And there were dwelling at Jerusalem Jews, devout men, out of every nation under heaven. Now when this was noised abroad, the multitude came together . . .

The original dispersal of the tribes came when the Northern Kingdom fell to the Assyrians as foretold by Isaiah (in that significant twenty-eighth chapter, for instance). The second dispersal came a century or so later, when the remaining tribes were exiled to Babylon. The Jews prospered so much in Babylon that, when the Exile ended, the majority chose to remain abroad rather than face the hardships of pioneering in the Promised Land. The Exile became voluntary. With their newly discovered commercial skills, the Jews migrated to country after country and settled down to run much of the business of the world. By the time of Christ, the Jews of the Dispersion controlled a significant unofficial commercial empire.

Wherever there was a quorum of ten men, the Jews established a synagogue, gathered for worship and religious instruction, and made a sharp difference between themselves and their Gentile neighbors, whom they despised. Devout men from the Diaspora, especially at the times of the annual feasts, found their way to Jerusalem.

Thus it was that on the day of Pentecost "there were dwelling at Jerusalem Jews, devout men, out of every nation under heaven." God had assembled a great multilingual Jewish congregation, and the phenomenon that accompanied the dramatic fulfillment of Pentecost in the upper room soon drew them together. The news flashed across the city, and, as Luke puts it, "the multitude came together."

b. THE AMAZEMENT (2:6b–11); THE CROWD RECOGNIZES THAT:

(1) THE DISCIPLES WERE LOCAL PROVINCIALS (2:6b–7)

. . . and were confounded, because that every man heard them speak in his own language. And they were all amazed and marveled, saying one to another, Behold, are not all these which speak Galileans?

It must have astonished them indeed. Suppose that today, at an international conference in some such country as Egypt, delegates from a score of countries were to be accosted by a dozen local peasants speaking to them fluently in their native dialects using flawless grammar, pronunciation, and local idioms. Certainly it would cause astonishment. People would ask, "How do they do it? Who taught them? What is it they are saying?"

All those who had been baptized with the Spirit on the day of Pentecost spoke with tongues. It was unique to this occasion. Moreover, they were Galileans, provincials from the backwoods, not educated Jews from the capital.

(2) THE DIALECTS WERE LINGUISTICALLY PURE (2:8–11a)

And how hear we every man in our own tongue, wherein we were born? Parthians, and Medes, and Elamites, and the dwellers in Mesopotamia, and in Judea, and Cappadocia, in Pontus, and Asia, Phyrygia, and Pamphylia, in Egypt, and in the parts of Libya about Cyrene, and strangers of Rome, Jews and proselytes, Cretes, and Arabians.

There were people present from the distant limits of the Parthian Empire in the East and from imperial Rome in the West. The languages and dialects of Asia, Africa, and Europe were instantly recognized. Nothing could have been more calculated to gain attention. Nothing will warm a man's heart more than to have someone speak to him in the language of his boyhood.

That is the practical point of "tongues" beyond the fact that it was a judgment sign to the Jews. It was a communication gift. It was intended to carry the gospel to the hearts of men in language they would understand. *That* kind of tongues make sense. If it were still available it would indeed be a gift worth coveting. Such seems to have been the nature of tongues on the day of Pentecost.

"Tongues" as it is practiced today and as it was being practiced in the Corinthian church (that most carnal of all Paul's churches and, incidentally, the only one in which any reference is made to tongues outside the limits of Palestine) is certainly not of this order. So then in Jerusalem, on the day of Pentecost, the dialects were linguistically pure. People heard and understood what was being said.

(3) THE DISCOURSES WERE LARGELY PRAISE (2:11*b*)

We do hear them speak in our tongues the wonderful works of God.

The expression *wonderful works* is "great things." The expression occurs on only one other occasion in the New Testament. When Mary learned she was to become the mother of the Lord, she burst into song. "For He that is mighty hath done to me *great things*" (Luke 1:49), she said.

The "wonderful works of God" proclaimed by the disciples doubtless dealt with the gospel story, beginning with the annunciation and ending with the ascension.

The gift of tongues was not intended to make the disciples feel good, superior, or personally edified. It was intended to make them a powerful witness. It was a supernatural gift designed to arrest the attention of the Jewish people and rivet their attention on the gospel.

c. THE ASSESSMENT (2:12–13)

(1) DOUBT (2:12)

And they were all amazed, and were in doubt, saying one to another, What meaneth this?

The more thoughtful members of the Jewish community were honestly perplexed. This was something quite outside their experience. They were used to organized religion: religion centered in Temple or synagogue, religion expressed in feasts and fasts and rules and regulations. This spontaneous outpouring of witness and praise by "Galileans" was beyond the scope of their experience. They were "amazed"—literally, dumbfounded.

(2) DERISION (2:13)

Others mocking said, These men are full of new wine.

Paul likens the filling of the Spirit to intoxication with wine (Eph. 5:18).

A man who is filled with alcohol has his whole personality changed as he is brought under the power of an alcoholic spirit and is turned into another man. The change in him is evident in his walk and talk. Just so, a person filled with the Holy Spirit is changed into another person, a Christlike person.

Some who were standing by mocked. The word is found in only one other place in the New Testament—of the Athenians who mocked Paul on Mars Hill (Acts 17:32). The world has always had its mockers. Men mock at sin, they mocked the Savior, they mock the saints. The derision of the unsaved is one of the devil's tools. It has held many a weak Christian in bondage and has kept many a person from Christ. The answer to mockery is the very thing at which this particular group of unbelievers mocked—the filling of the Spirit. That will make the feeblest believer bold.

2. *THE POWERFUL SERMON OF PETER (2:14–40)*

a. THE WORD OF EXPLANATION (2:14–21)

(1) PETER REJECTED THEIR SUPPOSITION (2:14–15)

But Peter, standing up with the eleven, lifted up his voice, and said unto them, Ye men of Judea, and all ye that dwell at Jerusalem, be this known unto you, and hearken to my words: For these are not drunken, as ye suppose, seeing it is but the third hour of the day.

Peter answered scorn with scorn. "Drunk!" he said, "How can these men be drunk? It is only nine o'clock in the morning." However, he wasted no time arguing the point. Having parried the Devil's thrust, Peter took the sword of the Spirit in hand and moved over to the attack.

He was going to prove that Jesus was indeed the Messiah. No message could have been more unwelcome to the Jews who had just murdered Him, so Peter, led by the anointing Spirit, began with something else.

(2) PETER RECITED THEIR SCRIPTURES (2:16– 21)

(a) THE FULFILLMENT OF JOEL'S PROPHECY (2:16)

But this is that which was spoken by the prophet Joel.

By beginning his message with an appeal to the Bible, Peter did several things. He lifted the thoughts of his listeners to higher ground; he gave an instant explanation to people who, whatever else they lacked of a spiritual nature, were, at least, thoroughly conversant with the Bible; and he vested his words with a ring of divine authority. Quoting the Scriptures allowed the Holy Spirit to do the speaking.

"*This* is *that!*" Peter said. Prophecy was being fulfilled. It had been fulfilled over and over again in the recent past in the life of Jesus. It was still being fulfilled.

(b) THE FACTS OF JOEL'S PROPHECY (2:17– 21), Having to Do with:

i. THE SPIRIT OF GOD: A PRESENT ADVENT (2:17–18)

Peter began by underlining three facts about Joel's well-known prophecy. First, the phenomenon that attracted the attention of the people was evidence of the Holy Spirit's prophesied advent.

And it shall come to pass in the last days, saith God, I will pour out of my Spirit on all flesh: and your sons and your daughters shall prophesy, and your young men shall see visions, and your old men shall dream dreams: And on my servants and on my handmaidens I will pour out in those days of my Spirit; and they shall prophesy.

Twice He said, "I will pour out." The first time, the expression evidently embraces the Hebrew world—"*your* sons, *your* daughters, *your* young men, *your* old men." The second time, the expression doubtless includes the heathen world, the great Gentile world so long passed by in favor of the Jewish people—"*my* servants, and *my* handmaidens." God's interests in this world have ever been wider than the narrow confines of Canaan. The evidence of a worldwide dispersal of Jewish people should have taught the Hebrews that.

"This is that!" Never before had there been such an outpouring of the Holy Spirit, not even among the Hebrew people. Occasionally in the past God had raised up a Moses or a Malachi, a David or a Daniel, even occasionally some obscure prophet or some godly woman, a Deborah, a Hannah, a Huldah. But never anything like this! Scores of people, all at once, in one place, in evident power, proclaiming the mighty works of God and in the languages of the Gentile world! What before had been restricted and rare was now made available to all.

This outpouring of the Spirit was without parallel in the past. It was to be accompanied by a corresponding outpouring of the Word of God. New revelations were to be made, new chapters added to the Bible. There would be visions and dreams and, above all, "prophecy" (twice repeated). The gift of prophecy was now given to the church as before it had been given to Israel. The gift of a prophet in the early church, like that of an apostle, was a foundational gift (Eph. 2:20), and like the gift of tongues, which so excited the people present at Pentecost, it would serve its purpose and become redundant once the witness to Israel as a nation was over and once the canon of Scripture was complete.

ii. THE SEVERITY OF GOD: A POSTPONED APOCALYPSE (2:19–20)

And I will show wonders in heaven above, and signs in the earth beneath; blood, and fire, and vapor of smoke. The sun shall be turned into darkness, and the moon into blood, before that great and notable day of the Lord come.

It is evident from this reference to the "day of the Lord" that Pentecost was only a partial fulfillment of Joel's prophecy. There were signs of God's wrath at Calvary—the sun was darkened, the earth shook, the rocks were rent. But, as the Lord made clear in His Olivet discourse, such signs as Joel indicated belong to the time of the second coming of Christ (Matt. 24:29–30).

It seems there is to be a second outpouring of the Spirit after the rapture of the church. According to Revelation 7 there will be a tremendous spiritual awakening among the Gentiles after the rapture. A countless host of Gentiles will from all nations be saved as a result of the witness of the 144,000 Hebrew evangelists (Matt. 24:14; Rev. 7:1–17). Still later, at the beginning of the millennial age, an even greater outpouring of the Spirit will take place.

Peter, however, has no hesitation in declaring that what was happening on that day of Pentecost was also a fulfillment of Joel's prophecy. "This is that," he said. It is a common feature of Bible prophecy that some predictions have a partial fulfillment followed later by another and complete fulfillment.

Calvary was a crime of such magnitude that God could have justly ushered in the apocalypse at once and wiped out the human race. Instead, He inserted into human history an age of grace, the church age, something not foreseen by the Old Testament prophets. It was this age that had now begun, an age during which the severity of God is being held back by the salvation of God, an age when the apocalypse (to be heralded by such signs as Joel envisioned) is postponed.

iii. THE SALVATION OF GOD: A PERMANENT ASSURANCE (2:21)

And it shall come to pass, that whosoever shall call on the name of the Lord shall be saved.

Thus Peter sounds the dominant note of this age of grace—salvation! Salvation centered in the name of Jesus! When He was born, the herald angel said, "Thou shalt call his *name* Jesus: for he shall save his people from their sins" (Matt. 1:21, emphasis added). John wrote, "As many as received him, to them gave he power to become the sons of God, even to them that believe on his *name*" (John 1:12). The name was anathema to the Jews. It is, however, the only name God honors for salvation.

b. THE WORD OF EXPOSITION (2:22–40)

(1) CONDEMNATION (2:22–24)

(a) JESUS WAS A RECOGNIZABLE MESSIAH (2:22)

Ye men of Israel, hear these words; Jesus of Nazareth, a man approved of God among you by miracles and wonders and signs, which God did by him in the midst of you, as ye yourselves also know.

Peter boldly proclaimed the saving name of Jesus. There was no excuse for rejecting Christ. He had presented His credentials to the whole nation with countless miracles. There had been numerous miracles in three earlier periods of Hebrew history—during the days of Moses and Joshua, during the days of Elijah and Elisha, and during the days of Daniel and his friends. Each of those times was a transitional point in Jewish history. Each time the miracles stopped as suddenly as they had begun, and each time they were replaced by the written Word. But there had never been anything like the miracles of Jesus. The New Testament records only thirty-six—on an average less than one a month for the three and one-half years of His public ministry—for God does not want us to rest our faith on miracles. But what miracles they were! He walked on the sea; He turned water into wine and multiplied loaves and fishes. He banished demons, disease, and death. He healed the sick, cleansed the leper, and raised the dead. And the miracles recorded are a fraction of those He actually performed. Several times the sacred historians simply lump miracles together, telling of the crowds of sick folk who came to Jesus with the comment, "And He healed them all." John ends the gospel narrative by saying that the world itself could not contain the books that could be written about Jesus and His signs.

So there was no excuse. Jesus was a recognizable Messiah. He was approved of God. He fulfilled all the criteria for the Messiah. He was of the tribe of Judah and of the family of David. He was born of a virgin and was born at Bethlehem. Out of Egypt God had called His Son. He lived as foretold and died and rose again as prophesied. There was no excuse for unbelief. The story of Jesus was known throughout the entire land.

(b) JESUS WAS A REJECTED MESSIAH (2:23)

i. GOD'S SOVEREIGN GOVERNMENT EXPLAINED (2:23a)

Him, being delivered by the determinate counsel and foreknowledge of God . . .

Peter spoke of God's sovereign government, for Jesus was delivered "by the determinate counsel and foreknowledge of God." Jesus Himself said, "No man taketh [my life] from me, but I lay it down of myself" (John 10:18). The death of Christ was foreknown of God in a past eternity. When God acted in creation, He also acted in redemption. Jesus is described as "the Lamb slain from the foundation of the world" (Rev. 13:8). God knew that, given a free will, man would sin; that His holiness would demand full payment for that sin; that His love would provide a free pardon for that sin; that in the fullness of time the Father would send the Son and that the Spirit would prepare His body; that God would become incarnate in Christ; and that, in the end, man would murder Him. All that was foreknown and taken into account by God's determinate counsel.

ii. MAN'S SOLEMN GUILT EXPLAINED (2:23b)

. . . ye have taken, and by wicked hands have crucified and slain.

God's foreknowledge does not absolve man from his fearful guilt. Men crucified the Christ. It was the most wicked thing ever done on this sin-cursed planet. And *they* had done it; *their* hands were stained with Jesus' blood. There was no escaping their guilt. They had murdered the Messiah, slain the very Son of the living God. There could be no greater guilt than that.

(c) JESUS WAS A RESURRECTED MESSIAH (2:24)

Whom God hath raised up, having loosed the pains of death: because it was not possible that he should be [held by] it.

"It is not possible!" That is the position taken by the agnostic and atheist when confronted with the resurrection of Christ. "It is contrary to nature, it defies natural law, it never happened, it is a lie propagated by the disciples who stole the body and faked an empty tomb."

God takes the same position when confronted with the unbelief of men regarding the resurrection. "God hath raised him up . . . because *it was not possible* that he should be holden of it." Hallelujah for such a glorious Divine impossibility! It was impossible for God to leave Jesus in the tomb.

It was impossible because He was sinless. "The wages of sin is death," says the Scripture. He did no sin, so obviously, He could not die. But die He did. He died because He was made sin for us, because He "bare our sins in his own body on the tree" (1 Pet. 2:24). Having thus paid the price of our sin, having suffered the extreme penalty and having discharged the debt, "it was not possible that He should be held" by death. The resurrection was part of that "determinate counsel and foreknowledge of God" (Acts 2:23), God's receipt to the believer for a debt paid in full.

What a message to herald to that guilty multitude who stood there on that Pentecost morning! What a message to be blazed across the world!

(2) CONFIRMATION (2:25-36)

(a) WHAT DAVID ACCURATELY FORESAW (2:25-28)

i. THE TIMELESS DEITY OF CHRIST (2:25-26a)

For David speaketh concerning him, I foresaw the Lord always before my face, for he is on my right hand, that I should not be moved: Therefore did my heart rejoice, and my tongue was glad. . . .

This is a quotation from Psalm 16:8-11. David sees the Lord on the cross in Psalm 22 and in Psalm 69; he sees Him risen and ascended in Psalm 16.

Many a time the Old Testament saints must have puzzled over Psalm 16 with its reference to death and preservation from corruption in the grave. How could "the Holy One" of the psalm, the Beloved One, the Messiah, possibly die, and how could He possibly escape the inevitable corruption of the grave if He did? As with so many other prophecies, suddenly all was clear. Psalm 16 had a literal fulfillment. The recent resurrection of Christ fulfilled the prophecy to the letter. It was a stunning blow to the now quickened consciences of Peter's listeners.

That glimpse of the resurrection of Christ had fortified David's soul and made him strong. He would never be moved because his Lord could never be moved. It made him sing: "Therefore did my heart rejoice and my tongue was glad . . ." David was so good a singer because he was so great a seer. There is nothing like a glimpse of heaven's viewpoint to put a hallelujah in the heart. To know that, in Christ, God has conquered not only sin and Satan, but the sepulcher as well should ring the joybells in each believing heart.

ii. THE TRIUMPHANT DEATH OF CHRIST (2:26b–28)

a. DAVID'S FAITH (2:26b)

Moreover also my flesh shall rest in hope.

The primary reference is to the body of Christ lying in the grave. Jesus knew He was going to be crucified. He also knew He would not see corruption in the grave and that He would rise again the third day. On a number of occasions He foretold those things to His disciples. As man, His confidence was in the Word of God, which He implicitly believed. However, by extension, the truth was David's, too, and ours. "My flesh shall rest in hope!" Christ's resurrection is the guarantee of ours.

b. DAVID'S FACTS (2:27)

Because thou wilt not leave my soul in hell, neither wilt thou suffer thine Holy One to see corruption.

The word *leave* is literally "forsake," or "abandon." At death the Lord Jesus committed His *spirit* to His Father in heaven. His *body*, touched now only by loving hands, was tenderly anointed with costly ointments, wrapped in linen, and laid to rest in a brand-new tomb belonging to Joseph of Arimathea. His *soul* went down into "hell" (Hades), the prison house of departed souls. He did not go there, however, as a victim of death but as a victor. There He proclaimed the triumph of the cross and "led captivity captive" (Eph. 4:8). He remained in those regions for three days and three nights "as Jonas was three days and three nights in the whale's belly" (Matt. 12:40), and then, on the third day, as He had so repeatedly proclaimed, He came forth in triumph. He could declare, "I am he that liveth, and was dead," and could add: "behold, I am alive for evermore, Amen, and have the keys of hell and of death" (Rev. 1:18).

The title *Holy One*, used by David (it occurs eight times in the New Testament and more than thirty times in the Septuagint, of which twenty-five times are in the Psalms) guaranteed that no corruption would taint the Lord's body during this time. That of course, was another miracle. "By this time he stinketh" (John 11:39), was Martha's startled cry when Jesus ordered the opening of Lazarus's grave. Lazarus had been in the tomb four days and had been buried with equal care. No taint of the grave's corruption, however, touched the body of God's Holy One.

David had his facts right. His eyes had been opened to see the resurrection of Christ, and that fact became the basis of his faith.

c. DAVID'S FEELINGS (2:28)

Thou hast made known to me the ways of life; thou shalt make me full of joy with thy countenance.

Facts, faith, then feeling: that is the Divine order. Feelings have their place, but we ought not depend on them. They can change from delight to despair, and, if we trust them, they will.

Jesus went to Calvary and into death, facing a time of anguish unparalleled in all the history of the world. Yet it was "for the joy that was set before him" that He "endured the cross" (Heb. 12:2). He knew the ways of life, knew His pathway led not just to the tomb but through the tomb. Now, "full of joy," He reigns in eternal bliss beyond the skies.

David entered into the goodness of that. It blessed his own soul. We can enter into the goodness too, and it will bless our souls.

This was the second great point, then, in Peter's sermon. He was confirming that Jesus accurately fulfilled Old Testament prophecies concerning the death, burial, resurrection, and ascension of the Christ.

(b) WHAT DAVID ACTUALLY FORETOLD (2:29–36)

i. THE INCORRECT INTERPRETATION OF DAVID'S WORDS (2:29)

Men and brethren, let me freely speak unto you of the patriarch David, that he is both dead and buried, and his sepulchre is with us unto this day.

So obviously, in writing Psalm 16, David was not expecting that the fulfillment of those marvelous statements would apply initially and primarily to him, and even if he had thought so, he would have been mistaken. For David died and experienced no resurrection. His tomb was a tourist attraction in Israel in Peter's day, as it still is.

So then, because those glorious truths were not fulfilled in David, they had to be prophetic; and if prophetic, they had to be fulfilled; and if they had to be fulfilled, in whom but in the Messiah? That the quoted passage was messianic in scope and content was obvious, and Peter's application of it to Jesus was correct, as must have been obvious to even the most obtuse. The crowd listening to Peter knew their Bible. They might have argued with Simon, but they could not argue with Scripture.

Having thus laid a general foundation for the interpretation of Psalm 16 by sweeping away as foolish any historical application, Peter went on to show:

   ii. THE INCONTROVERTIBLE INTERPRETATION OF DAVID'S WORDS (2:30–36)

      a. THE FORCE OF HIS PROPHECY (2:30–31)

         1. THE MESSIAH WOULD BE DAVID'S SON (2:30a)

Therefore being a prophet, and knowing that God had sworn with an oath to him, that of the fruit of his loins, according to the flesh, he would raise up Christ . . .

Peter was now going to draw out of Psalm 16 three things that must have gripped the heart of David as, having written the Psalm and failing to understand it, he came back to it again and again to ponder its truth.

First, one of his descendants would be the Christ. David was enough of a prophet to recognize the messianic character of the psalm, had sufficient spiritual sense to link it to the original Davidic covenant, and was able to grasp the essential fact that the psalm referred to that Son who would one day be born of his line. There was to be no allegorizing or spiritualizing of this prophecy. It was to have a literal fulfillment. The Messiah would be David's literal son, "the fruit of his loins, according to the flesh." One of David's descendants would be raised up by God to be Israel's Messiah.

Peter was now fencing in his listeners with the cold logic of prophetic truth literally fulfilled. There was no room for vague allegorical interpretation of this prophecy, just as there is no room for any such allegorizing.

         2. THE MESSIAH WOULD BE DAVID'S SOVEREIGN (2:30b–31)

He would raise up Christ to sit on his throne; he seeing this before spake of the resurrection of Christ, that his soul was not left in hell, neither his flesh did see corruption.

God had swept Saul aside and established a new dynasty in David. From David was to come the Messiah, who would sit on David's throne as David's Son and David's Lord. This has to be fulfilled as literally as the Scripture that prophesied that the Messiah would be David's Son. We could not take one literally and not the other.

Peter's logic was irrefutable. He was herding his listeners into a corner. He had already shown that Jesus was the promised Messiah, David's promised Son. But Jesus had *not* sat upon David's throne even though He had been born King of the Jews (Matt. 2). He had not been born in a palace and had never once come anywhere near a palace or David's throne. The Jews had murdered Him. They had said, "We will not have this man to reign over us" (Luke 19:14), and had handed Him over to Pilate to be crucified. He had been crowned indeed, but crowned with thorns, and He had died a death of ignominy and shame. When Pilate had said, "Shall I crucify your King?" they had said, "We have no king but Caesar" (John 19:15). And when Pilate had written His title and had it nailed to the cross: "This is Jesus of Nazareth, the King of the Jews," they had strenuously objected (19:19–21).

Christ had been crucified and not crowned; so how could He be David's Sovereign? Had the prophecy failed? How could He sit upon David's throne? The logic was inescapable. The resurrection was all part of the divine plan. That was the force of the prophecy of Psalm 16. David had seen it. Now they must see it. The Lord Jesus was God's one and only Savior, whether for David, them, or us.

b. THE FULFILLMENT OF HIS PROPHECY (2:32–36)
1. THE PRESENT WITNESSES (2:32)

This Jesus hath God raised up, whereof we all are witnesses.

Checkmate! Step by inescapable step Peter backed the Jews into a corner. That Jesus was the Messiah foreseen and foretold by David was an incontrovertible fact. That they had crucified Him and that God had raised Him was also incontrovertible. Peter had 120 witnesses to prove it. A man who could appear in court with that many witnesses of good character and ordinary ability would have no difficulty convincing judge and jury. Everybody knew Peter was telling the truth. The resurrection of Jesus was common knowledge in Jerusalem. Moreover, the event had taken place less than two months before. But he had the witnesses if they were wanted.

2. THE PROMISED WONDER (2:33)

Therefore being by the right hand of God exalted, and having received of the Father the promise of the Holy Ghost, he hath shed forth this, which ye now see and hear.

The coming of the Holy Spirit was the crowning proof. Jesus was not only alive from the dead by the power of God's hand, but He was now seated at the right hand of power in heaven. The outpouring of the Holy Spirit, long since foretold by Joel, was the proof that Jesus was now seated in the glory. He was the One who had thus sent the Holy Spirit to usher in a new age of grace. Instead of sending down wrath from heaven, He had sent down the Holy Spirit, and in such a way and on such a day as fulfilled the age-old symbols of Pentecost.

It all added up: the promised wonder of a new age, the age of the Holy Spirit, climaxed it all.

3. THE PROPHETIC WORD (2:34–35)

For David is not ascended into the heavens: but he saith himself, The Lord said unto my Lord, Sit thou on my right hand, until I make thy foes thy footstool.

Peter followed up with another verse of Scripture, another prophecy, another quotation from the Psalms, one he had once heard the Lord Himself quote with telling power. He quoted from Psalm 110:1, which clearly declared the deity of Christ. No Hebrew father would call his son "lord," but David did. "The Lord said unto my Lord!" David acknowledged that the One who would be born in his royal line would be his sovereign Lord. And that was the very One the Jews had rejected and crucified.

Now He had ascended into the heavens to sit at God's right hand, something it was patently obvious David had never done.

And what was the sovereign Lord of David doing now that He was seated on the very pinnacle of power? He was waiting for God to make His foes His footstool. So let the Jews not think they had won, that they had rid themselves of Him. They could expect fearful vengeance from the God whose Son they had slain if they persisted in their rejection.

All they had done fulfilled prophecy, for David had written in the prophetic word that his Son, his Lord, would have foes who would need to be dealt with from on high.

4. THE PUNGENT WARNING (2:36)

Therefore let all the house of Israel know assuredly, that God hath made that same Jesus, whom ye have crucified, both Lord and Christ.

They had crucified Him, God had crowned Him. They had entombed Him, God had enthroned Him. They had cast Him out, God had caught Him up. They had executed Him, God had exalted Him.

That is how Peter sums up this magnificent first sermon of his, the first sermon ever preached in the age of the church: Beware! The Lord is enthroned! "That same Jesus, whom ye have crucified, [is] both Lord and Christ."

That was the final twist of the Spirit's mighty sword in the guilty souls of those men: "Beware!"

Condemnation and confirmation now give place to:

(3) CONSOLATION (2:37–40)

(a) THE AGONY OF CONVICTION EXPERIENCED (2:37)

Now when they heard this, they were pricked in their heart, and said unto Peter and to the rest of the apostles, Men and brethren, what shall we do?

This is conviction. The enormity of their sin and guilt came home to their hearts. Conviction is the Holy Spirit's first work in a human heart. He convicts of sin, of righteousness, and of judgment to come—of the nature of sin, of the need for righteousness, and of the nearness of judgment. He makes people see their personal accountability before God for what they have done, and particularly for their rejection of Christ. They become desperate about their lost condition. It is doubtful if there can be genuine conversion without genuine conviction. Peter's whole Spirit-led sermon had been directed to this single end: producing conviction of sin.

All great evangelists have done the same. That is what made Alexander Whyte such a great preacher and explains why his books are still eagerly studied to this day by those who are charged to preach. Few people in modern times have dealt with sin as he did. Charles Finney's success as an evangelist rested on his awesome Holy Ghost ability to produce a soul-shattering conviction of sin in his hearers. Oftentimes his mere presence produced the result. The Welsh Revival did the same. People would fall down in the meetings overwhelmed by a sense of guilt.

So at Pentecost we have the prototype of all true evangelism—the agony of conviction was experienced. But God does not leave people there. The Jews instinctively felt that there was something they could do. "Men and brethren, what shall we do?" they said. In some ways this is an astonishing statement. They were thinking of what they had done—they had crucified the Lord of glory, murdered their Messiah, spat in the face of the very Son of the living God—and they wanted to know what they could do to make amends! He was beyond their reach, seated at God's right hand in heaven, "henceforth expecting till his enemies be made his footstool" (Heb. 10:13). Yet they said, "What can we do?"

Could they undo what they had done? Of course not! Yet they instinctively felt there was something they could do. Just as the people of Nineveh repented at the preaching of the prophet Jonah, who stalked their streets with a message of unmitigated doom, so the Jews listening to Peter came to the place of conviction and repentance. "What can we do?" All gospel preaching should begin with such a Spirit-anointed appeal to the conscience.

(b) THE ANSWER OF CONVERSION EXPLAINED (2:38–40)

i. A CONSCIOUS REPUDIATION OF THE GUILT OF THE HEBREW NATION (2:38 *a, b*)

a. SEPARATION—BY PERSONAL ACKNOWLEDGEMENT OF JESUS (2:38*a*)

Then Peter said unto them, Repent, and be baptized every one of you in the name of Jesus Christ . . .

The order of salvation in this verse is quite different from what we find anywhere else in the New Testament, for it was a unique situation. These were the people primarily responsible for the crime of Calvary. The Hebrew nation was being held accountable to God for their dreadful guilt. It was a nation without excuse, and its judgment would be sure. The whole issue before the people now, as since the days of John the Baptist, was Jesus Christ, Jesus the Messiah.

The first step for the people was to separate themselves from their horrendous national sin. There were two preliminary steps—repentance and baptism. That took them back to the beginning—back to John the Baptist, back to the original message to the nation, "Repent: for the kingdom is at hand" (Matt. 4:17). They knew their history; Peter did not have to labor that point. The leaders of Israel had rejected John, and now they had murdered Jesus. The people standing there in Jerusalem on Pentecost morning stood beneath the shadow of Calvary. They needed above all to repent; that is, they needed personally, as individuals, to repent of the enormous sin their nation had committed. Repentance is a change of mind, a deliberate turning away from a previous course of conduct. Those Hebrews had to thus deliberately repudiate the sin of the Hebrew nation.

But their repentance had to be expressed just as publicly as the national sin had been expressed, and the way to make their decision public was by baptism. That, again, took them back to the beginning—back to John the Baptist.

Only now the baptism was to be in the name of Jesus Christ. There could be no hedging on the issue for this people. It was absolutely essential that they be baptized to prove their repentance and to publicly proclaim their faith in the Lord Jesus Christ. There had to be a conscious repudiation of the guilt of the Hebrew nation by personal acknowledgement of Jesus.

b. SALVATION—BY PERSONAL ACCEPTANCE OF JESUS (2:38*b*)

. . . *in the Name of Jesus Christ for the remission of sins.*

This step would be a public acknowledgement of the fact that they were accepting Jesus as Savior from sin. It was another giant step forward. Up to this point, the Jewish nation had looked to the animal sacrifices offered in the Temple as the source of remission of sin. Even on that day of Pentecost, animals would be sacrificed in Jerusalem in accordance with a religious ordinance dating back fifteen hundred years.

Peter was proclaiming an end to all that. Jesus was God's sacrificial Lamb. Again, he was taking these Jews back to John the Baptist. John had pointed to Jesus and said: "Behold the Lamb of God, which taketh away the sin of the world!" (John 1:29). Jesus was God's Lamb. God, in grace beyond all human comprehension, had taken the crime of Calvary and turned it into a means for taking away their sins. So, by being baptized in the name of Jesus Christ, they would not only be repudiating the guilt of the Hebrew nation, but they would be acknowledging their personal acceptance of Jesus as God's Lamb, God's provision in salvation for their sin.

Baptism, in this case, was given special prominence because it was a special case. By their baptism they would be *personally* proclaiming their newfound faith in Christ, and at the same time they would be *publicly* protesting the guilt of the Hebrew nation to which they belonged.

The conscious repudiation of the guilt of the Hebrew nation would be followed by:

> ii. A CONSEQUENT RECEPTION OF THE GIFT OF THE HOLY SPIRIT (2:38c–40)
>> *a.* THE PROMISE (2:38c–39)

And ye shall receive the gift of the Holy Ghost. For the promise is unto you, and to your children, and to all that are afar off, even as many as the Lord our God shall call.

What a marvelous promise, in the light of Calvary! Again the clear allusion is to the ministry of John the Baptist, who promised the Hebrew people that the Messiah would baptize with the Holy Spirit.

However, Peter was not dealing here with the baptism of the Holy Spirit—that had already taken place in the upper room. The mystical Body of Christ had already been formed. There was no need for a repetition of that. From now on believers would be added to a baptized Body. The baptism of the Spirit guaranteed all believers a place in that Body. Peter spoke of the *gift* of the Spirit.

The gift of the Spirit is the inalienable right of every believer. It is his birthright in the family of God. All true believers have this gift. Paul says, "If any man have not the Spirit of Christ, he is none of his" (Rom. 8:9). It is wrong to pray for the gift of the Holy Spirit. How can you ask for something you already have?

When I was married I received a unique and marvelous gift—the gift of a wife, the gift of a woman to come and share her life with mine. When the preacher said, "Who giveth this woman away?" her father said, "I do." The preacher then said to me, "Will you accept this woman to be your lawful, wedded wife?" and I said, "I will." That moment I received the gift of a wife.

The Holy Spirit is a real person, the Third Person of the Godhead. When I became a Christian I received the gift of this Person into my life. I could not become a Christian without receiving the gift of the Holy Spirit, any more than I could become a married man without receiving the gift of a wife.

Moreover, we cannot receive a person by installments. It is wrong to ask God to give us more of His Holy Spirit. If we are truly saved, we already have the Holy Spirit in His totality. When I received the gift of my wife I did not get some hair one day, an eye and an arm another day, a leg and another arm some time later! I received the whole person. A person cannot be received in installments.

At the time of marriage we really do not know all that we are receiving as we accept another person to come share our life in a love relationship.

Marriage is largely the working out of that new relationship in the everyday affairs of life. Adjustments have to be made; life is forever changed.

Thus it is with the gift of the Spirit. Nobody, at the moment of conversion, can possibly know all that is involved in receiving the gift of the Holy Spirit, who comes to share His glorious life with him. The Christian life is the process of finding out, day by day, the vast dimensions of such a life. It is a learning, sharing experience. Countless changes have to be made to accommodate the marvelous Person who brings all the resources of deity with Him into a human life.

We receive the gift of the Holy Spirit because the Christian life is a supernatural life. The only person who ever lived that life was Jesus. Because we cannot live the Christ-life, He has sent His own Spirit, the Spirit of God, to come in and live that life in us.

That becomes very evident when we examine the names by which the Holy Spirit has revealed Himself in the New Testament.

He is the Spirit of *truth* (John 14:17), therefore we ought not to be deceived; of *faith* (2 Cor. 4:13), therefore we ought not to be discouraged; of *grace* (Heb. 10:29), therefore we ought not to be disgruntled; of *holiness* (Rom. 1:4), therefore we ought not to be defiled; of *wisdom* (Eph. 1:17), therefore we ought not to be daunted; of *power* (2 Tim. 1:7), therefore we ought not to be defeated; of *love* (2 Tim. 1:7), therefore we ought not to be discordant; of a *sound mind* (2 Tim. 1:7), therefore we ought not to be disturbed; of *life* (Rom. 8:2), therefore there should be nothing that savors of death about us; and of *glory* (1 Pet. 4:14), therefore we ought not to be dull.

All ten of those characteristics of the Holy Spirit are characteristics the Lord Jesus manifested in His humanity. He was never deceived, discouraged, daunted, or disturbed. He always manifested grace and wisdom, power and love. The gift of the Holy Spirit is what makes it possible for the supernatural life of the Lord Jesus to be reproduced in us day by day. The Holy Spirit, with our cooperation, lives that life in us and through us. Such is the genius of Christianity.

Now, says Peter, "the promise is unto you, and to your children, and to all that are afar off, even as many as the Lord our God shall call." To *you*—to those standing there, some of whom were guilty of shouting to Pilate, "Let Him be crucified!" (Matt. 27:23). "To your *children*," even though they had cried, "His blood be on us and on our children" (27:25). And it was "to as *many* as are *afar off*": it was by no means confined to the Hebrew people. "Even as many as the Lord our God shall call." That was a final statement, clear and unmistakable now, of the absolute deity of the Lord Jesus Christ. He was "the Lord"; He was "our God." His call was now going out. It was going out first to the Jews; later it would go out to the Samaritans; in time to all the world.

b. THE PLEA (2:40)

And with many other words did he testify and exhort, saying, Save yourselves from this [crooked] generation.

Swift and sure judgment was coming on that generation. It had been prophesied by Jesus (Matt. 23:36). Within less than forty years Jerusalem would be taken in one of the most terrible wars of history, the Temple would be burned to the ground, and the Jews dispersed. Beyond that, judgment awaited that generation at the great white throne. They were to save themselves. How? By coming to the Savior.

3. THE PHENOMENAL SALVATION OF PEOPLE (2:41–47)

a. A SAVED PEOPLE (2:41a)

Then they that gladly received his word . . .

Peter's sermon brought forth instant results. There was a mighty moving of the Holy Spirit on Peter's audience. The rest of the chapter describes what happened as people made their decision for Christ and stepped out of darkness into life; out of wrath and into grace; out of sin and into Christ; out of Judaism and into the church. Not all of them, it would sadly seem, but many. They not only received Peter's word, they also received it gladly.

That is always what happens when the work of conviction is done in a human heart by the Holy Spirit. None knew it better than John Bunyan. He describes his own spiritual experience in *Pilgrim's Progress.* As we see Pilgrim bowed beneath an enormous burden, making his agonizing way to Calvary, we see Bunyan himself. We see, too, Bunyan's relief when at last he came to the Savior, felt his burden lifted, and saw it run down that steep place into the open sepulcher. We hear his gladness, too, in Pilgrim's new song:

> Blest cross! Blest Sepulchre!
> Blest rather be,
> The One Who there was put to shame for me.

The Israelites who accepted Christ at Pentecost were the Israel of God, the true believing remnant. More Hebrews were added to their number as time went on, and, indeed, for the first half dozen years or so the church was entirely Jewish. The Lord was calling the true Israel out of all Israel. Thus too, for a time, the message in the Diaspora always went "to the Jew first." It was not until Peter's ministry in the house of Cornelius that Gentiles were added to the church. Shortly thereafter the Jews became a permanent minority in that church. First, however, the believing remnant of the old Israel became the charter members of the church.

b. A SEPARATED PEOPLE (2:41b)

They . . . were baptized.

Note the order of conversion in the case of the Jews. First they "gladly received" the truth concerning Christ, His deity and the hope of salvation in Him. Then they were baptized. From the first day of the church's history, and consistently through Acts and the epistles, baptism was believer's baptism. No other kind of baptism is ever considered in the New Testament. Baptism, as Peter was to later write, is "the answer of a good conscience toward God" (1 Pet. 3:21). Only a true believer in the Lord Jesus can have that.

It was a bold step to be thus publicly baptized in the name of the Lord Jesus. For many a Jew it meant persecution, to be cut off from family and friends and denied further place in the synagogue and in Jewish society. As it became increasingly clear that the church was not just another Jewish sect, and as official attitudes toward the church hardened, so the cost of baptism increased. The price of this first step of obedience remains high in many countries and cultures even today.

c. A STEADFAST PEOPLE (2:42)

And they continued steadfastly in the apostles' doctrine and fellowship, and in breaking of bread, and in prayers.

Four things marked the infant church. First, it was marked by *the truth*: they "continued steadfastly in the apostles' doctrine." The Holy Spirit was already beginning to fulfill Christ's promise that He would bring to the remembrance of the apostles all the teaching of Jesus and open their minds and hearts to new truth suited for the new age. First and foremost came the apostles' doctrine. It is no accident that this comes first. It always comes first. In all the epistles, precept comes before practice. *Experience must always be tested by doctrine, not doctrine by experience.*

Second, it was a company marked by *the tie*, that blessed "tie that binds our hearts in Christian love." They continued "in fellowship." New links of love were forged that day, a new community created. John wrote later: "We know that we have passed from death unto life, because we love the brethren" (1 John 3:14). The church is a body, the mystical Body of Christ. Union with the Head means union with the members.

Third, it was a company marked by *the table*. They continued in "breaking of bread." The ordinary communal meal would be included under "fellowship," but here we have reference to the Lord's Supper. The Lord's last request before He went to the cross was "This do in remembrance of me" (1 Cor. 11:24). The early disciples at once incorporated the Lord's Supper as one of the four cardinal practices of the church. It was the companion ordinance to baptism. In baptism we show our death with Christ; in breaking of bread we show His death for us.

And fourth, it was a company marked by *the throne*. "They continued steadfastly . . . in prayers." The name of Jesus opened up prayer opportunities never before known, for now we have instant access to the throne of grace. Every aspect of individual life and corporate life can now be related to the throne and to that great High Priest who sits at God's right hand.

d. A SANCTIFIED PEOPLE (2:43*a*)

And fear came upon every soul . . .

The church does not instill much fear today. The professing church accepts such low standards for its fellowship that lying, immorality, questionable doctrine, deception, and even perversion are allowed. We have forgotten the divine injunction "Be ye holy; for I am holy" (1 Pet. 1:16). We have forgotten that the believer's body and the corporate body of the church are alike the Temple of the Holy Spirit.

The infant church was holy. It was fresh from the hand of God, pristine in purity, untouched as yet by any wrongful act, so "fear came upon every soul." Those who were within feared—feared lest they defile and disgrace the holy fellowship of blood-washed saints. Those who were without feared—feared to join its ranks with sin-stained souls unwashed, uncleansed by the precious blood of Christ.

e. A SPECTACULAR PEOPLE (2:43*b*)

And many wonders and signs were done by the apostles.

The infant church had more than purity; it had power. The gift of the apostles included the power to work miracles. An ungrieved Holy Spirit poured out His power upon those men, and soon Jerusalem rang with stories of miraculous healings. It was as though Jesus of Nazareth were back, as though He were walking again—giving sight to the blind, making the deaf to hear, the dumb to talk, the dead to live, the lame to walk, cleansing the leper, casting out demons. And so He was. Only now it was His mystical Body that was the vehicle of divine power rather than the material body in which He had lived when in the flesh.

f. A SINGLE PEOPLE (2:44)

And all that believed were together, and had all things common.

It was a true body, each member caring for and nourishing each other member. Here we see the answer to the Lord's prayer:

That they all may be one; as thou, Father, art in me, and I in thee, that they also may be one in us: that the world may believe that thou hast sent me. And the glory which thou gavest me I have given them; that they may be one, even as we are one: I in them, and thou in me, that they may be made perfect in one; and that the world may know that thou hast sent me, and hast loved them, as thou hast loved me.

This was true ecumenicalism. The oneness of the early church was organic oneness, not organized oneness.

There was a mutual caring and concern for other believers. There was a spontaneous coming together of like-minded believers in love with the Lord, in love with each other, in love with lost souls.

g. A SACRIFICIAL PEOPLE (2:45)

And sold their possessions and goods, and parted them to all men, as every man had need.

When I was a lad in high school, I went once on a camping trip with some of the boys from school, organized by several of the teachers. During the day we helped the war effort by assisting farmers in the harvest fields. At night we sat around a campfire or played games.

One of the teachers was a communist. He used his influence to try to persuade us to espouse his social and political views. He appealed to the early church as being communistic—people shared. The motto was: From each according to his ability, to each according to his need. "That was the slogan of the early church," he said; "that is the slogan of communists today." The flaw in his argument is obvious. The sharing of the early church was spontaneous and motivated by Holy Spirit love. It was not a totalitarian system clamped on people against their will.

An open-air preacher was being heckled by a communist in the crowd. About that time a drunken derelict staggered past, a pitiable object, down at heel and arrayed in rags. The communist pointed to him. "Given the opportunity," he said, "Communism would put a new suit on that man. What does your Christianity do for him?" Said the preacher, "Given the opportunity, Christ would put a new man in that suit."

That was the secret of the mutual sharing of the early church. This was no government or ecclesiastical welfare program. This was not cold charity. This was the Body at work. This was the hand caring for the foot, the eye looking out for the ear. This was love, not law; compassion, not compulsion. The communist ideal is noble enough, but it breaks down because it leaves out God and relies on force.

h. A SPIRITUAL PEOPLE (2:46)

And they, continuing daily with one accord in the temple, and breaking bread from house to house, did eat their [food] with gladness and singleness of heart.

Spirituality is not something with which we clothe ourselves just on Sundays. Notice what the Holy Spirit links together: the Temple and the table. Those who were in love with the Lord found their way to the place of prayer. They went to the Temple because, as yet, it had not dawned upon those first believers that the Temple and its worship were obsolete. It would take Stephen to teach them that. The Temple court was a commodious and convenient place to meet for worship and for fellowship. The spiritual person will seek out the gathering place of God's people.

That spirituality will then spill over into the mundane aspects of life. It will bring people together in hospitality. The commonplace things of life, such as eating and drinking, will be sanctified into a sacrament. The joy of the Lord will add a new dimension of gladness to everything. Life will not be compartmentalized into the sacred and the secular, but both will be wedded in a marriage of blessing and bliss.

  i. A SINGING PEOPLE (2:47a)
Praising God, and having favor with all the people.
That was the keynote of the early church. The people were happy. No wonder their numbers grew. In the words of the hymn writer,

> Heav'n above is softer blue,
> Earth around is sweeter green!
> Something lives in every hue
> Christless eyes have never seen.
>   (George Wade Robinson, "I Am His, and He Is Mine")

There was no complaining, no criticizing, no envy, no strife. The fruit of the Spirit was evident everywhere—"love, joy, peace, long-suffering, gentleness, goodness, faith, meekness, temperance" (Gal. 5:22–23). What an attractive company of people it was—a company of people praising God!

  j. A SUCCESSFUL PEOPLE (2:47b)
And the Lord added to the church daily such as should be saved.
That is the only way anyone can be added to the church. The *Lord* adds to its members those He saves. "Except the Lord build the house, they labor in vain that build it" (Ps. 127:1). The church does not grow by adding to its rolls the names of baptized infants. It does not grow by high-pressure evangelism and doubtful professions of faith. It grows as the Lord adds saved people to its numbers. "The Lord added daily," says Luke. He has been adding to it daily ever since, sometimes by the thousands, sometimes a few here, a few there. Now a child at mother's knee, now an old man dying in his bed.

But we can be assured that there has never been a day since Pentecost when the Lord has not added to the church such as should be saved. He will go on doing that, adding and adding until the rapture.

II. TRIUMPH (3:1–4:37)

A. THE THRILLING OPPORTUNITY SEIZED (3:1–4:22)

1. THE MAN (3:1–8)
a. THE TRAGEDY IN HIS LIFE (3:1–3)
(1) HIS SERIOUS DEFECT (3:1–2a)

Now Peter and John went up together into the temple at the hour of prayer, being the ninth hour. And a certain man lame from his mother's womb was carried . . .

Peter and John! That was different. It used to be Peter and Andrew, James and John. Now it is Peter and John. Calvary had brought these men into closer fellowship with each other. By nature and temperament they were different. Peter was a doer, John was a dreamer; Peter was a motivator, John was a mystic; Peter had his feet on the rock, John had his head in the clouds. Peter would point to John and demand of the Lord, "And what shall this man do?" (John 21:21). John would quietly whisper to Peter in a moment of doubt, "It is the Lord" (21:7); John would outrun Peter to the tomb; Peter would push past John and rush right in; Peter would dash on out again, his mind in a whirl; John would walk away thinking deeply over the significance of those strangely ordered grave clothes. Peter and John were opposites. By nature they would get on each other's nerves, but now they walked together. We read, "Now Peter and John went up together into the temple." Before, they had been mutual disciples of Jesus, now they were members of a common body; before, they knew friendship, now they enjoyed fellowship.

It was prayer meeting time in the Temple, the place where the new believers in the Lord Jesus gathered in His Name. It was the ninth hour— three o'clock in the afternoon—the same magic moment when at Calvary the mysterious midday-midnight darkness had lifted (Matt. 27:45–46). It was the moment when the Sin-Bearer had dismissed His spirit, bowed His head, and died. It was the ninth hour, an hour to conjure up thoughts of Calvary, a fitting hour for two men who loved Jesus and who loved each other to find themselves arriving together at the place of prayer.

And there they met the man. Luke tells us of the tragedy in this man's life. He was a man lame from birth.

Think what that had meant to his parents. They looked upon their little baby and saw that his legs were not right. The defect became increasingly evident as the months passed. He could not stand, and he never learned to walk.

Think what that meant to the boy. He could never run and romp; never play games or join in the sports activities of his fellows. He had to be carried everywhere, as Luke the physician notes. There had never been a day in this man's life when he had not been a burden to somebody. He would not walk, and he could not work. All he could do was beg, sit there, and hope that his plight would provoke pity.

(2) HIS SAD DEPENDENCE (3:2b)

Whom they laid daily at the gate of the temple which is called Beautiful, to ask alms of them that entered into the temple.

If one had to beg, probably this was as desirable a spot as any. It was a place of *beauty*. The man was placed on the steps leading up to the Nicanor Gate through which Jews passed from the Court of the Gentiles to the Court of the Women. It was here that the famous barrier was erected known as "The Middle Wall of Partition," where announcements in Latin and Greek warned Gentiles, upon pain of death, to go no further. Nine gates led through this barrier, of which the Beautiful Gate was one.

From where he lay the lame man could contemplate the beauty of that gate. It is said to have been made of Corinthian bronze wrought with such rich ornamentation that it far exceeded in value gates plated with silver and set with gold. The lame man could also contemplate the beauty of the Temple itself. Herod had turned it into one of the wonders of the world. And, if the man was of a spiritual disposition he could contemplate "the beauty of holiness" (Ps. 29:2), of which all that other beauty was but a picture. There were worse places to beg.

It was, too, one would hope, a place of *bounty*. The man sat there "to ask alms of them that entered into the temple." If there was one place more than another where an able-bodied man might be presumed to have a generous feeling towards his less fortunate neighbor, surely it would be here. We note that the beggar's eyes were fixed on those going *into* the temple. On the way *in*, a person's thoughts would be more sharply focused on the nature and character of God, perhaps, than on the way *out*. The superstitious, hoping to propitiate God and secure His goodwill, might be more disposed to drop a coin or two in the beggar's palm. Or so the approaching worshiper might think.

If a man must beg, this man or his friends seem to have chosen a good spot.

(3) HIS SOLE DESIRE (3:3)

Who, seeing Peter and John about to go into the temple, asked an alms.

Had he ever seen them before? How long had he been there? Had Judas ever dropped some money in his palm in the name of Jesus? Had Jesus passed by that way when He was there? And if so, why had he not called out like blind Bartimaeus, "Thou Son of David, have mercy on me" (Mark 10:47)? The fact that he was lame from birth implies he had been a beggar for a long time.

Grinding poverty does not tend to lift a man's thoughts much higher than his pressing and continual material needs. All he asked of Peter and John was a coin or two to help him buy a crust of bread.

Here were two men who had leaped to fame in Jerusalem in these past few weeks. They were leaders of a revival that was the talk of the town. Thousands had come into new life in Christ since Peter preached at Pentecost. This poor beggar had no thought for that. All he knew was that he was hungry and poor and handicapped, that life had cheated him, and that if he did not get a coin or two he would go hungry to bed. His life had been reduced to that—to an outstretched palm, a pitiful look, and a wheedling plea.

b. THE TRANSFORMATION IN HIS LIFE (3:4–8)

(1) WE SEE HIM LOOKING (3:4)

And Peter, fastening his eyes upon him with John, said, Look on us.

What would he see? Two poor men, Galilean fishermen, but two men in touch with Jesus and filled with the Holy Spirit. They wanted him to see Jesus, but he was not ready for that yet. He must first see Jesus in them.

The poor lame man is a cameo of the human race. Men are born lame, with no standing before God. They stumble and fall through life. They have nothing. The very best person in the world, outside of Christ, is a hopeless spiritual cripple, born that way; the wealthiest man is a spiritual beggar.

And there he lay, his worn, woebegone face eagerly scanning the faces of others, hoping against hope for help, rarely lifting his thoughts much higher than the pity and charity of men.

There he lay at the Gate Beautiful, at the gorgeous gate of a dead religion, a religion that boasted of its law and of its legitimacy but that could do nothing for this lame man. It found him a beggar and left him a beggar. Such was religion.

"Look on us," said Peter, whose idea it was to redirect the beggar's thoughts from his rags and from his religion to the Redeemer.

"Look on us!" Dare we say that to those around us? Are we such a reflection of Christ that to look on us is to look, as it were, on Him?

(2) WE SEE HIM LISTENING (3:5–6)

And he gave heed unto them, expecting to receive something of them. Then Peter said, Silver and gold have I none; but such as I have give I thee: In the name of Jesus Christ of Nazareth rise up and walk.

He expected to receive something: not much, perhaps, because they were obviously poor men; but something.

Peter's first words must have dashed his hopes. "Silver and gold have I none." He turned his pockets inside out. If he had had a coin, however small, it would have gone into the beggar's outstretched hand. And probably that would have been that. The man wanted money, and money is what he would have received. But he needed a miracle, and though Peter had no money, he could provide the miracle. How different from the church today.

We recall the oft-told story of Thomas Aquinas when he visited Pope Innocent II and found him counting a large sum of money. "Ah, Thomas," said the Pope, "the church can no longer say, 'silver and gold have I none.' " "That is true, Your Holiness," said Aquinas, "but then, neither can it now say 'Arise and walk.' "

Peter was poor, but he was exceeding rich towards God: "Such as I have give I thee," he said. "In the Name of Jesus Christ of Nazareth rise up and walk." He redirected the man's look away from himself to Jesus and offered him a new life in Christ. He need never beg again.

Jesus Christ of Nazareth! The begger had heard of Jesus. All Jerusalem had heard of Jesus. Since Pentecost all he had heard, as he sat there in his need, were people talking about Jesus. Some said He was a blasphemer, crucified for His sins and His body stolen away to substantiate rumors of a resurrection. Others said He was alive from the dead, ascended into heaven, enthroned on high. Others talked about the newly formed ecclesia of those who believed in Him. Since Pentecost thousands had believed. They thronged the Temple courts, for that was where they met.

"In the Name of Jesus Christ of Nazareth rise up and walk," said Peter. We see the lame man listening. Nobody had ever talked to him like that before. He had heard people talking *about* Jesus; Peter asked him to put his faith in Jesus. To help him, Peter held out his hand.

(3) WE SEE HIM LEAPING (3:7–8a)

And he took him by the right hand, and lifted him up: and immediately his feet and ankle bones received strength. And he leaping up stood, and walked, and entered with them into the temple, walking, and leaping . . .

This was no gradual cure, it was instantaneous. Nor did Peter build a basilica and dedicate a shrine for the man's crutches—to become crutches to other men's faith. No! There was better evidence than that. There was a man himself leaping, trying out his new ankles, jumping all around.

He was no longer chained to charity. He was free! All Jerusalem was before him. The world was before Him. He could run home. He could hop, skip, and jump wherever he wished. Where did he go? With the believers, of course! He accompanied them into the Temple, to the place of fellowship and prayer. That is always a good sign in a life touched and transformed by the name of Jesus.

(4) WE SEE HIM LAUGHING (3:8*b*)

. . . *and praising God.*

That was spiritual discernment. He was not praising Peter, he was praising God! He did not regard Peter as someone special, though naturally he was grateful to him. He did not kiss the hand through which the life-transforming power flowed. He praised God.

As Paul would put it later to the Corinthians, who were apt to make much of men: "Who then is Paul, and who is Apollos, but ministers by whom ye believed, even as the Lord gave to every man?" (1 Cor. 3:5). This lame man had Pauline insight.

So much for the man.

2. *THE MULTITUDE (3:9–11)*

a. THEIR ASTONISHMENT (3:9–10)

And all the people which saw him walking and praising God: And they knew that it was he which sat for alms at the Beautiful Gate of the temple: and they were filled with wonder and amazement at that which had happened unto him.

They knew what his life had been like before. He had evidently been a bit of a character, beggar though he was. Everybody knew him, knew his wretched way of life, knew exactly where he was to be found. He was as much a fixture as the Beautiful Gate itself. Now here he was showing off, for all the world to see, the miracle that had been wrought in his life. They met him where they had never met him before, never indeed ever expected to meet him—in the Temple praising God. The Holy Spirit marks down their astonishment.

The world is always astonished at the evidence of new life in Christ. Here is a man, a woman, who comes into the blessing of salvation. Suddenly all is changed. That person is missing from his old haunts. The bar, the poolroom, the racetrack know him no more. He is found instead in the company of the people of God, in the place where God's saved ones gather to sing the praises of the Lord Jesus. He is walking new paths and praising the living God.

The miracle of salvation is intended to provide astonishment.

b. THEIR ASSEMBLY (3:11)

And as the lame man which was healed held Peter and John, all the people ran together unto them in the porch that is called Solomon's, greatly wondering.

The prayer meeting was over. Peter, John, and the healed man came from the Temple, back through the Beautiful Gate, and made their way in an easterly direction across the outer court towards Solomon's colonnade.

Notice what the healed man was doing. He was hanging on to the believers. Good for him! That is the thing to do! A new believer will not go far astray if he does that. When I was a lonely soldier, moved from place to place, surrounded by godless men and ceaseless temptation, that is what I learned to do—hang on to the Lord's people. My first concern in a new town was to locate a company of the Lord's people. My most eager expectation in any unit of the army was to find another believer.

We can picture the man as he walked out of the Temple, right past the Gate Beautiful. He must have cast a passing glance at the spot where only that morning he had sat, a prisoner to his misery and woe. Do you think he said to Peter, "Thanks for everything, Peter, but I'm going back now to my old way of life. I have a sentimental attachment to the spot over there. All I know is begging. Say hello to me when you come back again"? Not he! He hung on to Peter and John until he was well past that benighted spot haunted by so many bitter memories of his past.

The evidence of this transformed man walking away from his past drew a crowd. They came running. There is nothing like a changed life to draw a crowd. This healed man could not preach, but he could draw a crowd, and he wisely left the preaching to Peter. Nowadays we would make a nine-day wonder of this man—put him up to give his testimony, put him on a talk show or on TV. We would arrange a speaking itinerary for him and generally stunt his growth in the deeper things of God. Peter had more sense. When the crowd gathered he did not so much as ask this man to say a word. *He* was the one anointed to preach.

3. *THE MESSAGE (3:12–26)*

a. THE REJECTION OF CHRIST (3:12–15 17a)

(1) THE SADNESS OF IT (3:12–13)

And when Peter saw it, he answered unto the people, Ye men of Israel, why marvel ye at this? or why look ye so earnestly on us, as though by our own power or holiness we had made this man walk? The God of Abraham, and of Isaac, and of Jacob, the God of our fathers, hath glorified his Son Jesus; whom ye delivered up, and denied in the presence of Pilate, when he was determined to let him go.

Peter wasted no time in turning the gathering of the crowd to full advantage.

First he denied that he and John were anything out of the ordinary in themselves, that their "goodness" had anything to do with the lame man's cure. In one slashing statement Peter demolished all the claims of so-called "holy men," the idea of trusting in "saints" to work miracles, the notion that people can accumulate merit and from the treasury of their goodness can work miracles for others.

Peter directed everyone's attention to Christ. Indeed, in this short sermon, he made ten direct references to Christ. All attention was turned away from the lame man and from the apostles to Jesus. Peter was not going to elevate himself. He was going to lift up the Lord Jesus. It was not his supposed goodness that was at issue. It was their fearful guilt.

With terrible swiftness he plunged the sword of conviction into their souls. He did not have to talk about the healing of the lame man. The whole country had been filled with such healings for three-and-one-half years. God's Servant Jesus had been abroad in the land.

And what had they done? They had rejected Him. Pilate was willing to release Him, had determined to release Him, but they had browbeaten Pilate into crucifying Him. In a flash, Peter had the crowd at Calvary, face to face with their crime.

(2) THE SERIOUSNESS OF IT (3:14)

But ye denied the Holy One and the Just, and desired a murderer to be granted unto you.

Could crime be greater? Jesus was the Holy One. Isaiah had seen Him surrounded by the singing seraphim who hid their faces in their wings because they dared not look on Him, and who awoke the echoes of the everlasting hills with their ceaseless chant: "Holy, Holy, Holy" (Isa. 6:3). Jesus was the Holy One, the One who dwelt in the Holy of Holies in heaven and who came to earth to live a holy life.

He was "the Just One," the righteous One, the One who never deviated from the good and the right way. He had lived His life before them. "Which one of you convinceth Me of sin?" (John 8:46), He could say. "I do always those things that please the Father" (8:29). Pilate said: "I find in him no fault at all" (18:38). The dying malefactor said: "This man hath done nothing amiss" (Luke 23:41). Peter, who had lived with Him for more than three years, said that He did no sin" (1 Pet. 2:22).

He was the One the Jews had forced Pilate to crucify. "Ye . . . desired a murderer to be granted unto you," he charged, taking them back to the trial before Pilate less than two months ago and conjuring up before them the mob scene in which some of them had played their part. The Holy One, or Barabbas? And they chose the murderer. Could crime be greater?

(3) THE SINFULNESS OF IT (3:15*a*)

And killed the Prince of life . . .

Jesus was the Prince of life, the Author of life ("Prince" here is used in the same sense as in Heb. 2:10). Life from nothing began through Him. It was His idea; He was its Creator and Sustainer. There was not a man, woman, or child in that audience who did not owe life itself to Him. The very breath they breathed was in His hand. This One, the Prince, the Author of life, had come into the world as a man, and they had killed Him. Could crime be greater?

The enormity of their sin had to be brought home to them. Not indeed that they were worse than we. Any rejection of Christ in any age is a manifestation of the same spirit.

Having dealt thus bluntly with the rejection of Christ, Peter dealt with:

b. THE RESURRECTION OF CHRIST (3:15*b*–18)

(1) THE PROOF OF IT (3:15*b*)

Whom God hath raised from the dead; whereof we are witnesses.

The great debate in Jerusalem was, "What happened to the body?" It was sealed in the tomb, that was certain. The empty tomb had confounded the Sanhedrin. They had silenced the soldiers with "large money" (Matt. 28:12). The price of a slave could buy Judas, but it took handsome bribes to tie the tongues of the guard. Frightened half out of their wits by the sight of an angel, they had been frightened clean out of the other half by the scowls of the Sanhedrin. "The disciples stole the body," they said.

"We did not steal the body," said the disciples, "but we know where it is!" All the authorities needed to do was arrest those men, put them on public trial, and extract from them a confession as to when and where they had seen that body. That they did not dare to do. That was the last thing they wanted. We can picture such a trial:

Judge to Guards: "What happened to the body you were guarding in the tomb, sealed with the governor's seal?"

Guards: "While we slept, the disciples came and stole the body."

Judge: "You slept!"

Guards: "Yes, your honor."

Judge: "Is that what you were paid to do?"

Guards: "No your honor."

Judge: "How do you dare make such an admission? What is the penalty for sleeping on guard?"

Guards: "Death, your honor."

Judge: "But you were asleep?"

Guards: "Yes, your honor."

Judge: "Does the governor know about this?

Guards: "We expect so, your honor."

Judge: "Then why have you not been arrested?"

Guards: (Embarrassed) "Can't say, your honor."

Judge: "But you were *asleep*?"

Guards: "Yes, your honor."

Judge: "If you were asleep when it happened, how could you possibly know what happened to the body?" (Laughter in court)

Guards: (Embarrassed silence.)

Judge: "Your testimony is worthless. We shall have to have a full investigation of your story to see if you are committing perjury. I am going to bind you over for trial. Bailiff, put these men in custody."

Bailiff: "Very good, your honor."

(The disciples take the stand and are sworn in.)

Judge: "You claim you have seen the body."

Disciples: "Yes, your honor."

Judge: "All of you?"

Disciples: "Yes, your honor."

Judge: "Are you the only ones who have knowledge of its whereabouts?"

Disciples: "No, your honor."

Judge: "Who else has seen this body?"

Disciples: "There are hundreds, your honor. We know of one occasion when five hundred people saw it at once."

Judge: "Where is this body?"

Disciples: "In heaven, your honor."

Judge: "What do you mean, in heaven?"

Disciples: "God has raised Jesus from the dead. He appeared to us and to others in His resurrection body on numerous occasions and in various places over a period of forty days between the Feast of First Fruits and Pentecost. He ate with us, allowed us to touch Him, came and went, appeared and disappeared at will. Then ten days before Pentecost we walked with Him through Jerusalem, out of the city gate, down across the Kedron, up past the Garden of Gethsemane to the brow of Olivet. From there He returned to heaven. We watched Him rise. We saw the cloud receive Him out of our sight. We know where His body is, your honor. It is in heaven. God has raised Jesus from the dead, of which we are witnesses."

It is obvious that the last thing the Jewish authorities wanted was to arrest the disciples, put them on trial, subject them to cross-examination, and receive their formal testimony to the momentous events that had shaken all Jerusalem.

But truth will out. Now those men, emboldened by the Holy Spirit, were giving their witness to the world. The credibility of their witness would be upheld in any court of law in the civilized world were they to be put on trial and cross-examined by the rules of evidence that hold good in our courts today.

(2) THE POWER OF IT (3:16)

And his name, through faith in his name, hath made this man strong, whom ye see and know: yea, the faith which is by him hath given him this perfect soundness in the presence of you all.

So they had crucified Him, and God had raised Him. Now in *His* name salvation is offered to men, salvation by faith. In those early days the message of the church had to be authenticated with miracles. This man's faith in the saving name of Jesus was authenticated by his physical healing.

Miracles that occurred from time to time in the early church were designed to demonstrate that "all that Jesus began to do and teach" (1:1), as recorded in the gospels, He was still doing and still teaching in the church. The things He had done and taught when here in His material body, He was still doing and teaching in His mystical Body. The Jewish context of the sign miracles is usually in evidence because "the Jews require a sign" (2 Cor. 1:22). By the time Paul arrived at Corinth, however, his great concern was not to cater to the Jewish sign-seeking or to Greek intellectualism but to "preach Christ crucified, unto the Jews a stumbling block, and unto the Greeks foolishness" (1:23).

(3) THE PROPHECY OF IT (3:17–18)

And now, brethren, I [know] that through ignorance ye did it, as did also your rulers. But those things, which God before had shown by the mouth of all his prophets, that Christ should suffer, he hath so fulfilled.

He charged them and their leaders with ignorance of the Scriptures— just as Jesus had once done when the Sadducees asked Him a foolish question to ridicule the doctrine of resurrection. Jesus had replied: "Ye do err, not knowing the Scriptures, nor the power of God (Matt. 22:29).

The Jewish people prided themselves on their knowledge of the Scriptures. All they had, however, was the kind of rabbinic teaching espoused by Hillel and Gamaliel, which made a great show of scholarship but was far from the truth of God. Jesus charged the rabbis with being "blind leaders of the blind" (Matt. 15:14).

The Jews were ignorant of the true significance of the Scriptures. When Jesus talked to that thoughtful ruler of the Jews, Nicodemus, about the need for the new birth, that man, grown old in his devotion to Judaism, twice asked the question, "How?" Jesus said, "Art thou a master of Israel, and knowest not these things?" (John 3:10).

There was some excuse for the ignorance of people like Pilate, Gentiles, "aliens from the commonwealth of Israel, and strangers from the covenants of promise" (Eph. 2:12). There was no excuse for the Jews. They were looking for a Messiah, but they wanted a *militant* Messiah, one who would smash the power of Rome and make Jerusalem the capital of a new world empire. They were not interested in a *meek* Messiah. What they were looking for was a *ruler*; God sent them a *Redeemer*. They wanted a *sovereign*; God sent them a *Savior*. Their Scriptures prophesied both, but they blindly overlooked such references to the Sufferer as were to be found in Psalm 22, Psalm 69, and Isaiah 53.

It was the ignorance and unbelief of the Jews that had helped fulfill those old prophecies—which, of course, God had foreseen and foretold (Isa. 53:1).

It was the inability of the Jews to distinguish between the two comings of Christ that caused all their confusion about the prophetic Scriptures and teaching concerning the Christ. So Peter spoke of:

  c. THE RETURN OF CHRIST (3:19–26)

  (1) PETER WOOS THEM TO REPENTANCE (3:19–21)

  (a) THE TIMES OF REFRESHING (3:19)

Repent ye therefore, and be converted, that your sins may be blotted out, when the times of refreshing shall come from the presence of the Lord.

The term *times of refreshing* refers to those Old Testament prophecies that promised that before the return of Christ there would be an outpouring of the Spirit and that many Jews would repent and turn to God in preparation for the millennial kingdom (Deut. 30:1–3; Joel 2:28–32; Zech. 12:10–14).

If the Jews had repented then and there, the initial fulfillment of such prophecies, as were evidenced at Pentecost, would have blossomed into a complete fulfillment, and the return of Christ could have taken place within a generation. A few individuals did repent, but the leaders of Israel and the mass of the people both in the homeland and in the Diaspora rejected God's second call and the ministry of the Holy Spirit as adamantly as they had rejected the ministry of Christ Himself.

But the national principle was clear: no repentance, no refreshing. The individual principle was the same: no repentance, no refreshing. Those who did repent came at once into the good of that refreshing poured out at Pentecost. Those who repent today still do. They are baptized into the mystical Body of Christ.

(b) THE TIMES OF RESTITUTION (3:20–21)

And he shall send Jesus Christ, which before was preached unto you: whom the heaven must receive until the times of restitution of all things, which God hath spoken by the mouth of all his holy prophets since the world began.

This is a further call to the nation of Israel to reverse their decision, taken on the eve of Passover, to get rid of Jesus. God had reversed that decision, for although they had rejected Him, heaven had received Him. Yes, and would receive Him until, in the long-prophesied purpose of God, the times of restitution arrived.

The word *restitution* comes from a word meaning "to restore to a former state," "to fulfill," or "to establish." Peter's words tell us that the Lord Jesus will remain in heaven until the time comes for the establishment of all that God has spoken through the prophets.

The prophets speak of the restoration of Israel to the land and of the restoration of the theocracy under David's greater Son. The fulfillment of those and other prophecies, however, is much wider than the mere restoration of the kingdom of Israel, although it includes that. It includes the regeneration (Matt. 19:28) and the renovation of all nature.

Had Israel as a nation repented at the preaching of Peter, the centuries between then and now would have been telescoped. The evangelization of the nations would have been swift. Possibly Nero would have become the Antichrist, and Christ would have returned. But it was not to be. Israel remained obdurate in unbelief.

So Peter wooed them to repentance—in vain, as we shall see.

(2) PETER WARNS THEM OF RETRIBUTION (3:22–24)

(a) THE APPEAL TO MOSES AS PROPHET (3:22–23)

For Moses truly said unto the fathers, A prophet shall the Lord, your God, raise up unto you of your brethren, like unto me: him shall ye hear in all things whatsoever he shall say unto you. And it shall come to pass, that every soul, who will not hear that prophet, shall be destroyed from among the people.

Peter's quotation was from Deuteronomy 18:15, 19, a passage known by heart by his hearers. It was a clear messianic prophecy. The appeal to Moses was an appeal to an unimpeachable authority, and the application of the prophecy was so clear as to barely need mentioning.

That prophet had come! The Sanhedrin had once half suspected that John the Baptist was that prophet (John 1:21–23), but John had denied the claim and had pointed to the One who was to follow him, of whom he was the forerunner.

Jesus was that prophet. For three and one-half years He had crossed and recrossed the land preaching and teaching and performing miracles. They had all heard Him. They had heard all that He had to say to them. He was God's fullest and final revelation of Himself.

And hearing they had not heard. "This people's heart is waxed gross," Jesus had declared, "and their ears are dull of hearing, and their eyes they have closed; lest at any time they should see with their eyes, and hear with their ears, and should understand with their heart, and should be converted, and I should heal them (Matt. 13:15).

Therefore destruction was imminent. Moses, whom they revered above all men except perhaps Abraham, had said so. They had treated that prophet in a far worse way than their fathers had treated Moses. Death and damnation stared them in the face.

(b) THE APPEAL TO MANY OTHER PROPHETS (3:24)

Yea and all the prophets from Samuel and those that follow after, as many as have spoken, have likewise foretold of these days.

Samuel was the last of the judges and the first of the prophets. Not all the prophets were writing prophets in the sense that Isaiah and Amos and the rest were. Peter says "as many as have *spoken*." For Samuel did not specifically write prophecies such as those to which Peter refers, but he certainly may have spoken them. In any case, it was Samuel who anointed David and who certainly did speak of the establishment of the Davidic kingdom (1 Sam. 13:14; 15:28; 16:13; 28:17), and it was through great David's greater Son that all those prophecies were to be fulfilled.

Peter was speaking to an audience thoroughly familiar with the messianic prophecies. He did not need to pile up quotations to prove his point. They could recall them for themselves. Suffice it to say that there was unanimous testimony among the prophets that Messiah would be rejected and that He would return; but woe to those who rejected Him.

Finally:

(3) PETER WAKENS THEM TO RESPONSIBILITY (3:25–26)

(a) AS JEWS (3:25)

Ye are the children of the prophets, and of the covenant which God made with our fathers, saying unto Abraham, And in thy seed shall all the kindreds of the earth be blessed.

That only aggravated their sin and increased their responsibility. There was no excuse for what they had done in murdering their Messiah. Of all people on earth, they should have known who and what manner of Man it was who moved among them, healing their sick, casting out demons, cleansing their lepers, raising their dead. Their responsibility was inescapable. They were children of the prophets, they were Abraham's seed.

      (b) REGARDING JESUS (3:26)

Unto you first God, having raised up his Son Jesus, sent him to bless you, in turning away every one of you from his iniquities.

Here was the wonder of it! God had stayed His hand. Twelve legions of angels with drawn swords were waiting to execute God's wrath upon human-kind for the torture and crucifixion of heaven's Beloved, but judgment was being stayed, and God was giving them another chance. Mercy held the scepter. They could be saved from all their sins. God was willing to bless rather than curse, but they must turn to the Jesus whom they had rejected and whom God had raised up.

Such was the message. The story now turns to

    4. THE MASTER (4:1–22)

      a. THE GLORY OF HIS NAME (4:1–12)

        (1) THE ANGER OF HIS FOES (4:1–7)

          (a) IT WAS FOCUSED (4:1–2)

And as they spake unto the people, the priests, and the captain of the temple, and the Sadducees, came upon them, being grieved that they taught the people, and preached through Jesus the resurrection from the dead.

There was a sudden interruption. The Temple authorities had been watching the growing crowd with increasing apprehension and had caught snatches of Peter's message with growing alarm. The time had come for them to put a stop to it.

We note first how their anger was focused. The lead was taken by the priests and by the Sadducees—the priests because of *where* Peter was preach-ing and the Sadducees because of *what* Peter was preaching.

The captain of the Temple was an important Jewish official. He was a member of one of the families of the chief priests and, in regards to the Temple, was outranked only by the high priest himself. He commanded a guard of handpicked Levites.

The Sadducees were a key Jewish sect in New Testament times. They were aristocratic, wealthy, and influential. The high priest was usually chosen from their ranks. They collaborated with the occupying Roman power, and at this time they dominated the Sanhedrin. In theology they denied the super-natural, the existence of spirits, and the possibility of resurrection.

The Sadducees were the party that now led the nation of Israel in its second rejection of Christ. The rejection of Christ as recorded in the gospels was fomented by the Pharisees; in Acts it was led by the Sadduccess. The Sadduccess found themselves in a particularly vulnerable position. The resurrection of Christ had publicly disproved their liberal theology. Rather than confess themselves wrong, they led in the persecution of the church and spearheaded this second and fatal national rejection of Christ. They hated Christ, hated His very name, hated Him for His resurrection. Their anger was focused on Peter and John, who were publicly preaching Jesus and the resurrection.

Such are most of us when our pet theories are challenged and proved false. Instead of saying "I'm wrong," we tend to dislike intensely those who refute us. The anger of the Sadduccees was focused now on a couple of humble fishermen, former followers of Jesus. It appeared that they would not be hard to crush.

(b) IT WAS FUTILE (4:3–4)

And they laid hands on them, and put them in hold unto the next day; for it was now eventide. Howbeit many of them which heard the word believed; and the number of the men was about five thousand.

It was three o'clock in the afternoon when all this began. Hours had elapsed, and now it was eventide. But what eventful hours! Would that the church could have more such eventful hours. Three thousand were saved at Pentecost—thousands more were now added. Luke, counting only the men (the word he uses excludes women and children) gives us a total of 5,000. The arrest of Peter and John could not stop the Holy Spirit from going on with the work.

Because it was getting late, the authorities locked up the two apostles for the night. All that night news would be coming in of rejoicing among the thousands who had been born again that day. The whole city must have been humming with the news. The story of the healing, excerpts from Peter's sermon, the joy of those who had been so deeply convicted but who were now in the family of God rang through the city. What a stir there must have been.

(c) IT WAS FORMIDABLE (4:5–7)

i. THE QUORUM (4:5–6)

And it came to pass on the morrow, that their rulers, and elders, and scribes, and Annas the high priest, and Caiaphas, and John, and Alexander, and as many as were of the kindred of the high priest, were gathered together at Jerusalem.

This was a gathering of the Sanhedrin. It was convened in the council chamber in a building just west of the Temple precincts at the near end of a bridge that spanned the Tyropoean Valley.

What an impressive crowd it was that gathered there that day to intimidate two Galilean fishermen. Luke's use of the polysyndeton (the repetition of the word "and") draws attention to "each and every one."

The Sanhedrin was composed of seventy-two members—the high priest being the president of the court. The Sadducees, who dominated it, threw their weight on the side of the chief priest. A powerful minority was made up of Pharisees, a party to which most of the scribes (the professional expositors of the law) belonged.

Annas was the previous high priest. He had held the office for nine years, having been installed by Quicinius, the Roman legate of Syria. The fact that he was no longer the high priest made little difference to his power. From the time of his deposition in A.D. 15 until the fall of Jerusalem in A.D. 66, five of his sons, a grandson, and son-in-law occupied the office.

Caiaphas was the son-in-law of Annas. He had been installed by Valerius Gratus, the procurator of Judea, in A.D. 18. Caiaphas had held sway for eighteen years and continued in office all through the period of Pilate's term as procurator.

Just a couple of short months before, that unscrupulous pair had played a leading role in getting rid of Jesus. Now they wanted to get rid of the church.

Little or nothing is known of John and Alexander beyond the assumption they were members of the high priest's clan.

ii. THE QUESTION (4:7)

And when they had set them in the midst, they asked, By what power, or by what name, have ye done this?

And there it was, out in the open, the crux of everything: the question of the *name*. Peter could not have been asked a better leading question. Unwittingly they handed him his text on a silver platter. Thus God makes the wrath of man to praise Him. The anger of Jesus' foes is used to introduce the glory of His Name.

(2) THE ANSWER OF HIS FRIENDS (4:8–12)

(a) ITS POWER (4:8–10)

Then Peter, filled with the Holy Ghost, said unto them, Ye rulers of the people, and elders of Israel, if we this day be examined of the good deed done to the impotent man, by what means he is made whole; be it known unto you all, and to all the people of Israel, that by the name of Jesus Christ of Nazareth, whom ye crucified, whom God raised from the dead, even by him doth this man stand here before you whole.

What boldness! "What have we done wrong? Is it wrong to do something good? Is it not a good deed to make a lame man whole? Are we being arrested and put on trial for doing a good deed? Who made him whole? Jesus did, Jesus Christ, Jesus the Messiah, Jesus of Nazareth. You want to know where the power came from to make a lame man leap? It came from Jesus Christ of Nazareth. That is the Name we used.

"And who is this Jesus of Nazareth? You know well enough who He is. You crucified Him"—that would offend the Pharisees and the two high priests—"God raised Him from the dead" (that would infuriate the Sadducees).

Peter had now put the cat in with the pigeons. This is the same Peter who a couple of months before had trembled before a slip of a girl and denied his Lord with oaths and curses, frightened lest he, too, be arrested and crucified. This new boldness was the result of the resurrection and the filling of the Holy Spirit.

They wanted a name? Peter gave it to them with an added measure of unpalatable truth.

(b) ITS POINT (4:11–12)

Without waiting for the dumbfounded court to reply, Peter went on with his sermon, intent on driving home his point. He had the knife in their consciences now, and he was going to give it three sharp twists. He spoke about:

i. THEIR GUILT (4:11a)

This is the stone which was set at nought of you builders.

They knew the quote well. It was from Psalm 118:22, a recognized messianic prophecy. They had heard this text referred to by Jesus, at the end of His damning parable of the vineyard in which He had so graphically portrayed these "builders" (Mark 12:10). The symbol of a stone for the Christ was too well known to need elaboration. Isaiah had spoken of Christ as "a stone of stumbling" (Isa. 8:14) over which many would fall and be broken. Daniel had visualized the Christ as a stone descended from heaven (Dan. 2:35).

How the members of the Sanhedrin must have writhed at this apt quotation: "*This* is the stone which was set at nought of you builders." Could accusation be sharper?

ii. CHRIST'S GLORY (4:11b)

. . . which is become the head of the corner.

Although they refused to admit it, the resurrection of Christ was a proved fact and common knowledge in Jerusalem. As for Christ's ascension, enough people had witnessed that, too, to make it likewise a matter of general knowledge. Doubtless the Sanhedrin, through its agents and spies, had heard about it. In any case Peter made sure that they heard about it now. This Jesus Christ of Nazareth, whom they crucified, this Stone which they, the builders, had rejected, had become the headstone of the corner. He had ascended to the right hand of the Majesty on high. Could glory be greater?

iii. GOD'S GRACE (4:12)

Now comes one of the greatest gospel texts in the New Testament:

Neither is there salvation in any other; for there is none other name under heaven given among men, whereby we must be saved.

Not the name of Confucius, Buddha, or Allah, not the name of many or any of God's choicest saints. Not the name of Abraham or Moses. Only in the name of Jesus is salvation to be found.

The name of Jesus, by which the lame man had been healed; the name they hated, was the only name by which they could be saved. They could be saved. They *must* be saved. But first they must turn to the very Jesus they had crucified and slain. God would save even them on those terms. Could grace be greater?

Thus Peter extols the glory of His name.

b. THE GREATNESS OF HIS FAME (4:13–22)
(1) THE DILEMMA OF THE RULERS (4:13–16)
(a) WHAT THEY SAW (4:13–14)
i. THE MEN WHO HAD BEEN WITH JESUS (4:13)

Now when they saw the boldness of Peter and John, and perceived that they were unlearned and ignorant men, they marvelled; and they took knowledge of them, that they had been with Jesus.

There was no denying the skillfulness with which Peter had handled the Scriptures. He was far more effective than the rabbis, trained as they were in the subtleties of theological argument. Peter used the Scriptures like a sword to stab through all their defenses and to pierce them to the very heart.

Nor was there any denying the boldness of Peter and John. Everything in their surroundings should have overawed these two peasants. They were standing in the impressive surroundings of the nation's supreme court, facing the nation's richest, ablest, most aristocratic, educated, and powerful men. They were a couple of country bumpkins who should have stood there mumbling apologetically, with shuffling feet and downcast eyes. Instead they looked more like what they really were, ambassadors from the courts of heaven. They stood as those who had an ultimatium to present—surrender or war.

Nor was there any denying the ultimate fact: these men had been with Jesus. They talked as Jesus had talked. No higher compliment could have been paid to these two Spirit-filled men than that. Their enemies identified them with Jesus. They "marvelled." They saw something else; they saw:

ii. THE MAN WHO HAD BEEN BROUGHT TO JESUS (4:14)

And beholding the man which was healed standing with them, they could say nothing against it.

There was the lame man—healed. He was still with Peter and John, identifying himself with those who had led him to the Lord. He had done that in praise in the Temple; he would do it in prison, too. He could easily have slipped away in the crowd after being healed, but not he! He wanted to be with the Lord's people.

Now, without saying a word, he added his testimony—the silent, unanswerable testimony of a transformed life.

"Two are better than one," said the Old Testament proverb, "and a threefold cord is not quickly broken" (Eccl. 4:9, 12). All the worldly might and sophistication of the men who constituted the Sanhedrin were confounded by the simple witness of a couple of Galilean fishermen and a Jerusalem beggar. Thus God uses the weak things to confound the mighty.

Such was the dilemma of the rulers. They had expected an easy victory over these nobodies. Instead of nobodies they had been confronted with the Holy Spirit living in the hearts of three of heaven's somebodies.

(b) WHAT THEY SAID (4:15–16)

But when they had commanded them to go aside out of the council, they conferred among themselves, saying, What shall we do to these men? for that indeed a notable miracle hath been done by them is manifest to all them that dwell in Jerusalem; and we cannot deny it.

There it was, out in the open. The miracle was the talk of the town. Everybody in Jerusalem knew that particular beggar. He had occupied the prime begging concession in Jerusalem. He had been there, right where everyone passed going in and out of the Temple, for years. Now he was whole, and his healing was publicly linked with the name of Jesus, the One this very same body of men had sought to silence forever.

The simplest thing would have been to deny that the man had been healed, but that was patently impossible.

This lame man had begged at the Beautiful Gate for a long time, and Jesus must have passed him on numerous occasions. He had healed others. But though other lame men had been made to walk, Jesus had made no attempt to heal this particular lame man. Now the whole world knew why. It had not been God's time. This man was to be healed later by the *risen* Christ, through a member of His Body, for the greater glory of God. What a light that sheds on the mystery of God's providential dealings with the sons of men.

(2) THE DECISION OF THE RULERS (4:17–22)

(a) IT WAS DESPOTIC (4:17–18)

i. THEIR OPPOSITION TO THE SALVATION OF GOD (4:17a)

But that it spread no further among the people, let us straitly threaten them . . .

Threats that would have swiftly cowed Peter at one time frighten him no more. Peter filled with the Holy Spirit was a different person from Peter filled with his own good resolutions.

Satan always resorts to force when other methods fail. The great concern of the Sanhedrin was not to get to the truth but to stop the truth from spreading. Peter had just preached the truth of salvation to those men. "We must stop it from spreading," they said. How blind! That blindness spelled the doom of the nation. In less than forty years Jerusalem, the Temple, and the nation would feel the full weight of Roman arms and the horror of seige, massacre, and deportation.

Nor could they stop the truth from spreading. Already it had taken wings. Soon groups of believers would be springing up wherever newly convinced and committed believers went.

ii. THEIR OPPOSITION TO THE SON OF GOD (4:17b–18)

. . . that they speak henceforth to no man in this name. And they called them, and commanded them not to speak at all nor teach in the name of Jesus.

Jewish hatred of the name of Jesus has not softened in nearly two thousand years. One has only to read the distortions concerning Christ in books written by some Jewish historians, or see how the name of Jesus is used in novels written by unbelieving Jews, to see that.

Indeed, that is where the attack centers—on the name of Jesus. Satan hates and fears that name and does everything he can to belittle it and blaspheme it. However, the day is coming when every knee in earth and heaven and hell will bow to the name of Jesus and when every tongue will confess Him as Lord.

(b) IT WAS DEFIED (4:19–22)

i. PROMPTLY SO (4:19–20)

But Peter and John answered and said unto them. Whether it be right in the sight of God to hearken unto you more than unto God, judge ye. For we cannot but speak the things which we have seen and heard.

This is the first instance in the New Testament of civil disobedience. If the authorities thought that they could stifle Christianity merely by making it illegal to mention the name of Jesus, they were in for a rude awakening. It was now a question of which authority was to be obeyed—that of the Sanhedrin or that of the Savior.

In the New Testament, governmental authority is always upheld, even when it is despotic. "The powers that be are ordained of God" (Rom. 13:1). That is the rule. "Obey them that have the rule over you" (Heb. 13:17). Jesus taught, "Render unto Caesar the things which are Caesar's," even though the

Caesar be a Tiberius, a Caligula, or a Nero. But He added, "And [render] unto God the things that are God's" (Matt. 22:21).

There are times when Caesar so abuses his power as to command that we do something morally or spiritually wrong. That is where the believer draws the line, even at the cost of imprisonment or death. He firmly but respectfully refuses to bow to the dictates of subordinate human authority in matters where it trespasses on divine authority.

Thus Peter very bluntly tossed the Sanhedrin's mandate back in their faces. He told them to decide for themselves whether they had any moral or spiritual right before God to issue such a command—but in any case believers had no intention of obeying it.

ii. PROPERLY SO (4:21–22)

So when they had further threatened them, they let them go, finding nothing how they might punish them because of the people; for all men glorified God for that which was done. For the man was above forty years old, on whom this miracle of healing was showed.

When Jesus was born this man was a little lad of some seven years, hopelessly crippled, excluded from the fun and games of other boys and girls, unable to help at home, unable even to attend school unless someone should carry him. When Jesus came to Jerusalem as a boy of twelve, this man would have been nineteen or twenty—Jesus, bright-eyed, eager, just entering his teenage years; this man leaving them woefully behind. He had no work, no hopes, no prospects beyond begging. Had he already taken up his place at the Gate Beautiful? Had Jesus looked at him with eyes full of compassion during those days He haunted the Temple precincts? Had He talked to him? Had He said to him, "Cheer up! One day you will be well and whole"?

And, in a moment, through the power of the name of Jesus, he was healed! All Jerusalem knew it and rejoiced and gave God the glory. All Jerusalem except the Sanhedrin.

So we may picture Peter and John leaving the Sanhedrin determined to go on preaching Jesus. On the one hand there were thrills at the glorious power of that lovely name and at the joy that filled Jerusalem; on the other hand there were threats from an evil body of men at present intimidated by the crowd but determined now to pursue a collision course with judgment.

B. THE THREATENING OPPOSITION SCORNED (4:23–27)

1. THE FELLOWSHIP (4:23–30)

a. FELLOWSHIP IN SUFFERING (4:23)

And being let go, they went to their own company, and reported all that the chief priests and elders had said unto them.

The proverb says, "Birds of a feather flock together." "Being let go, they went to their own company," says Luke. Of course they did. We see that principle at work all the time. When restraints are removed we gravitate to our own kind. That is one of the incidental proofs that we love the Lord—we love His people.

Peter and John now related to the whole body of believers the experience of the last few hours—the arrest and arraignment and, above all, the arrogance of the Sanhedrin. The battle lines were now clearly drawn. Perhaps the infant church expected nothing less, but probably the believers had hoped that the whole nation would now repent and receive Christ. It was not to be. In the new fellowship of the Body of Christ if one member rejoiced all rejoiced, so the lame man was received with open arms; if one member suffered all suffered, so the bullying of Peter and John became the bullying of all. It was God's first sovereign move to begin separating the church from Judaism, though of course the first Jewish believers had no inkling of that.

> b. FELLOWSHIP IN SUPPLICATION (4:24–30)
>> (1) PRAISE (4:24–28)
>>> (a) FOR GOD'S OMNIPOTENCE (4:24)

And when they heard that, they lifted up their voice to God with one accord, and said, Lord, thou art God, which has made heaven, and earth, and the sea, and all that in them is.

The whole congregation of believers now gave themselves over to prayer. The first note struck was praise. They praised God for being what He is; omnipotent, the Creator of the universe.

That helped put things into perspective. The Sanhedrin had power; God had almighty power. The Sanhedrin could threaten, but it could not go one step beyond the permissive will of a God who can create suns and stars, seas and shores. We have a God who holds in His hand all the forces of nature, all the factors of space, matter, and time, all the possibilities and eventualities in the universe.

The threats of the Sanhedrin seemed rather weak compared with that— rather like a two-year-old with a plastic toy hammer threatening the village blacksmith.

>>> (b) FOR GOD'S OMNISCIENCE (4:25–28)
>>>> i. IN PROPHETIC FOREKNOWLEDGE (4:25–26)

Who by the mouth of thy servant David hast said, Why did the heathen rage, and the people imagine vain things? The kings of the earth stood up, and the rulers were gathered together against the Lord, and against his Christ.

This is a quotation from Psalm 2, which we recognize as a prophetic and messianic psalm. We would see its final fulfillment at Armageddon; the infant church saw its initial fulfillment at Calvary. Calvary and Armageddon are two critical phases of the world's planned opposition to Christ. They represent the world's attitude to His two comings.

The first time He came, He came in weakness, and God allowed men to do their worst to His Beloved. The next time He will come for war, in all the power of His might. The first time His glory was veiled; the next time it will be displayed in dazzling splendor. The first time they shed His blood; the next time He will shed theirs. Both times the world's opposition is organized, official, and determined.

God was not taken by surprise by Calvary. David (and many others) foretold it. The world's opposition to God's Son was foreseen and predicted. The title nailed to the cross proclaiming Jesus of Nazareth to be the king of the Jews was not only derisive, it was inclusive. It was written in Greek, the language of this world's culture; in Latin, the language of this world's power; and in Hebrew, the language of this world's only revealed religion. The whole world endorsed the crime of Calvary.

ii. IN PROPHETIC FULFILLMENT (4:27–28)

For of a truth against thy holy child Jesus, whom thou hast anointed, both Herod, and Pontius Pilate, with the Gentiles, and the people of Israel, were gathered together, for to do whatsoever thy hand and thy counsel determined before to be done.

This is in keeping with the previous affirmation that God was omnipotent, Creator of all things. Now He is affirmed to be omniscient as well, aware of all that would happen if His "holy child Jesus" were to live on this rebel planet Earth. The description of Jesus as God's "Holy Child" pictures Him as seemingly helpless in the hands of brutal men. It is a title that aggravates the wickedness done to Him.

The culpability of the whole human race is mentioned. There was *individual guilt*—"both Herod, and Pontius Pilate." Herod Antipas, who was a king of the Jews, mocked Jesus; Pontius Pilate, a Gentile ruler, murdered Jesus. Herod scorned Him because he was angry; Pilate sentenced Him because he was afraid. The motive for rejecting Christ is different, the result is the same. There was *corporate guilt*—"the Gentiles, and the people of Israel." Pilate and the soldiers who executed his sentence represented the whole Gentile world; the people of Israel were represented by their leaders and by the mob that howled for the death of Jesus and that gathered at Golgotha to watch Him die.

Thus Psalm 2 had its initial fulfillment. The world united against that "holy child Jesus." We see that "holy child" in Gethsemane crying, "Abba, Father" (Matt. 14:36), *Abba* being an Aramaic word, the word of an infant—we would use the word "daddy" to convey its meaning. Was ever a sight so sad? Heaven's Beloved, weeping His heart out in the lonely darkness of that garden, gazing in "sore amaze" (14:33) into the depths of the cup being offered to Him and crying, "Daddy!" That was the holy child Jesus. Later, on the cross, again in the dark, there rang out that dreadful cry, "My God, my God, why hast thou forsaken me?" (15:34). That was Emmanuel's orphan cry. There He hung, God's "holy child Jesus," with the whole world united against Him.

At the same time, although not for one moment absolving men of their guilt, it was all done in accordance with a plan worked out in eternity—"to do whatsoever thy hand and thy counsel determined before to be done." It was all foreknown and foretold. God turned that horrible scaffold upon which men murdered their Maker into a stage upon which He demonstrated the wonder of His saving grace. Well might we sing with George Bennard:

> In the old rugged cross
> Stained with blood so divine,
> A wondrous attraction I see;
> For 'twas on that old cross
> Jesus suffered and died
> To pardon and sanctify me.

> ("The Old Rugged Cross")

Thus God converted that gallows into a means of grace, so that the cross that meant a horrible death to Jesus now means life everlasting to us.

(2) PRAYER (4:29–30)

(a) THE DANGER (4:29a)

And now, Lord, behold their threatenings.

Praise gave way to prayer. The Sanhedrin's threats were real. Because they had murdered Jesus, might they not also massacre them? The future loomed black with visions of imprisonment, beating, stoning, and crucifixion. It was no use denying those possibilities, just because of the omnipotence and omniscience of God. Jesus had warned them, "In the world ye shall have tribulation" (John 16:33). A world that had crucified Him was not likely to coddle them.

(b) THE DESIRE (4:29b–30)

i. FOR COURAGE (4:29b)

And grant unto thy servants, that with all boldness they may speak thy word.

The danger did not lie with the Sanhedrin but with self. The subject of their prayer was not the force the enemy could muster but the fear they had to master. They did not expect the power of the Sanhedrin to go away, and they did not ask for some miraculous intervention to deal with the armed might of the foe. They did not even pray for the conversion of those blind and guilty men. They simply asked God to give them courage to carry on with the task of telling abroad the tidings of the gospel.

ii. FOR CONFIRMATION (4:30)

By stretching forth thine hand to heal; and that signs and wonders may be done by the name of the holy child Jesus.

The second thing they desired was that their testimony be accompanied by "signs," that is, by the evident blessing of God. They were jealous for the honor of the name of Jesus.

The apostolic gift included the gift of healing and the gift of miracles. Those sign gifts were especially relevant when the church was still in its infancy, when its testimony was primarily to the Jews, and when it needed such special accrediting from on high. So in the very early days the sign gifts were much in evidence. As time wore on, even in the apostolic age, they became much less prominent. By the end of the apostolic age, with the witness of the church fully established and with the New Testament Scriptures complete, the sign gifts seem to have disappeared. That does not mean, of course, that God no longer heals in answer to prayer or that God no longer works miracles when His people seek His face. Such an assertion would be foolish, for God is "the same yesterday, and to-day, and for ever" (Heb. 13:8). His ear is not heavy that it cannot hear, nor is His arm shortened that it cannot save. It is not that healing and miracles have ceased; it is that the *gift* of healing and the *gift* of performing miracles has ceased; the sign gifts have ceased. Miracles and healings continue, though now, for the most part, they are of a spiritual rather than of a physical nature.

Such, then, was the prayer. We see the believers gathered together in the fellowship of the Body of Christ, sharing in all that had happened, wholly one in Christ.

2. THE FILLING (4:31)

a. THE SPECTACULAR SIGN (4:31a)

And when they had prayed, the place was shaken where they were assembled together.

The answer to their prayer was instantaneous. The Holy Spirit was present in power, and the whole meeting place shook. The shaking of that house was symbolic of the shaking now taking place in the house of Israel. The whole nation trembled on the brink of a Millennium or an Armageddon. Old ideas, systems, theologies, prejudices, and power structures in Israel were being shaken to the very foundations by the proclamation of the name of

Jesus. Many were fleeing to God's new house, the church. Others were determined to shore up the tottering old house at all costs. One only has to look at the Talmud and at rabbinic Judaism to see how they did it (see John Phillips, *Exploring the World of the Jew* [Chicago: Moody, 1981]). When the old house collapsed with the destruction of the Temple, they built another in which ritual law was replaced by rabbinic law and from which Christ was to be permanently excluded.

b. THE SPIRITUAL SIGN (4:31b)

And they were all filled with the Holy Ghost, and they spake the word of God with boldness.

No mention is made of tongues in connection with this filling of the Spirit. Indeed, tongues are rarely mentioned in Acts at all (except on several key occasions) and only once outside the book of Acts. The filling of the Spirit is to enable us to speak the Word of God with boldness under the controlling influence of the Holy Spirit Himself.

Again there was an instantaneous answer to prayer. They prayed for boldness to speak the Word; it was given at once. We need never doubt that such a prayer will be given top priority in heaven.

3. THE FAMILY (4:32–37)

a. ITS MYSTICAL ONENESS (4:32)

And the multitude of them that believed were of one heart and of one soul; neither said any of them that aught of the things he possessed was his own; but they had all things common.

Here was the kind of ecumenical movement God had in mind for His church, the kind of oneness for which Jesus prayed (John 17). It existed only for a very brief time. The visible church was not exempt from the law of deterioration and decline, which affects all things in this world of sin. Soon divisions would come, strong personalities would attract a following, jealousies would divide, false teaching would force separations. Never again would the church be so unanimously united in heart and soul. Certainly no man-made ecumenical formulas and organizations can produce such unity. It has to be of the heart. Movements based on compromise of essential doctrine and on administrative machinery might well produce a world church, but it will be a harlot church, not the bride of Christ.

For the moment, however, the church was one. The love and unity was soon seen spilling over into a sharing of everything.

We must remember that this was devotion, not doctrine, at work. Nowhere in the epistles is this kind of Christian commonwealth advocated as a rule of faith and practice. It was unique to the Jerusalem church at a golden moment in time. Soon the fires of mutual love and concern would die down, and Paul would have to be begging in his Gentile churches for money for "the poor saints which are at Jerusalem" (Rom. 15:26).

From time to time similar experiments have been made by Christian communities, often in times of persecution. They flourish for a while, but when the original impetus is spent, they fade away.

b. ITS MINISTERIAL ONENESS (4:33)

And with great power gave the apostles witness of the resurrection of the Lord Jesus: and great grace was upon them all.

Far from silencing the apostles, the action of the Sanhedrin only spurred them on. It drove them to their knees, and the Holy Spirit drove them to their feet. Grace and power flowed through them. No foe could daunt them, no fear could haunt them. And it was the resurrection they preached. *Historically* it was undeniable and unprecedented. There had been nothing like it in all of the long annals of time. It was the most awesome demonstration of Divine power to be exhibited on the planet since the Fall of man. The fact that it irritated the Sadducees was of no importance at all. *Theologically* it was the very essence of the new faith. It authenticated the message of the church, vindicated all the claims of Christ, and demonstrated that salvation was complete and that the new faith was not some idle religious ideal but a solid and glorious reality. *Apologetically* it was unanswerable. The only answer the enemies of Christ could employ was violence. After all, as Paul later said to King Agrippa, "This thing was not done in a corner" (Acts 26:26).

c. ITS MATERIAL ONENESS (4:34–37)

(1) SPONTANEOUS EXPRESSION OF THAT ONENESS (4:34–35)

Neither was there any among them that lacked: for as many as were possessors of lands or houses sold them, and brought the prices of the things that were sold, and laid them down at the apostles' feet: and distribution was made unto every man according as he had need.

This is the basic philosophy of Communism, and a noble ideal it is in many ways. But Communism breaks down because of the selfishness of the human heart and because it is administered by ambitious men intoxicated with power and enforced by the ruthless application of raw power.

Here we see the real thing at work. The motivation was Christian love—the manifestation a common, voluntary sharing. There has never been such a visible demonstration of the oneness of the Body of Christ. The whole Christian community was intoxicated with the love of Christ. The mutual care, concern, and compassion was a miracle of grace. What a company it must have been! No wonder so many wanted to become part of it. This is a lonely world, especially for the old, the infirm, the weak, the poor. Here was a company that cared. People flocked to it. No laws were passed by the apostles making such sharing mandatory. That would have converted Christianity into a religion. The only principle that operated was love. There had to be a spontaneous expression of that love. We would do well in our own church fellowships today to recapture some of this sharing, caring spirit.

(2) A SPECIFIC EXAMPLE OF THAT ONENESS (4:36– 37)

And Joseph, who by the apostles was surnamed Barnabas, (which is, being interpreted, the son of consolation,) a Levite, of the country of Cyprus, having land, sold it, and brought the money, and laid it at the apostles' feet.

We are going to hear more of this man. He was a Cypriot Jew, one of the Dispersion. He was a Levite, from a family in Israel devoted to the handling of sacred things. According to the Mosaic law, Levites were not supposed to hold property, but were to live off the freewill offerings of the tribes. They were to live by faith. What law could not do, love did. Joseph Barnabas, constrained by the love of Christ, sold his property and put the proceeds at the apostles' feet.

Barnabas, who had relatives in Jerusalem (Acts 12:12; Col. 4:10), had already attracted the attention of the apostles. The name means either Son of Consolation, which would indicate something of the man's *grace*, or it means Son of Exhortation, which would indicate something of this man's *gift*—he had the gift of prophecy. Perhaps the vagueness is deliberate. From what we learn later of this man, he was both a son of consolation and a son of exhortation. Grace and gift were well wedded in his soul.

III. TREACHERY (5:1–42)

A. THE SPIRITUAL ATMOSPHERE OF THE CHURCH (5:1–10)

1. THE SATAN-INSPIRED DECEPTION (5:1–2)

a. WHAT THE CULPRITS DECIDED (5:1–2a)

But a certain man named Ananias, with Sapphira his wife, sold a possession, and kept back part of the price, his wife also [knowing of] it.

The "buts" in the Bible are the hinges on which great doors swing. They always mark a decisive change in the story. Thus far the church triumphant had been marching forward in victory. Satan was unable to conquer it, so next tried to corrupt it. He used that tactic with Balaam and with Achan. He used it on Samson, on David, and on Solomon. He used it again, with devastating results, when Constantine embraced Christianity and made it a state religion.

No doubt Ananias and Sapphira wanted to bask in some of the glow that surrounded Barnabas. They too had property; they too sold it. But then came that fateful family conference. They decided to keep back part of the price. Little did they realize the cost of that decision. Their conversation was overheard in heaven, as all such conversations are.

b. WHAT THE CULPRITS DID (5:2b)

And brought a certain part, and laid it at the apostles' feet.

So far so good. They still had time and opportunity to explain. "Peter, this is just a percentage of the price. We did not feel we could give it all." The Holy Spirit wants our all; He will use, however, whatever we give. But He will not be party to pretense. For us to pretend that we are more holy, more dedicated, more spiritual than we are is an offense to Him. "Ye shall be holy; for I am holy" (Lev. 11:44) was the great edict of the law. Peter later quoted that command in his first epistle—doubtless with the memory of Ananias and Sapphira in his mind.

It was, then, Satan-inspired deception. The serpent had once again entered the Garden of Eden, and Ananias and Sapphira had eaten of the forbidden fruit. The love of money became the root of all evil.

It was amazing how often it has been so. It was love of money that inspired Simon Magus to make his wicked overture to Peter, that motivated Elymas the sorcerer, that led to the persecution of the missionaries at Philippi and again at Ephesus, that gripped the sordid soul of Felix, and that ruined the church at Laodicea. It was love of money that turned Judas into a traitor, Gehazi into a leper, and Achan into a deadly hindrance to Israel. Let us beware of the *love* of money. Money itself is not evil; it is very useful. It was the love of money that did the damage here.

2. THE SPIRIT-INSPIRED DETECTION (5:3–10)

a. THE FIRST EXPOSURE (5:3–6)

(1) THE SOURCE OF THE WICKEDNESS (5:3)

But Peter said, Ananias, why hath Satan filled thine heart to lie to the Holy Ghost, and to keep back part of the price of the land?

It came like a thunderbolt. The Holy Spirit knew all about the trick. He had been present in their home, had heard their conversation, knew the market price of that property, knew all about their conspiracy. He was there when the land was put up for sale; there when the bargain was struck; there when the deed of sale was signed. He knew how much was paid for the property, and He was present when the bank deposit was made. He knew how much the conniving couple had decided to give and how much was still in the bank. He was present when Ananias kissed his wife good-bye that morning. He saw the knowing look that passed between them. He walked beside Ananias all the way to the church, prodding his conscience, troubling his soul. He stood sadly and silently by as the deception was consummated, and

Ananias gave his gift. Then He flashed the whole lying picture into unsuspecting Peter's mind, gave him an instantaneous gift of discernment, and told him what to do.

How inexpressibly solemn! How easily we forget that the Lord God, the Holy Spirit, knows all the mundane details of our lives.

(2) THE SUBSTANCE OF THE WICKEDNESS (5:4*a*)

While it remained, was it not thine own? and after it was sold, was it not in thine own power? why hast thou conceived this thing in thine heart?

That was it. Ananias was under no obligation to give. No pressure was brought to bear upon him. He was a free agent. He did not have to sell his property, and once it was sold he was under no constraint to give his money to the Lord's work. He was free to keep it all, give part of it, or give it all. No pledges had been signed. God is as great a respecter of our property as He is of our persons. He covets no man's money. What is not freely given out of a spirit of generosity and integrity, He neither needs nor wants.

(3) THE SERIOUSNESS OF THE WICKEDNESS (5:4*b*–6)

(a) THE SERIOUSNESS DECLARED (5:4*b*)

Thou hast not lied unto men, but unto God.

Sin is always serious. However, its seriousness is always in proportion to the dignity of the person against whom the sin is committed. It is a serious matter to tell a lie; it is more serious to tell a lie to a judge; it is serious beyond words to lie to God.

Deception was at the root of Ananias's sin. The idiom of Satan's language is the lie, deception his stock in trade. This first attack on the church from within was in keeping with his character and his method. It was by deception he conquered Eve. But his lies cannot live even for an instant in the presence of God. All of a sudden this act of treachery was not only exposed as high treason against God, but it appeared cheap and tawdry as well.

(b) THE SERIOUSNESS DEMONSTRATED (5:5–6)

And Ananias hearing these words fell down, and gave up the ghost: and great fear came on all them that heard these things. And the young men arose, wound him up, and carried him out, and buried him.

"Thou hast . . . lied . . . unto God!" Those were the last words Ananias ever heard on earth. As Peter spoke, Ananias dropped dead where he stood. Not a penny of his purloined money did he ever spend.

A wholesome fear gripped the whole community. What heart-searching must have followed, what inner conviction, what inner examination of motives. Word of what had happened spread swiftly through the fellowship of the Lord's people and throughout the city. The Holy Spirit had acted swiftly. He had done something the Lord Jesus had never done. He had struck down a human being in judgment. It was a warning. It was one of those occasions when God makes an example out of a case in order to fully reveal what He thinks of a matter. It was thus He struck down Sodom and Gomorrha for their sins, smote Uzzah, smote King Uzziah and King Jeroboam. It is a good thing God does not so smite every case. God exercises patience and grace in the face of much human sin. However, from time to time He makes a summary example to remind us that He *is* holy. Most of us have some of Ananias about us—the desire to be thought better or more holy or more spiritual than we are.

b. THE FURTHER EXPOSURE (5:7–10)

(1) SAPPHIRA'S FALSE CONFIDENCE (5:7–8)

(a) HER DREADFUL IGNORANCE (5:7)

And it was about the space of three hours after, when his wife, not knowing what was done, came in.

We can picture the sudden tension. Sapphira had been about her business, cleaning up her home, perhaps, visiting with some friends, doing her shopping. Three hours had passed. Her husband was dead, and the young men had just finished burying him and were on their way back, and Peter had had time to think through what had just happened. He took a very serious view of the matter, for he had no doubt that God had acted in judgment upon one of the believers. He knew what he had to do next, and we cannot suppose he relished it. Sapphira's name means "beautiful," and if she lived up to her name it must have been even more unpleasant for Peter.

Now she was coming. Peter heard her pass the time of day with those present as she entered, all unaware of her sudden, awful widowhood—unaware, too, of the tension all about her, the restraint in the voices of those to whom she spoke. She was basking in thoughts of smug complacency over the donation she and her husband had just made to the church funds. She probably thought that the looks she was getting were a tribute to their generosity. The atmosphere was pregnant with the coming storm, but Sapphira suspected nothing. In she came, in complete ignorance of what had just happened.

(b) HER DREADFUL INSISTENCE (5:8)

And Peter answered unto her, Tell me whether ye sold the land for so much? And she said, Yes, for so much.

This is one of those times when the written word is weaker than the spoken word. One wonders with what tone of voice Peter said that. Impulsive Peter! Did he carefully control his features? Did he use a flat, even tone? One can be sure there was nothing impulsive about this question. He had had three hours to think about it.

And she gave him the lie. The words came out so easily. Was she not even surprised at such a question? Did she not sense that something was wrong? Was she an accomplished liar? Or was this the answer of desperation as she suddenly detected the subtle change in the atmosphere but determined to be loyal to Ananias and the story upon which they had agreed?

Whatever the reason, the lie rang out in the room, as heaven wept and hell laughed.

(2) SAPPHIRA'S FEARFUL CONDEMNATION (5:9–10)

(a) THE NATURE OF HER SIN (5:9a)

Then Peter said unto her, How is it that ye have agreed together to tempt the Spirit of the Lord?

We are not to presume on the grace of God. "Thou shalt not tempt the Lord thy God" (Matt. 4:7)—so said Jesus when Satan urged Him to cast Himself down from the pinnacle of the Temple because God's angels would hold Him up according to a promise of God. We are not to put God to the test. Nor must we put the Holy Spirit in a position where His wisdom and His power war with His mercy and His grace.

Perhaps Ananias and Sapphira did not see their sin in that light when they planned their deception. We rarely see our sin in its true light. We have pretty euphemisms for it, clever rationalizations, light-hearted ways to diminish its seriousness and consequences. Peter put their sin in its true light as sin against the Spirit of God. That they had deceived him and the church was nothing compared with their sin against God. Thus the nature of sin stands exposed—all sin, their sin, our sin. Sin is a serious business.

(b) THE NATURE OF HER SENTENCE (5:9b–10)

Behold, the feet of them which have buried thy husband are at the door, and shall carry thee out. Then she fell down straightway at his feet, and yielded up the ghost: and the young men came in, and found her dead and, carrying her forth, buried her by her husband.

The sentence was death, with no time for repentance. Sapphira stood there, heard the news that her husband was already dead and buried, collapsed on the spot, and died. Within the hour she was in her coffin in the tomb beside her husband.

The story of Ananias and Sapphira was over. The church had purged itself of sin. The measures it took were drastic but effective. "A little leaven leaveneth the whole lump" (Gal. 5:9). The infant church rid itself of that leaven the moment it was introduced into the loaf, but it would be insinuated back in again before the church had grown much older. For now, however, it was clean. The Holy Spirit had acted in judgment; He could now act again in blessing.

B. THE SPECTACULAR ATTENDANCE OF THE CHURCH (5:11–16)

1. ITS ABSOLUTE PURITY (5:11–13)

And great fear came upon all the church, and upon as many as heard these things. And by the hands of the apostles were many signs and wonders wrought among the people; and they were all of one accord in Solomon's porch. And of the rest durst no man join himself to them: but the people magnified them.

The news of what had happened spread quickly through the Christian community and throughout the city. Here was an unrecognized dimension. The church was not only a happy place, a place where one could learn of sins forgiven and peace with God, where people could gather to sing and share all things in common. It was also a holy place. Let people beware.

According to some authorities, this is the first mention of the church in the Greek text. The word itself has both a Gentile and a Jewish ancestry. To the Greeks *ecclesia* described an assembly of citizens in a Greek city (Acts 19:32, 39, 41). In the Septuagint, the Greek translation of the Hebrew Scriptures, it was used to denote "the congregation of the Lord," the Jewish nation in its religious character. In the early church the word was used to describe "the called-out ones," the community of believers in the Lord Jesus. The judgment of Ananias and Sapphira reinforced the concept of the separated nature of the believers.

The ungrieved Holy Spirit now gave further evidence of His grace. It was no part of His sovereignty to frighten people away from the gatherings of God's people. A fresh outbreak of miracles proved that. What a place Solomon's porch must have been in those days! What enormous crowds must have congregated there!

But just the same, there was a new note of caution. The idly curious, those who simply wanted the fringe benefits of Christianity, kept their distance. The "mixed multitude" that always wants to get what it can from a new movement without making any real commitment to its truths was scared off.

Down through the centuries the church has been greatly weakened and sadly misrepresented by the coming into its ranks of countless multitudes of those who profess to be Christians but who have never been regenerated by the Holy Spirit. The result is what we call Christendom. The Holy Spirit's discipline delayed the process for a while, and He had exemplified the fact that the church can enjoy His presence in power only if it exercises self-discipline and keeps itself pure. Very rarely, any more, does a local church act in discipline against moral and doctrinal evils in its midst. It has no power because the world looks at church members and sees no difference between them and itself. So, instead of making an impact on society, the church is ignored and treated as of no account.

2. ITS ABUNDANT PROGRESS (5:14)

And believers were the more added to the Lord, multitudes both of men and women.

This is another of those progress reports we find scattered throughout the book of Acts. What a success story was being written! In heaven the Lord could see that the anguish of Calvary was bringing souls to new birth. An ungrieved Holy Spirit was doing His work unhindered and unhampered, and souls were being saved.

Nor has He changed. His work on earth is vast. It is carried on in all parts of the world by a multitude of believers. Every day He adds new souls to the church. If we could see that vast work as heaven sees it, we would be encouraged. The Holy Spirit is at work. If He is not working thus in our midst, perhaps there is sin somewhere that is choking the channel.

3. ITS APOSTOLIC POWER (5:15–16)

Inasmuch that they brought forth the sick into the streets, and laid them on beds and couches, that at the least the shadow of Peter passing by might overshadow some of them. There came also a multitude out of the cities round about unto Jerusalem, bringing sick folks, and them which were vexed with unclean spirits: and they were healed every one.

It reads just like the story of Jesus all over again, like a paragraph out of the gospels. This was God proving to Israel that the church was indeed the mystical Body of Christ and that the apostles were His accredited messengers. "The Jews require a sign" (1. Cor. 1:22), says Paul. Well, signs enough were being given.

The news spread far and wide. Huge crowds gathered from all around the city and from the surrounding communities. Peter's shadow was as much an instrument of the Spirit's power as the hem of His garment had been an instrument of the Savior's power. The apostolic gift of healing and miracles is no longer with the church because the need for it has passed. The poor, the sick, the tormented are still here indeed, and God still answers prayer. From time to time God does work a miracle, does heal the sick, does free a demented soul. But the gift of miracles has gone with the apostles because it was a transitional gift and directed specifically to Israel.

What then of those today who claim to have the gift of healing? Take away the psychosomatic healings, the outright chicanery, the showmanship, the deliberate Satanic deception, and the money to be made, and little if anything is left. We would be much more impressed if these "healers" would walk the wards of our hospitals and cure the sick folk there with such evident demonstrations of power that the whole medical world would stand back awed and amazed. "They were healed every one," says Luke. That was apolostic healing.

C. THE SUDDEN ATTACK UPON THE CHURCH (5:17–22)

1. AN INEFFECTIVE DETENTION (5:17–26)

a. THE APOSTLES ARE FETTERED (5:17–18)

(1) WHY THEY WERE IMPRISONED (5:17)

Then the high priest rose up, and all they that were with him, (which is the sect of the Saduccees), and were filled with indignation.

Imagine the high priest, supposedly the spiritual leader of Israel, infuriated because sick people were being healed and because Satan's hold over peoples' lives was being broken. Truly no hatred is like religious hatred.

The Holy Spirit was giving the leaders of Israel the signs they always craved, and the response was fury. Truly the nation was ripe for judgment. Nor was this simply the high priest. This was the entire Sadduccean leadership of the Sanhedrin. Nor was it just personal spite. It was organized, deliberate opposition to the truth and grace of God.

(2) WHERE THEY WERE IMPRISONED (5:18)

And laid their hands on the apostles, and put them in the common prison.

They were now treated like common felons and locked up overnight. On the morrow the Sadducees intended to take more severe measures to put an end to the new movement. They had its leaders now, safely under lock and key in Jerusalem prison.

b. THE APOSTLES ARE FREED (5:19–21a)

(1) DELIBERATELY—BY A MIRACLE (5:19)

But the angel of the Lord by night opened the prison doors, and brought them forth . . .

This was a clear case of divine intervention. Some have suggested the apostles were set free by a messenger (the same Greek word as "angel"), that this was some kind of an inside job. But there seems to be no valid ground for doubting that it was a genuine miracle, that the apostles were set free by an angel—especially in light of Peter's later experience recorded in chapter 12.

The whole transitional period was packed with supernatural happenings. God was accrediting His church to the Jewish people. The miraculous release of the prisoners was one more hammer blow at the conscience of such of the Sanhedrin as would listen. The Sadducees, who were now taking the lead in opposing Christianity, denied the supernatural. What could be more fitting than that the Holy Spirit should force them to confront it? Sadly, many were quite willing to rationalize even these multiplied and manifest miracles. If they could explain away the resurrection of Christ, no doubt they could rationalize this escape, too.

(2) DESIGNEDLY—FOR A MINISTRY (5:20–21*a*)

[The angel said,] Go, stand and speak in the temple to the people all the words of this life. And when they heard that they entered into the temple early in the morning, and taught.

The apostles had not been liberated by the angel in order to flee but so they could preach. Back they were sent to the Temple, to the place where they had been arrested.

(c) THE APOSTLES ARE FOUND (5:21*b*–25)

(1) THE ASSEMBLING OF THE SANHEDRIN (5:21*b*)

But the high priest came, and they that were with him, and called the council together, and all the senate of the children of Israel, and sent to the prison to have them brought.

Quite unaware of what had happened, Caiaphas called a special session of the Sanhedrin. He surrounded himself with members of his own party, men who were with him. Having thus marshaled his forces, he was ready to insist that firmer steps be taken against the ringleaders of the objectionable cult. It was time to make good on the threats they had hurled at Peter and John.

We can picture the men assembling. There would be the usual greetings between acquaintances: "Shalom, Ananias!" "Shalom, Caiaphas!" There would be the usual buzz of small talk, the normal coming together here and there of little groups, all eagerly discussing the miracles of the past few days and their connection with Jesus of Nazareth. Doubtless many shades of opinion would be freely aired between friends. Now that the arrest had been made, however, it was time to take sides once and for all. Many a glance would be directed at wise old Gamaliel.

The gathering was called to order, and, as the various members took their seats, the officers were sent to bring the prisoners. While awaiting their arrival, views were no doubt aired about the momentous decision about to be made.

(2) THE ASTONISHMENT OF THE SANHEDRIN (5:22–25)

(a) THEIR DISMAY (5:22–23)

But when the officers came, and found them not in the prison, they returned, and told, saying, The prison truly found we shut with all safety, and the keepers standing without before the doors: but when we had opened, we found no man within.

The cage was still locked and guarded, but the birds had flown. Naturally the officers of the Sanhedrin would have conducted an immediate though doubtless cursory examination of the locks, the guards, and the premises to see if there was any explanation. The surprise of the guards would have been as great as that of the officials. There would be no doubting the genuineness of their astonishment. The prison was empty. A dozen men had gone, and nobody knew where they were. There was nothing for it but to go back emptyhanded to the Sanhedrin and make the unwelcome report.

(b) THEIR DOUBTS (5:24)

Now when the high priest and the captain of the temple and the chief priests heard these things, they [were perplexed concerning them how] this would grow.

Their doubts were not concentrated on the miracle. They had come to the place where there was no further use in denying or doubting miracles. It was an age of miracles; they were happening every day, the whole city was agog at them, and the evidence for them was overwhelming. They would have convinced any but the most stubborn and determined unbelievers.

What these men, the supposed spiritual guides of Israel, doubted, was their ability to put a stop to them and to the spread of Christianity.

That is what Israel had come to. No wonder the lot was now being cast for the inevitable judgment of God, for "a man convinced against his will, is of the same opinion still." That is exactly where the religious leaders of Israel stood. They had opposed John the Baptist, they had crucified Christ, and now they would fight the apostles. They might have doubts as to whether they could win, but they would go down fighting.

(c) THEIR DILEMMA (5:25)

Then came one and told them, saying, Behold, the men whom ye put in prison are standing in the temple, and teaching the people.

Nothing could be worse from the standpoint of the high priest and his crowd. They had made a fatal mistake in rejecting Christ. The resurrection of Christ not only was their indictment, it was a source of acute embarrassment. Those ignorant fishermen, followers of Christ, were doing all the things Jesus had done. They were attracting an enormous following. Threats and imprisonment did not work. They did not dare make martyrs of them by killing them, even if they had sufficient power to make such a clean sweep. And now those men were right back in the Temple, the private preserve of the high priest and his party (or so they presumed), doing the very thing the Sanhedrin had told them not to do.

Such was their dilemma.

d. THE APOSTLES ARE FETCHED (5:26)

Then went the captain with the officers, and brought them without violence: for they feared the people, lest they should have been stoned.

It was a touchy business, and well the arresting officers knew it. If the apostles had been bent on resisting arrest, an ugly riot could easily have been sparked. It was no part of Christianity, however, to defy constituted authority except in the one area of proclaiming the gospel.

The Temple police did not know that, however, and handled the arrest with kid gloves.

2. THE INEFFECTIVE DISCUSSION (5:27–39)
a. THE CRIMINAL CHARGE (5:27–28)

And when they had brought them, they set them before the council; and the high priest asked them, saying, Did we not [strictly] command you that ye should not teach in this name? And behold, ye have filled Jerusalem with your doctrine, and intend to bring this man's blood upon us.

That was a guilty conscience speaking. They had already brought that blood upon themselves when they had incited the mob to shout, "His blood be on us, and on our children" (Matt. 27:25). The apostles, however, had no desire to bring the blood of Christ to the door of these men. Their desire was to bring that blood to their hearts, that they might be saved from their sin.

As for their command, it was an unconstitutional violation on their authority. They knew it, and the apostles knew it.

The Sanhedrin was no longer up against unlearned Galilean fishermen; it was up against the Holy Spirit, who was empowering them. The leaders of Israel were now set on their collision course with God's wrath, and nothing could be further from their thoughts than repentance and conversion to the Lord Jesus Christ.

b. THE COUNTER CHALLENGE (5:29–32)
(1) THE QUESTION OF LOYALTY (5:29)

Then Peter and the other apostles answered and said, We ought to obey God rather than men.

There was a higher court in Israel than the Sanhedrin: the Supreme Court of Heaven. The God of heaven had sent His Son into the world; He had sent His Spirit into the world; He had now sent His servants into the world. The Sanhedrin had no authority to forbid them to preach in the name of Jesus. They knew it. The apostles knew it. It was simply a question of loyalty. From the apostles' standpoint, there was no more to be said. They derived their authority from God; let the Sanhedrin bow to that. But John and the others had not finished. They were now going to put the shoe on the other foot and accuse the Sanhedrin. The Sanhedrin had accused them of wanting to bring the blood of Jesus on their heads, but they had already brought it on their own heads.

(2) THE QUESTION OF LIABILITY (5:30–32)

(a) THE TRUTH ABOUT THE CROSS (5:30)

The God of our fathers raised up Jesus, whom ye slew and hanged on a tree.

No greater crime could be imagined than that brought about by the Sanhedrin. They had sinned against "the God of our fathers," the true, living, ancestral God of Israel who had revealed Himself and His purposes in so many ways to the fathers of the nation. Some excuse, perhaps, could be found for the Romans; none could be found for them.

What they had done was criminal—"Whom ye slew and hanged on a tree." The Sanhedrin had taken a sardonic satisfaction in the mode of Christ's death. The law said, "He that is hanged [on a tree] is accursed of God" (Deut. 21:23). They did not know that Christ was deliberately bearing in His body the curse so that blessings might flow. Now, with twisted logic, the Sanhedrin saw the death of Christ by hanging as evidence that He was accursed. Some Jews refer to Jesus still as *Taluy* ("the hanged one").

(b) THE TRUTH ABOUT THE CHRIST (5:31–32)

Him hath God exalted with his right hand to be a Prince and a Saviour, for to give repentance to Israel, and forgiveness of sins. And we are his witnesses of these things, and so is the Holy Ghost, whom God hath given to them that obey him.

Their hatred of Christ was arrant folly. The resurrection proved them wrong. Jesus was both Sovereign and Savior.

A note of wistful pleading now entered the defendants' reply. There was still time for repentance for Israel, but time was running out. This was one of the last chances the Sanhedrin would have to officially reverse its rejection of Christ. Peter warned them that they were now dealing with the Holy Spirit. Moreover, God's message to Israel had passed into new hands. No longer was the Sanhedrin custodian of the truth—the apostles were; no longer was the nation of Israel the depository of God's message to men—the church was.

But they could be blessed if only they would obey Him.

c. THE CLEAR CHOICE (5:33–39)

(1) MURDER (5:33)

When they heard that, they were cut to the heart, and took council to slay them.

The knife had gone deep. At this point in the Spirit's convicting work, a person either repents or reacts. With the Sanhedrin there was an immediate reaction. How to get rid of the disciples—that was the question. It would call for delicate handling, as had the recent case of Jesus. There was the mob to be considered. A mob could always be manipulated, but this time there were a dozen men to kill, not just one. Moreover, the movement seemed to have taken deep roots.

But murder was an alternative. The fury of the high priest and his supporters was such that it was considered a good, workable solution to the problem.

Although the nation was now trembling on the brink of the precipice, it was to be given one more chance. That chance would not last long. Just two chapters later we see these same men, again "cut to the heart" by the unanswerable logic of Stephen, taking the nation to its final plunge.

Just now, however, another voice was heard.

(2) MODERATION (5:34–39)

(a) GAMALIEL'S REPUTATION (5:34)

Then stood up one in the council, a Pharisee, named Gamaliel, a doctor of the law, had in reputation among all the people, and commanded to put the apostles forth a little space.

To muster sufficient votes for a death sentence, the high priest needed the support of the Pharisees on the court.

The Pharisees constantly found themselves in opposition to the Sadducees. The Sadducees were the liberal theologians of the day, given to Hellenizing Jewish life; the Pharisees commanded the loyalty of the scribes, the popular teachers of the law, most of whom belonged to their party. The Pharisees were themselves divided into two chief theological schools, that of Shammai and that of Hillel, whose views were to prevail in the end. Both schools, although giving lip service to the Scriptures, were more concerned with tradition and rabbinical wrangling than with truth. However, it was easier for a Pharisee to become a Christian than for a Sadducee, who had to repudiate his entire liberal theology.

The chief exponent and disciple of the Hillel school in the Sanhedrin at the time was Gamaliel the Elder. As head of the Hillel school he had many disciples of his own, not the least of whom was Saul of Tarsus.

This was the man who now took the floor to lead the Sanhedrin to saner counsel. He ordered the officers to take out the prisoners while he made his own views known.

(b) GAMALIEL'S REASONING (5:35–37)

i. BE WARY (5:35)

And said unto them, Ye men of Israel, take heed to yourselves what ye intend to do as touching these men.

Gamaliel, at least, was not carried away with the clamor. He was as much a Christ-rejector as the rest of them, but he was not about to commit a rash act in the heat of passion. His chief concern was to cool the hot tempers that were now controlling the Sanhedrin. It was all very well to vote for a clean sweep of the leadership of this new movement, but that was a dangerous course. Who could tell what the next miracle might be? Who could predict the reaction of the mob? Who could ensure the acquiescence of the Romans? Who could be sure that that solution might not invite disaster?

i. BE WISE (5:36–37)

For before these days rose up Theudas, boasting himself to be somebody; to whom a number of men, about four hundred, joined themselves: who was slain; and all, as many as obeyed him, were scattered, and brought to nought. After this man rose up Judas of Galilee in the days of the taxing, and drew away much people after him: he also perished; and all, even as many as obeyed him, were dispersed.

Nothing is known for certain about the first of these insurrectionists, Theudas. We do know that when the detested Herod the Great died in 4 B.C., numerous would-be liberators surfaced in Palestine, and Theudas might have been one of them.

More is known about Judas of Galilee, who led a revolt against Rome in A.D. 6 at the time when the Romans reduced Judea to the status of a Roman province. Publius Sulpicius Quirinius in A.D. 6–7 ordered a census to determine how much money the new province of Judea could be expected to contribute to the imperial coffers. (This is not the same census Luke records [2:2], which was imposed by Caesar Augustus at the time of Christ's birth, at the time when Quirinius was governor of Syria.) Judas, from Gamala in Gaulanitis (Golan of the Old Testament), led a revolt against Rome that was crushed. The rallying call of Judas was that, because God was Israel's King, it was high treason to pay tribute to Caesar. Although the Romans crushed the revolt, the movement lived on in the party of the Zealots. Gamaliel seems to have played down the whole thing in this speech.

(c) GAMALIEL'S RESTRAINT (5:38–39)

i. WHAT HE CONSIDERED A PROBABILITY (5:38)

And now I say unto you, Refrain from these men, and let them alone: for if this counsel or this work be of men, it will come to nought.

That seems to have been Gamaliel's personal view. Like other recent movements originated by zealous but misguided men, this whole movement would probably come to nothing if they left it alone. It would lose its drive and fade away, or, perhaps, it would go too far, attract the attention of the

Romans, and be forcibly repressed, as had happened on the two occasions he gave as his examples. In any case, it would be best for the Sanhedrin not to get involved. Let time or Rome take care of it.

i. WHAT HE CONSIDERED A POSSIBILITY (5:39)

But if it be of God, ye cannot overthrow it; lest haply ye be found even to fight against God.

It was a sane and sobering reminder, the last one the Sanhedrin was to get, of the possibility that this new movement *was* of God. How else could they account for the miracles of Jesus, for His resurrection, for the miracles now being performed by those illiterate Galilean peasants? The implications in this line of reasoning were so revolutionary that Gamaliel himself shied away from it. Still the possibility was there. Let them beware. Let them be wise.

3. THE INEFFECTIVE DISSUASION (5:40-42)

a. PUNISHMENT (5:40)

And to him they agreed: and when they had called the apostles, and beaten them, they commanded that they should not speak in the name of Jesus, and let them go.

The law of Moses permitted flogging—"forty stripes save one" was the usual formula (based on Deut. 25:3). So the Sanhedrin vented its spite and asserted its power by giving each of the apostles a thrashing accompanied by the useless warning to desist from further mention of the name of Jesus.

b. PRAISE (5:41)

And they departed from the presence of the council, rejoicing that they were counted worthy to suffer shame for his name (or "the name," as some texts have it).

Far from being discouraged or intimidated by their beating, the apostles saw in it a share in Christ's sufferings. Singing and rejoicing, they wended their way back to their own people, thrilled that they had been counted worthy to be persecuted for His name's sake. If any of the Sanhedrin spies reported this reaction to the high priest and his crowd, it must have filled them with further fury, not to mention an overwhelming sense of frustration. What can you do with men who, when you have flogged them, thank God for the favor you have bestowed on them?

c. PROCLAMATION (5:42)

And daily in the temple, and in every house, they ceased not to teach and preach Jesus Christ.

They did it *incessantly.* Every day they spent their time spreading the good news of the gospel. They did it *insistently.* Back they went to the

Temple, for public meetings where the crowds were thickest, and also into every house for private meetings throughout the city. They did it *instructively*. It was Jesus Christ who was the theme of their teaching and preaching.

The Sanhedrin had now lost two rounds in its fight against the church.

Part Three:

The Forward Emphasis: Stephen (6:1—12:25)

I. NEW VOICES (6:1–8:40)

A. The First Ministers (6:1–7)
1. Division (6:1)
   a. Growth (6:1a)
   b. Grievances (6:1b)
2. Addition (6:2–6)
   a. The Meeting (6:2a)
   b. The Motion (6:2b–5a)
      (1) The Motion Proposed (6:2b–4)
         (a) The Priorities (6:2b)
         (b) The Practicalities (6:3)
         (c) The Primacies (6:4)
      (2) The Motion Passed (6:5a)
   c. The Men (6:5b–6)
      (1) Chosen (6:5b)
      (2) Charged (6:6)
3. Multiplication (6:7)
   a. Its Scope (6:7a)
   b. Its Significance (6:7b)
B. The First Martyr (6:8—7:60)
1. Stephen, the Tremendous Worker (6:8– 15)
   a. His Divine Enablement (6:8–14)
      (1) The Wonders He Performed (6:8)
      (2) The Words He Proclaimed (6:9–14)
         (a) How He Engaged His Foes (6:9–10)
         (b) How He Enraged His Foes (6:11–14)
            i. How They Incited the Mob (6:11)
            ii. How They Indicted the Man (6:12–13)

iii. How They Insulted the Master (6:14)

b. His Divine Enoblement (6:15)

2. Stephen, the Truthful Witness (7:1–53)

  a. His Excellent Approach (7:1–8)

    (1) He Talks about Abraham's Faith (7:1–5)

      (a) The Revelation that Was Made to Abraham (7:1–3)

      (b) The Response that Was Made by Abraham (7:4–5)

        i. The Positive Response (7:4)

        ii. The Passive Response (7:5)

    (2) He Talks About Abraham's Future (7:6–8)

      (a) The Government of God (7:6–7)

        i. God's Omniscience (7:6)

        ii. God's Omnipotence (7:7)

      (b) The Grace of God (7:8)

        i. The Covenant Conveyed to the Pilgrim (7:8a)

        ii. The Covenant Confirmed to the Patriarchs (7:8b)

  b. His Extensive Appeal (7:9–50)

    (1) How Israel Had Treated Their Saviors (7:9–36)

      (a) Their Rejection of Joseph, the One Who Settled Them in Egypt (7:9–16)

        i. How Joseph Was Resented (7:9)

        ii. How Joseph Was Raised (7:10)

        iii. How Joseph Was Revealed (7:11–16)

          a. The Famine That Brought Them to Joseph (7:11–12)

          b. The Forgiveness That Bound Them to Joseph (7:13–14)

            1. His Kindness Declared (7:13)

            2. His Kindness Demonstrated (7:14)

          c. The Faith That Blessed Them in Joseph (7:15–16)

      (b) Their Reaction to Moses, the One Who Saved Them from Egypt (7:17–36)

        i. The Fearful Bondage of Israel (7:17–19)

          a. The Time (7:17a)

          b. The Tension (7:17b–18)

          c. The Terror (7:19)

        ii. The Foolish Bigotry of Israel (7:20–28)

          a. The Savior's Birth (7:20)

          b. The Savior's Background (7:21–22)

    c. The Savior's Brethren (7:23–28)
     1. The Manifestation of Moses (7:23–25)
     2. The Mediation of Moses (7:26)
     3. The Misinterpretation of Moses (7:27–28)
   iii. The Further Burdens of Israel (7:29–34)
    a. While Moses Was Learning (7:29)
    b. While Moses Was Looking (7:30–31)
    c. While Moses Was Listening (7:32–34)
     1. To a Living God (7:32–33)
     2. To a Loving God (7:34)
   iv. The Fatal Blindness of Israel (7:35–36)
    a. Moses Had Been Sent to Save Them (7:35)
    b. Moses Had Been Sent to Separate Them (7:36)
  (2) How Israel Had Treated Their Scriptures (7:37–43)
   (a) The Scriptures Delivered to Israel (7:37–38)
    i. A Word About Their Messiah (7:37)
    ii. A Word About Their Mandate (7:38)
     a. Their Gathering (the Church) (7:38*a*)
     b. Their Guide (the Angel) (7:38*b*)
   (b) The Scriptures Disobeyed by Israel (7:39–43)
    i. Their Rebellion Against the Leadership God Gave (7:39–40)
    ii. Their Rebellion Against the Laws God Gave (7:41–43)
     a. Their Initial Apostasy (7:41)
     b. Their Increasing Apostasy (7:42–43)
  (3) How Israel Had Treated Their Sanctuaries (7:44–50)
   (a) The Tabernacle (7:44–45)
    i. Its Heavenly Significance (7:44)
    ii. Its Holy Sojournings (7:45)
   (b) The Temple (7:46–50)
    i. The Builder (7:46–47)
    ii. The Building (7:48–50)
     a. A Cramped Concept of God (7:48)
     b. A Correct Concept of God (7:49–50)
 c. His Explosive Application (7:51–53)
  (1) They Had Accused Him of Reviling the Holy Place—He Accused Them of Resisting the Holy Ghost (7:51)
  (2) They Had Accused Him of Slighting Moses, the Man of God—He Accused Them of Slaying Jesus, the Messiah of God (7:52)

(3) They Had Accused Him of Blaspheming the Law—He Accused Them of Breaking the Law (7:53)

3. Stephen, the Triumphant Warrior (7:54–60)

  a. His Convicting Voice (7:54)

  b. His Complete Vindication (7:55)

  c. His Continuing Valor (7:56–59)

    (1) His Final Testimony (7:56)

    (2) His Final Trial (7:57–58)

      (a) How They Stopped Him (7:57)

      (b) How They Stoned Him (7:58)

    (3) His Final Triumph (7:59)

  d. His Crowning Victory (7:60)

C. The First Missionary (8:1–40)

  1. A New Foe: Emphasis—Persecuted Christians (8:1–4)

    a. The Magnitude of the Persecution (8:1–4)

      (1) Its Focus (8:1–2)

        (a) An Explosion (8:1a)

        (b) An Exception (8:1b)

        (c) An Example (8:2)

      (2) Its Fury (8:3–4)

        (a) The Manner of the Persecution (8:3)

        (b) The Ministry of the Persecution (8:4)

  2. A New Field: Emphasis—Preaching Christ (8:5–25)

    a. Philip's Fruit in the Gospel (8:5–8)

      (1) Revival (8:5–7)

        (a) His Gospel Preaching (8:5)

        (b) His Great Power (8:6–7)

          i. They Were Convicted by What He Said (8:6a)

          ii. They Were Convinced by What They Saw (8:6b–7)

      (2) Rejoicing (8:8)

    b. Philip's Fame in the Gospel (8:9–14)

      (1) Simon Magus Hears the News (8:9–13)

        (a) His Deceptions (8:9)

          i. His Method (8:9a)

          ii. His Motive (8:9b)

        (b) His Disciples (8:10–12)

          i. Why They Followed Him (8:10–11)

          ii. Why They Forsook Him (8:12)

        (c) His Decision (8:13)

(2) Simon Peter Hears the News (8:14)

c. Philip's Fellowship in the Gospel (8:15–25)

    (1) Dispensing the Gift of the Holy Spirit (8:15–17)

        (a) Ending the Historic Isolation of the Samaritans by the Jewish Community (8:15–16)

        (b) Ensuring the Happy Identification of the Samaritans in the Christian Community (8:17)

    (2) Detecting the Guilt of Simon Magus (8:18–24)

        (a) Simon's Conclusions (8:18–19)

            i. What He Discerned (8:18*a*)

            ii. What He Decided (8:18*b*)

            iii. What He Desired (8:19)

        (b) Simon's Condemnation (8:20–23)

            i. Peter's Godly Indignation (8:20)

            ii. Peter's Godly Intuition (8:21)

            iii. Peter's Godly Injunction (8:22)

            iv. Peter's Godly Insight (8:23)

        (c) Simon's Concern (8:24)

    (3) Declaring the Gospel of Jesus Christ (8:25)

3. A New Follower: Emphasis—Personal Contact (8:26–40)

  a. Foreknowledge (8:26–31)

    (1) The Strange Command (8:26)

    (2) The Sacred Cause (8:27–28)

        (a) The Eunuch's Social Status (8:27)

        (b) The Eunuch's Spiritual State (8:28)

    (3) The Strategic Contact (8:29–31)

        (a) The Command (8:29)

        (b) The Compulsion (8:30)

        (c) The Complaint (8:31)

  b. Fact (8:32–35)

    (1) The Text that Engaged the Eunuch (8:32–33)

        (a) The Silence of the Lamb (8:32)

        (b) The Slaughter of the Lamb (8:33)

    (2) The Truth that Eluded the Eunuch (8:34–35)

        (a) The Question Asked (8:34)

        (b) The Question Answered (8:35)

  c. Faith (8:36–38)

    (1) Faith Exercised (8:36)

    (2) Faith Expressed (8:37)

    (3) Faith Exhibited (8:38)

114

    d. Feeling (8:39)
      (1) The Messenger Was Removed from His Sight (8:39a)
      (2) The Message Was Ringing in His Soul (8:39b)
    e. Faithfulness (8:40)

Part Three:

The Forward Emphasis: Stephen (6:1–12:25)

I. NEW VOICES (6:1—8:40)

A. THE FIRST MINISTERS (6:1–7)

1. *DIVISION (6:1)*
   a. GROWTH (6:1*a*)
   And in those days, when the number of the disciples was multiplied . . .
   The consternation of the Sanhedrin was well founded from their point of view. The new movement was growing, and growing rapidly. It was no longer a matter of addition—it was multiplication. People were flocking to the meetings of the church, and great numbers were becoming disciples. Because the chief meeting place was still the Temple court, the evidence of this growth must have been a daily source of frustration to the high priest and his friends.
   Growth and size, however, do not solve all problems. Often the bigger the church, the bigger the problems, something that now proved itself to be the case. Satan again attacked the church from within, and again it was the question of money. This time, however, it involved not just a couple of individuals but a whole segment of the church.
   b. GRIEVANCES (6:1*b*)
   There arose a murmuring of the Grecians against the Hebrews, because their widows were neglected in the daily ministration.
   There were two kinds of Jews within the fold of the church, as there were two kinds in Jewish society in general in those days. There was always a degree of tension between the two groups just as in the State of Israel today there is tension between Ashkenazi Jews and Sephardic Jews. In the New Testament world there were Hellenist Jews and Hebrew Jews. The Hebrews were Aramaic-speaking and mostly native-born Palestinians; the Hellenists were Greek-speaking Jews of the Dispersion, especially of the Greco-Roman

world. The Hebrews tended to be narrow and rigid, with few interests outside their own small world; the Hellenists were generally much more ready to recognize the better features of the great Gentile world beyond the confines of the Promised Land. Tensions between Hebrews and Hellenists went back a long time, to the very beginnings of the Hellenist period, when the brilliant world of Greek thought and culture burst upon the Jews and threatened to destroy Judaism, both with its philosophy and by its persecution.

Now the tension had come into the church. There was great concern for the poor in the early church. Wealthy men like Barnabas often donated their estates to the common fund to help care for such. Widows made up a fairly large segment of the poor. The daily distribution of charity was in the hands of the Hebrew believers. The Hellenist believers, rightly or wrongly, conceived the idea that there was discrimination against their widows. Tension developed and came to a head. Satan's goal was to divide the membership and discourage the leadership, but he was to be foiled by the spirit of wisdom in the apostles.

2. ADDITION (6:2–6)

a. THE MEETING (6:2a)

Then the twelve called the multitude of the disciples unto them . . .

The apostles were determined to nip the thing in the bud. Moreover, although they had the authority to make an arbitrary decision, they wisely chose to involve the whole church in the momentous change now about to be made in the way the affairs of the local church were to be run.

There is no doubt that the local church is to be ruled by its elders. The local church is not a democracy—it is ruled by its Spirit-appointed elders. At the same time, it is not a dictatorship. So here we have the first hint of that happy blending of apostolic authority and congregational activity working towards a united decision—which should characterize all local church affairs.

b. THE MOTION (6:2b–5a)

(1) THE MOTION PROPOSED (6:2b–4)

(a) THE PRIORITIES (6:2b)

And said, It is not reason that we should leave the word of God, and serve tables.

That was plain common sense. There was no point in the apostles doing something anyone could do when they could do things no one else could do. It was not a question of position but of priorities. It was not that the apostles thought it beneath their dignity to run the errands of the church; it was simply a matter of putting first things first. Nobody expects the director of a giant corporation to work in the mailroom. Serving tables was impor-

tant, but the apostles sensibly decided that since they could not do everything, they would concentrate on what they had been called to do—minister
the Word.

(b) THE PRACTICALITIES (6:3)

*Wherefore, brethren, look ye out among you seven men of honest
report, full of the Holy Ghost and wisdom, whom we may appoint over this
business.*

The criterion for public office in the church was not business acumen,
financial success, or organizing ability. Nowadays those are the qualities
many churches would look for. The apostles had other and more significant
criteria. A successful man might not be a spiritual man. On the other hand, a
spiritual man might not be a sensible man. So we note the criteria. A man
successful in business might qualify, but just because a man is wealthy does
not mean he is not spiritual, so the criteria must include other things.

First, he had to be a *good* man. That was of paramount importance. Paul
says that "for a good man some would even dare to die" (Rom. 5:7). He had
to be a man who commanded the love and respect of others because of his
personal integrity and unblemished character, a man who avoided evil and
who devoted himself to the well-being of others. Then, too, he had to be a
godly man "full of the Holy Ghost," and he had to be a *gifted* man, "full of
. . . wisdom." Not all good men and not all godly men are wise. He had to be
a man who made sensible decisions.

These were the practicalities, and they still are. God wants His church to
be served by such men. No man has any right to any church office, however
humble, if he is not qualified for that office by these three criteria. No wonder
the money squabbles in the Jerusalem church came to such a swift end when
"waiting on tables" was handed over to seven such men. It was a sensible
precaution, too, to have seven men, because that divided the work load and
kept money matters above suspicion.

(c) THE PRIMACIES (6:4)

*But we will give ourselves continually to prayer, and to the ministry of
the word.*

All men must pray and all can have a share in the ministry of the Word,
but not all are called to give themselves wholly to such spiritual ministry. The
apostles were. Down through the ages since Pentecost, God has seen to it that
His church has been served by such men, called and equipped by His Holy
Spirit and dedicated to a purely spiritual ministry. It is not a profession into
which one enters as a matter of personal preference, such as the medical or
legal profession. One does not graduate from high school and choose the
church as a profession; one is called to the work by the Holy Spirit.

(2) THE MOTION PASSED (6:5a)

And the saying pleased the whole multitude.

The observation and suggestion of the apostles was so sensible and so fair that it was picked up unanimously by the church as a whole.

   c. THE MEN (6:5b–6)

     (1) CHOSEN (6:5b)

And they chose Stephen, a man full of faith and of the Holy Ghost, and Philip, and Prochorus, and Nicanor, and Timon, and Parmenas, and Nicolas a proselyte of Antioch.

The dispute was between the Hellenists and the Hebrews. The Hellenists had complained of real or imagined discrimination. It is significant that all the deacons now chosen by the people had Hellenist names, the inference being that they were all Greek-speaking Jews. What a tremendous act of grace! It would be comparable in American society to a similar situation arising between blacks and whites in a Southern church—the blacks complaining of discrimination, and the whole church, without hesitation, appointing in all-black board of administrators.

The first mentioned was Stephen, of whom it is said that he was "a man full of faith and of the Holy Ghost." He was to demonstrate that very shortly.

Next was Philip, always to be distinguished from the apostle Philip. We often call Philip the deacon "Philip the evangelist." His evangelistic gifts were soon to be made manifest in the church.

Indeed, these first two men illustrate Paul's comment: "They that have used the office of a deacon [servant] well purchase to themselves a good degree, and great boldness in the faith which is in Christ Jesus" (1 Tim. 3:13). Stephen became the first martyr of the church, and Philip became its first missionary.

Prochorus is not so well known. According to tradition, he became secretary of the apostle John, then bishop of Nicomedia and, ultimately, a martyr.

We know nothing of the next four, which illustrates the general principle that much of the work of God is carried on by unknown, unsung individuals who faithfully carry out the tasks entrusted to them, quite content to leave the limelight to others.

Luke himself adds a note about the last on the list. He tells us that Nicolas was not even Jewish but a proselyte, and that he came from Antioch, a city soon to leap to prominence in the history of the church. Some think Luke was from Antioch. Some of the church Fathers have linked this Nicolas with the cult of the Nicolaitans (Rev. 2:15), which was castigated by the Lord for its compromise with idolatry and immorality. The cult of the Nicolaitans certainly seems to derive its name from "Nicolas." Its chief purpose seems to have been to dilute the decisions made at the Jerusalem Conference (Acts 15:29) in order to make it easier for Christians in a pagan world to meet the requirements and demands imposed by society and the Caesar. It is by no means certain that this chosen deacon had anything to do with that movement; in view of his high reputation in the Jerusalem church it seems unfair to saddle him with such compromise.

(2) CHARGED (6:6)

Whom they set before the apostles: and when they had prayed, they laid their hands on them.

The laying on of hands was a common Jewish practice, as we learn from the Old Testament. When an Israelite brought a sacrifice to the altar, he was required to identify himself with his offering by laying his hands on its head (Lev. 1:4). The apostles thus formally identified themselves with these delegates in this familiar way. In so doing they imparted no special gift, unction, or ability—the seven already had all they needed for their work. They simply gave them public accreditation to function on their behalf and on behalf of the whole church. Thus Satan's attempt to discourage the leadership and divide the membership failed. The leaders were more encouraged than ever because they now had more time to devote to the more spiritual side of the work, and the members were more united than ever, happy that a potential breach had been so amicably healed.

3. MULTIPLICATION (6:7)

a. ITS SCOPE (6:7a)

And the word of God increased; and the number of the disciples multiplied in Jerusalem greatly . . .

How this must have infuriated the Sanhedrin! Every convert to the new movement weakened its position still further. The new evidence of unity in the church made it possible for the Holy Spirit to pour out even greater blessing. Luke does not simply say that the disciples in Jerusalem multiplied; he says that they multiplied greatly.

It is always thus in times of revival. Revival spreads like a prairie fire driven before the wind. People are attracted by its note of joy and enthusiasm and are eager to have a share in the blessing.

b. ITS SIGNIFICANCE (6:7b)

And a great company of the priests were obedient to the faith.

And no wonder. They, more than anyone else, knew that the old-fashioned Judaism, of which they were the most visible and venerable representatives, was finished. There had been a day, not long before, when some of them had gone into the Temple as usual to trim the lamps in the Holy Place, and they had been stopped cold in their tracks. The Temple veil had been rent in two—from top to bottom! No human hand had done that. The veil was as thick as a man's hand, and, besides, no Jew would have dared commit such sacrilege. But the awesome fact was evident. The veil was rent.

For the first time the priests could look beyond the golden altar into the holiest of all and see the sacred Ark with the outspread wings of the cherubim. They could see where, generation after generation, the high priest on the Day of Atonement had sprinkled the blood. They had stood and stared.

The priests compared notes. The rending of the veil had happened the very moment Jesus of Nazareth had died. For a while they resisted the irrefutible evidence of the collapse of Judaism, but now a great company of them became obedient to the new faith.

There was a problem with this, however. The influence of these priests would tend to tie the new movement closer to traditional Judaism. For even though these good men could see that Jesus was indeed the Messiah and that the rending of the veil signaled the end of an era, old traditions die hard. In any future confrontation between Hebrews and Hellenists the influence of these men would all be on the side of a conservative, Judaistic type Christianity, dedicated to preserving as much of the old order as could be conserved. They would want the new wine to be kept in the old bottles.

B. THE FIRST MARTYR (6:8—7:60)

    1. STEPHEN, THE TREMENDOUS WORKER (6:8–15)

        a. HIS DIVINE ENABLEMENT (6:8–14)

            (1) THE WONDERS HE PERFORMED (6:8)

And Stephen, full of faith and power, did great wonders and miracles among the people.

Stephen now took the stage. He was soon to be martyred. He seems to have stood in contrast with that "great company of the priests" (6:7) who were obedient to the faith—as though, by proximity and contrast, the Holy Spirit would emphasize again the vital difference between formal belief and dynamic faith.

Up to now, the sign-gifts seem to have been exercised only by the apostles. Now one of the newly appointed deacons began to manifest the extraordinary powers that so excited the people of that day. This, too, must have further inflamed the radicals in the Sanhedrin. It must have been frustrating in the extreme to see the movement spreading in defiance of threats and thrashings, to see the defection of large numbers of the ordinary priests, and now to see an increase in the signs and wonders associated with Jewish Christianity. Soon Jerusalem became the scene of verbal encounter as apologists for the old faith took up active opposition to Christianity.

(2) THE WORDS HE PROCLAIMED (6:9–14)

(a) HOW HE ENGAGED HIS FOES (6:9–10)

Then there arose certain of the synagogue, which is called the synagogue of the Libertines, and Cyrenians, and Alexandrians, and of them of Cilicia and of Asia, disputing with Stephen. And they were not able to resist the wisdom and the spirit by which he spake.

Synagogue worship seems to have had its roots in the Babylonian Exile. Jews congregated in synagogues to hear the Scriptures read and expounded. They became common gathering centers of the Jews, especially in the lands of their dispersion. Any sizable town with a Jewish population had its synagogue, sometimes several.

The "synagogue of the Libertines" in Jerusalem seems to have been attended by Jews from various parts of the Dispersion. The mention of Jews from Cilicia suggests that this was the synagogue attended by Saul of Tarsus when he was in Jerusalem. Jews from this synagogue engaged Stephen in hot debate over the question of the messiahship of Jesus and the continued relevance of the Temple. Stephen's able handling of the Scriptures was such that not even the keenest Jewish apologists could defeat him. Again and again they retired from the debate thoroughly beaten.

Unable to defeat Stephen in debate, they soon resorted to violence.

(b) HOW HE ENRAGED HIS FOES (6:11–14)

i. HOW THEY INCITED THE MOB (6:11)

Then they suborned men, which said, We have heard him speak blasphemous words against Moses, and against God.

Hired informers were now engaged to distort Stephen's words in the most damaging way possible. He was accused of blasphemy against Moses, presumably because he challenged the permanence of the Mosaic law; and of blasphemy against God, presumably because he challenged the permanence of the Temple. The Jews would see in these two accusations a threat to their whole religious system. The accusations were very clever and were calculated to arouse the fiercest passions among the Jewish people.

ii. HOW THEY INDICTED THE MAN (6:12–13)

And they stirred up the people, and the elders, and the scribes, and came upon him, and caught him, and brought him to the council. And set up false witnesses, which said, This man ceaseth not to speak blasphemous words against this holy place, and the law.

It was Calvary all over again. The nation, having officially rejected the Son of God, was now going to officially reject the Spirit of God with the same trumped-up charges, the same use of false witnesses, the same use of the mob, the same lawless murder of the victim. With the death of Stephen the nation finally crossed the line that led to the destruction of the Temple and the dissolution of Jewish national life for the next two thousand years.

Stephen was arrested, and the charge brought against him was one the Sanhedrin knew it could exploit to the full. This time the high priest and his party would be in the driver's seat, and the mob would be on their side.

iii. HOW THEY INSULTED THE MASTER (6:14)

For we have heard him say, that this Jesus of Nazareth shall destroy this place, and shall change the customs which Moses delivered us.

One can almost hear the tone of contempt in the words "this Jesus of Nazareth." Yet Jesus had foretold the destruction of the Temple and had done so as a prophet and with perfect accuracy. Stephen saw much further than most of his contemporaries, even in the church. He had grasped the truth that along with the divinely announced destruction of the Temple came an inevitable change in all forms of worship. The Old Testament Levitical system was over. There was to be a higher and more spiritual form of worship linked to the unseen realities in heaven and anchored to the finished work of Christ at Calvary. Many Jewish Christians might continue to worship in the Temple, but its day was done. It would remain for the apostle Paul to bring to full flower and fruit the seed-truths now being sown by the farsighted, Spirit-filled Stephen.

b. HIS DIVINE ENOBLEMENT (6:15)

And all that sat in the council, looking stedfastly on him, saw his face as it had been the face of an angel.

Having heard the indictment, the Sanhedrin turned to see how Stephen was reacting to the deadly charges. They saw the face of an angel. As the face of Moses had shone with the light of another world when he came down from the mount, so now the face of Stephen shone. It was not hate they saw there, nor horror, but heaven.

The sight of that angelic face must have burned like a red-hot iron into the soul of Saul of Tarsus. That face, we cannot doubt, haunted him until he saw the face of Jesus, which thereafter filled his vision.

2. STEPHEN, THE TRUTHFUL WITNESS (7:1–53)

a. HIS EXCELLENT APPROACH (7:1–8)

(1) HE TALKS ABOUT ABRAHAM'S FAITH (7:1–5)

(a) THE REVELATION THAT WAS MADE TO ABRAHAM (7:1–3)

Then said the high priest, Are these things so? And he said, Men, brethren, and fathers, hearken; The God of glory appeared unto our father Abraham, when he was in Mesopotamia, before he dwelt in Charran, and said unto him, Get thee out of thy country, and from thy kindred, and come into the land which I shall shew thee.

Stephen was not concerned with an acquittal. He knew the character and determination of his foes. He was a marked man. His concern was to unravel the false from the true in the twofold charge laid against him and also to show the true nature of Christianity.

He began his defense with Abraham, for that was where the life of faith began for the Jews. Moreover, the revelation of God to Abram was quite independent of Moses or the Temple. God, restricted to neither a special person nor a special place, can reveal Himself when and where He wills, as He did to Abram in Ur of the Chaldees. Moreover, there is movement and progress in God's dealings with people. Abraham was to become a pilgrim and a stranger on earth. The faith is not static, not rooted to an institution, however venerable. It was a clever beginning.

Stephen began, then, with God's revelation to Abraham, a manifestation so convincing that Abraham pulled up stakes at once and left his homeland to follow where God might lead. Stephen would come back to this again in his defense: there must always be a willingness to move when God moves; we are all too prone to get wedded to tradition.

(b) THE RESPONSE THAT WAS MADE BY ABRAHAM (7:4–5)

i. THE POSITIVE RESPONSE (7:4)

Then came he out of the land of the Chaldeans, and dwelt in Charran: and from thence, when his father was dead, he removed him into this land, wherein ye now dwell.

Abraham left Ur and settled in Haran, a flourishing city in the upper Euphrates Valley. Settling in Haran was a compromise and seems to have been influenced by Abraham's father, Terah. God, however, had no intention of allowing Abraham to settle anywhere in Mesopotamia. Accordingly, Abraham was uprooted once more and sent on his way to Canaan.

ii. THE PASSIVE RESPONSE (7:5)

And he gave him none inheritance in it, no, not so much as to set his foot on: yet he promised that he would give it to him for a possession, and to his seed after him, when as yet he had no child.

Stephen was still undermining the notion that the Temple was a permanent institution. Abraham had no tangible possession even in Canaan. His faith was exercised along purely spiritual lines. He had the promise but not the place, not owning even a foot of land in Canaan. God wanted Abraham's faith to be in Him alone. Stephen was underlining the purely spiritual roots of the Hebrew faith and pointing to the purely spiritual nature of New Testament Christianity, which takes little or no account of sacred shrines and holy places.

(2) HE TALKS ABOUT ABRAHAM'S FUTURE (7:6–8)
(a) THE GOVERNMENT OF GOD (7:6–7)
i. GOD'S OMNISCIENCE (7:6)

And God spake on this wise, That his seed should sojourn in a strange land; and that they should bring them into bondage, and entreat them evil four hundred years.

Not only was Abraham not to have a permanent holding in the Promised Land, but his descendants would actually leave the land altogether. They would settle in Egypt, where they would run afoul of a great oppressor and God would have to intervene in judgment. Moreover, some four hundred years would pass before God's promise of the land to Abraham would be made good. All this must have been a tremendous test of Abraham's faith. It was an implied rebuke, too, to those who thought that biblical belief had to be tied to a Temple. At the very beginning of Jewish national life, and for four long centuries, the chosen people were not even in the Promised Land! They were a persecuted and ill-treated minority in Egypt. The high priest and his party could hardly escape the drift of Stephen's argument. Abraham's faith rested on the bare Word of God and in the omnipotence and omniscience of the One who made the promise.

ii. GOD'S OMNIPOTENCE (7:7)

And the nation to whom they shall be in bondage will I judge, said God: and after that shall they come forth, and serve me in this place.

God is well able to safeguard His own promises. Time and distance make no difference to Him. The might of an anti-Semitic world super-power could not foil His purposes. Humanly speaking, all the power lay with Pharaoh. He had the standing army, the secret police, the concentration camps. God was not impressed. When He struck in His own immutable purposes, all the might and stubbornness of Pharaoh could not delay the fulfillment of God's pledge to Abraham. Blow after blow was aimed at Pharaoh's pride and power until, at last, the redeemed Hebrews came indeed into the Promised Land. All that was foreseen of God and foretold to His friend Abraham.

(b) THE GRACE OF GOD (7:8)
i. THE COVENANT CONVEYED TO THE PILGRIM (7:8a)

And he gave him the covenant of circumcision.

One sign Abraham did have—circumcision. God took the cutting edge of the knife and brought it to bear on all that spoke of the reproductive energy of the flesh. Abraham was taught, symbolically, to bear in his body the marks of the Lord Jesus. No fleshly energy would bring the promises of God to pass. Abraham was to look beyond himself to God and to teach his seed to do the same.

ii. THE COVENANT CONFIRMED TO THE PATRIARCHS (7:8*b*)

And so Abraham begat Isaac, and circumcised him the eighth day; and Isaac begat Jacob; and Jacob begat the twelve patriarchs.

There was no Temple; there was no law. The essential faith of the fathers was transmitted from generation to generation in simple dependence on the Word of God. It went on like that for generations and for centuries, and could have gone on like that forever. The law, no doubt, was very functional as a means for defining limits of behavior. It provided ritual illustrations of divine truth. The Temple, too, was equally functional as a rallying point for the faith. But neither law nor Temple was essential. The patriarchs had managed well enough without them, even under circumstances calculated to make the boldest believer tremble. Christianity was a return to the original. It could dispense with rules and rituals because it had the reality in Christ.

b. HIS EXTENSIVE APPEAL (7:9–50)

(1) HOW ISRAEL HAD TREATED THEIR SAVIORS (7:9–36)

(a) THEIR REJECTION OF JOSEPH, THE ONE WHO SETTLED THEM IN EGYPT (7:9–16)

i. HOW JOSEPH WAS RESENTED (7:9)

And the patriarchs, moved with envy, sold Joseph into Egypt: but God was with him.

Stephen now changed his angle of attack to show that the Jewish people, right from the start, had resisted God's plans for them.

Their unbelief had begun with their treatment of Joseph, one of the great types of Christ in the Old Testament. As the Sanhedrin had rejected Jesus, so the patriarchs rejected Joseph, and for the same reason—envy. Pilate well knew that it was for *envy* that the Jewish leaders had delivered Jesus to him for judgment (Matt. 27:18). The Jews were running true to type. The sons of Jacob united to get rid of Joseph; the children of Israel united to get rid of Jesus. The patriarchs resented Joseph because of his goodness. Moreover, their badness was highlighted by that goodness. As a jeweler will place a diamond on black velvet and shine a bright light upon it so that its faces and facets might blaze against the light-absorbing background, so Joseph's goodness stood out in brilliant contrast to their wickedness. And thus, too, it was with Jesus, although Stephen had no need to draw the obvious parallel.

ii. HOW JOSEPH WAS RAISED (7:10)

And delivered him out of all his afflictions, and gave him favour and wisdom in the sight of Pharaoh king of Egypt; and he made him governor over Egypt and all his house.

Joseph was rejected of his brethren, sold for the price of a slave, handed over to Gentiles, falsely accused, and made to suffer for sins not his own. He was cast out by the Gentiles and put in the place of death. He took possession of the keys of the prison and ruled there as he ruled everywhere.

Nor could that place of death hold him. He came forth in triumph to be exalted to the right hand of the majesty. He was given a name that was above every name, that at the name of Zaphnath-paaneah ("Savior of the World," [Gen. 41:45]) every knee should bow and every tongue confess that Zaphnath-paaneah was lord to the glory of the Pharaoh. In Egypt he ruled not only over all that land, symbolic of the world, but also over all of Pharaoh's house, symbolic perhaps of Israel as God's house.

Stephen had no need to tell all that story or to make all the obvious applications of that story to Christ. The members of the Sanhedrin could see where Stephen was leading them. For God had delivered Jesus, just as He had delivered Joseph from the prisonhouse of death in which they had placed Him. Now He was high and lifted up and far beyond the reach of their petty spite, and He was destined to rule the world.

iii. HOW JOSEPH WAS REVEALED (7:11–16)

a. THE FAMINE THAT BROUGHT THEM TO JOSEPH (7:11–12)

Now there came a dearth over all the land of Egypt and Chanan, and great affliction: and our fathers found no sustenance. But when Jacob heard that there was corn in Egypt, he sent out our fathers first.

All worked together for good, as Joseph later told his brethren. "Ye sold," he said; "God sent" (Gen. 45:4, 7). "As for you, ye thought evil against me; but God meant it unto good . . . to save much people" (50:20). God was able to take their rejection of Joseph and make it, in the end, an instrument of worldwide salvation—which is, of course, just what He did through Jesus at Calvary. The cross represents the greatest tragedy in man's dealings with God, the final expression of sin. At the same time it represents the greatest triumph in God's dealings with men. For God took our sins and, in Christ, nailed them all to the tree (Col. 2:14). Men meant it for evil; God meant it for good.

In the meantime, God set in motion a chain of circumstances designed to bring Joseph's kinsmen to His feet. The rejection of Joseph meant the beginning of sorrows for the chosen people. A famine came. The time of Jacob's trouble came. The circumstances of life frowned upon the chosen people, and they began to look for a savior. And, all unknown to them in their unbelief, they were being driven to Joseph.

It is only with the full light of the New Testament thus shining upon the Old Testament page that we can appreciate to the full the cleverness of

Stephen's speech. For what had happened in Joseph's day will all be repeated, on a grander scale, to drive the Jews at last to Jesus.

b. THE FORGIVENESS THAT BOUND THEM TO JOSEPH (7:13–14)

And at the second time Joseph was made known to his brethren; and Joseph's kindred was made known unto Pharoah. Then sent Joseph, and called his father Jacob to him, and all his kindred, threescore and fifteen souls.

Again, Stephen did not dwell on all the details that his hearers knew by heart. The Old Testament parallel is exact. Joseph, now at the right hand of the Pharaoh, with a Gentile bride to share his exaltation, began to work sovereignly to bring about the repentance and restoration of his brethren. His discipline was harsh, or so it seemed to those who in their blindness failed to recognize him, but all was motivated by the most marvelous forgiveness and love, and all was designed to bring them to the place where they said, "We are verily guilty concerning our brother" (Gen. 42:21). All was planned, too, to bring them to Judah's forthright confession. Then Joseph, in one of history's most emotional scenes, made himself known: "I am Joseph" (45:3).

Nor was that all. When the reconciliation was complete he gathered the chosen family to himself and associated them with him in his world government, as all nations came to him. The divinely planned parallels in all this to the not-too-distant future experiences of the Jewish people are evident. At last they will see in Jesus their Messiah, look on Him whom they pierced, and not only repent but also share in His millenial reign.

c. THE FAITH THAT BLESSED THEM IN JOSEPH (7:15–16)

So Jacob went down into Egypt, and died, he, and our fathers, and were carried over into Sychem, and laid in the sepulchre that Abraham bought for a sum of money of the sons of Emmor the father of Sychem.

For neither Joseph nor Jacob lost sight of one supreme fact. All God's promises to His Old Testament people were to be fulfilled in Canaan. That blazed through both in Jacob's and Joseph's insistence on being buried in Canaan.

All that, of course, the Sanhedrin knew, and Stephen knew they knew. The relevance of it lay in the fact that soon the Hebrew people would again be driven out of the Promised Land to begin that period of worldwide wandering that has only now just begun to end. The Sanhedrin did not believe that, but Stephen, his faith resting solidly on the prophetic Scriptures and the teachings of Jesus, knew it would be so. The Jews must be reminded that their coming exile would end in a return to the Promised Land. They must never lose sight of Canaan, no matter where they might settle in the years of their exile.

So with incisive comment and many an enlightened inference, Stephen showed how Israel rejected Joseph, the first of the many saviors sent to them by God.

Then he approached one of the central characters in Hebrew history: Moses, a man whose name shone in the Jewish firmament with a brightness rivalled only by that of Abraham.

> (b) THEIR REACTION TO MOSES, THE ONE WHO SAVED THEM FROM EGYPT
> (7:17–36)
>> i. THE FEARFUL BONDAGE OF ISRAEL (7:17– 19)
>>> a. THE TIME (7:17a)

But when the time of the promise drew nigh, which God had sworn to Abraham . . .

God's eye is ever on the clock. He does things according to set times and never forgets a date or misses an appointment. There are set times, predetermined in heaven, at which God acts. The Scriptures may be studied profitably from that standpoint. A vast wealth of evidence proves it so. When God created the sun and moon He ordained that they might be "for signs, and for seasons" (Gen. 1:14) and deliberately introduced a time factor into human affairs. Thus the sun governs our days and our years, and the moon divides them into months.

The book of Daniel strikes that time note constantly. There was the prophecy of the seventy years, for instance, which alerted Daniel to the near end of the Babylonian captivity, and the subsequent prophecy of the seventy "weeks." Messiah was to be "cut off" after sixty-nine of those weeks.

In the book of Revelation we find continuing reference to a period described as "a time and times, and half a time," (Rev. 12:14), described elsewhere in the book as "forty and two months" (11:2; 13:5) and even more specifically as 1260 days. That period is related to the second half of the seventieth week of Daniel. When the Beast sets up his image in the Temple, the Jews will be able to begin their countdown to the full return of Christ based on that significant time factor.

Jesus, after His resurrection, remained here forty days and, at His ascension, told the disciples to wait for the coming of the Holy Spirit "not many days hence" (Acts 1:5). Nothing was hurried beyond its time. It was fifty days between Passover and Pentecost. The mathematical precision with which the types connected with Passover, Firstfruits, Unleavened Bread, and Pentecost were kept leads us to expect a like mathematical precision, even in the matter of dates, for the fulfillment of Trumpets, Atonement, and Tabernacles.

Thus the years of the Egyptian exile ran their course. As the time drew near for prophecy to be fulfilled, God made the first of His moves. It was not one that we would have expected, had it not already been foretold to Abraham (Gen. 15:13–14).

b. THE TENSION (7:17b–18)

The people grew and multiplied in Egypt, till another king arose, which knew not Joseph.

There was a change of dynasties in Egypt. National gratitude can be short-lived, especially when the debt is owed to a foreigner. A new regime came to power, and the throne was occupied by a new pharaoh. Biblical historians are divided as to who this pharaoh was. Those who espouse the theory of a late exodus fix on Rameses II (1301–1234 B.C.) as the pharaoh of the oppression. Those who hold to the theory of an earlier exodus see Thutmose I (1528–1508 B.C.) as the king in question.

The rapid multiplication of the Hebrews in Goshen not unnaturally caused great alarm. They were an indigestible lump in the body politic of Egypt. They had their own tightly-knit social order, their own religion, however diluted, their own national goals, economy, and aspirations, and their own history and identity. A few of them would have made no difference, but when their numbers began to climb into the millions the Egyptians viewed them with increasing alarm. Tension began to build. What if they allied themselves to a foreign foe? The fact that they were shepherds added to the fear. Memories of the Hyksos shepherd kings (1730–1570 B.C.) still remained.

c. THE TERROR (7:19)

The same dealt subtilly with our kindred, and evil entreated our fathers, so that they cast out their young children, to the end they might not live.

Pharaoh's solution to what Hitler called "the Jewish question" was along the same lines—genocide, the systematic murder of a race. Goshen became a ghetto, the Nile was Pharaoh's gas chamber, the crocodiles his means of disposing of the bodies. Pharaoh's plans were longer range than Hitler's, but just as effective. Every male Hebrew born from the date of the decree was to be cast into the river. It is hard to think of a reign of terror more heartless. Imagine the horror and heartache in every Hebrew home at the prospect of their newborn sons being torn away by a member of Pharaoh's Gestapo and flung living or dead into the Nile.

Such was the fearful bondage of Israel. With a few brief words, Stephen set the stage for another act in Israel's history of rejecting her saviors.

ii. THE FOOLISH BIGOTRY OF ISRAEL (7:20–28)

a. THE SAVIOR'S BIRTH (7:20)

In which time Moses was born, and was exceeding fair, and nourished up in his father's house three months.

The story was too familiar to need comment. Jochebed, the mother of Moses, hit on an ingenious plan to rescue her baby from Pharaoh's murderers. She thought, *What does God do to save a people under the sentence of death?* and then perhaps she remembered Noah and his ark. Noah had gone right through the judgment, safe in the ark of God's providing. Jochebed decided to make a little ark. She put her baby in the ark and then put the ark in the judgment water. She was calling on God to honor her faith. Stephen adds a note of considerable interest. He says that Moses was "exceeding fair." He was, in other words, an extraordinarily good-looking child—one can hardly imagine Pharaoh's daughter being too interested in an extremely ugly baby.

b. THE SAVIOR'S BACKGROUND (7:21–22)

And when he was cast out, Pharaoh's daughter took him up, and nourished him for her own son. And Moses was learned in all the wisdom of the Egyptians, and was mighty in words and in deeds.

Moses was hidden at home for three months. "When she could no longer hide him" (Ex. 2:3), Jochebed resorted to the stratagem of the ark. Stephen says he was "cast out."

Then it was that Pharaoh's daughter "took him up." Those who espouse the theory of a late exodus have trouble identifying this daughter of Pharaoh, but those who embrace the theory of an early exodus have no trouble at all. She stands out on the pages of history as one of the most remarkable women of all time—the daughter of a Pharaoh, the wife of another, the stepmother of a third, and a Pharaoh herself for some twenty years.

She was Hatshepsut. Her father was Thutmose I (1528–1508 B.C.), during whose reign Moses was born (1527 B.C.). Hatshepsut became the wife of Thutmose II (1508–1504 B.C.), who reigned for only a few years. Hatshepsut then seized the throne for herself (1504–1483 B.C.) and, as his stepmother and regent, managed to keep Thutmose III off the throne for twenty-one years, by which time that vigorous and imperious young man harbored a fierce but impotent rage against his powerful stepmother. When he did ascend the throne upon her death, he reigned (1483–1450 B.C.) with a force and fury that made him one of the greatest of all the empire-building pharaohs. In his rage against Hatshepsut he obliterated her monuments, some of which he simply plastered over—preserving for us a considerable documentary of the period. Then he proceeded to pulverize the surrounding nations, especially the tribes of Canaan (making Joshua's task that much easier some years later). During the reign of that energetic Pharaoh, Moses was in the backside of the desert. Thutmose III was succeeded by Amenhotep II (1450–1423 B.C.) in whose reign the Exodus took place (1447 B.C.).

If that dating for the Exodus is correct, then Hatshepsut was the princess who adopted Moses. She is certainly an ideal candidate and just the kind of woman who would defy the Pharaoh's law, which decreed that the Hebrew foundling should be drowned.

Stephen tells us that Moses was "learned in all the wisdom of the Egyptians." Hatshepsut had her adopted son groomed for the throne, to which doubtless she would have elevated him in time had not Moses heard and heeded the call of God to be Israel's savior. He gave up a throne to step down to Israel's need—just as did our Lord.

Stephen also tells us that Moses was "mighty in words and in deeds."

Moses was mighty in words. When God called him to become Israel's Kinsman Redeemer, Moses replied, "I am not eloquent" (Ex. 4:10), but that was after he had spent forty years in the desert solitudes. Perhaps he was referring to the Egyptian language, which he had probably not spoken much in all that time. Or perhaps the reference "mighty in words" is to his writing skills, which were certainly of a high caliber. His eloquence is evident in all his writings and never more so than in the book of Deuteronomy, which contains ten of his magnificent monologues.

He was also mighty in deeds. Josephus has it that while a member of Pharaoh's court Moses led a campaign against the Ethiopians (*Antiquities* 2:10).

In any case Moses, like Jesus, increased in wisdom and in stature and acquired the ability and discipline necessary for the great ministry of becoming savior to his people.

c. THE SAVIOR'S BRETHREN (7:23–28)

1. THE MANIFESTATION OF MOSES (7:23–25)

And when he was full forty years old, it came into his heart to visit his brethren the children of Israel. And seeing one of them suffer wrong, he defended him, and avenged him that was oppressed, and smote the Egyptian: for he supposed his brethren would have understood how that God by his hand would deliver them: but they understood not.

The Hebrews in Egypt were blind to the redemptive purposes of God in the birth and background of Moses. They were envious of him and of the position he occupied in life as compared with theirs. They could not see that he had been set apart from them to be their savior. "They understood not," Stephen says, with obvious application to the sad parallel being reenacted in Israel by the Jews of his day. Jesus, by birth and background, was set apart from His "kinsmen according to the flesh" (Rom. 9:3) by virtue of His essential position in life as God's own Son. They "understood not." Blindness, as Paul would put it later, had happened to Israel.

Moses, however, when the moment came, identified himself with his oppressed people. "It came into his heart to visit his brethren," the Holy Spirit says. This was not a thought that came into his head; this was a yearning that came into his heart. Redemption, after all, is the thought of God's heart towards us. It was not curiosity that took Moses from the palace to Goshen; it was kinship. He wanted to be identified with his brethren—so much so that he struck a blow for them against the oppressor.

Thus it was that the Lord Jesus, in the fullness of time, identified Himself with Adam's ruined race in the waters of Jordan and then went into the wilderness to strike a deathblow at Satan. After the Lord's temptation, a tremendous upsurge of demon possession seems to have taken place in Israel as Satan's desperate answer to the now-manifested and identified Savior.

2. THE MEDIATION OF MOSES (7:26)

And the next day he shewed himself unto them as they strove, and would have set them at one again, saying, Sirs, ye are brethren; why do ye wrong one to another?

Moses wanted his brethren to know that God had not only raised him up to be their Kinsman-Redeemer, but also to bring them peace. The petty squabbles of that downtrodden people grieved him greatly. He sought to bring about reconciliation, but his ministry was regarded as meddling.

When Jesus came He found the children of Israel in just such a state. The nation was torn by warring factions. The Pharisees, the Sadducees, the Zealots, the Herodians, and the Essenes were all at odds with each other, and all were under the heel of Rome, the great oppressor. Jesus came preaching peace. In the Sermon on the Mount He taught a loftier way of life: "Blessed are the poor in spirit . . . blessed are the meek . . . blessed are the merciful . . . blessed are the peacemakers" (Matt. 5:3, 5, 7, 9). His message fell on deaf ears.

3. THE MISINTERPRETATION OF MOSES (7:27–28)

But he that did his neighbor wrong thrust him away, saying, Who made thee a ruler and a judge over us? Wilt thou kill me, as thou diddest the Egyptian yesterday?

These scornful words fell from the lips of him "that did his neighbor wrong." He had no desire for Moses' ministry of reconciliation. He it was who took the lead in rejecting Moses. The reaction to Moses was now out in the open, accompanied by a veiled threat. Thus Moses, like Christ, "came unto his own, and his own received him not" (John 1:11). Moses was misunderstood. They thought he had stooped down from the great heights in which he lived to lord it over them, to take advantage of his position, to make them feel even more wretched in their miserable condition, to judge them; whereas he had come to identify himself with them and to save them. The sneering words of this embittered Hebrew showed how deep was the resentment and jealousy harbored against him. When the Jews delivered Jesus to Pilate, Pilate "knew that for envy they had delivered him" (Matt. 27:18). With consummate skill Stephen touched just those notes that struck the chord he wanted. He showed how Israel treated the saviors God had given. But he had not finished yet by any means. He now showed:

iii. THE FURTHER BURDENS OF ISRAEL (7:29–34)

a. WHILE MOSES WAS LEARNING (7:29)

Then fled Moses at this saying, and was a stranger in the land of Madian, where he begat two sons.

The offer of salvation for Israel was postponed. The Israelites had rejected Moses; God left them to their burdens and to those who oppressed them. He had not abandoned them forever, but He left them for the time being to reap the fruits of their rejection of the savior He had provided.

In the meantime, the focus remained on Moses. Moses learned the lessons of a new type of life. His heart was with his people, but his home was now far away. His mode of living was forever changed. There could be no turning back the clock to conditions as they were before he first visited his brethren. Now, in a different land, he found a Gentile bride and entered into a new joy as sons were born to him. Israel may have rejected him, but his heart was warmed as the Gentiles received him and as he saw fruit among them.

We cannot miss the continuing parallel with the life of the Lord. After Israel's final rejection of Him, a rejection the Sanhedrin was about to consummate in the murder of Stephen, God left Israel, as a nation, to its burdens and to its foes. In the meantime the Lord took His journey to that distant land. He has taken a Gentile bride (the church) and is rejoicing in the fruit that is coming to Him from among the Gentiles. He is bringing new sons into glory. The rejection of Jesus has not foiled God's plans but furthered them.

In heaven the Lord Jesus is learning the joys of His new life. His coming into this world slammed the door on all the past. There could be no turning back. The second Person of the Godhead has taken on humanity. That can never be changed. He has carried His battle-scarred body to that distant land, and He is seated at God's right hand as the Man Christ Jesus. He is learning there all the mysteries of that new mode of being into which we cannot pry and about which we can only wonder.

b. WHILE MOSES WAS LOOKING (7:30–31)

And when forty years were expired, there appeared to him in the wilderness of mount Sina an angel of the Lord in a flame of fire in a bush. When Moses saw it, he wondered at the sight: and as he drew near to behold it, the voice of the Lord came unto him.

The burning bush symbolized the nation of Israel in the fierce fire of the Pharaonic persecution. The Old Testament tells us that the bush was not consumed. God was in the bush. Israel, in the fire down there in Egypt, could not perish because God was in their midst. Moses now had his attention drawn to the dire plight of God's earthly people, for the time had come for him to move. There was to be a second coming of Moses as Israel's Kinsman-Redeemer, a coming as a flame of fire, a coming in judgment to take vengeance on Israel's foes.

Again we have the studied parallel. The Lord Jesus is still Kinsman to the Hebrew people. He will yet be their Redeemer. The time will come when the "bush" will burn again in the dreadful fires of the Great Tribulation. The Lord Himself will be watching, His eyes fixed upon their suffering, knowing that the moment of His final return is at hand.

c. WHILE MOSES WAS LISTENING (7:32–34)

1. TO A LIVING GOD (7:32–33)

Saying I am the God of thy fathers, the God of Abraham, and the God of Isaac, and the God of Jacob. Then Moses trembled, and durst not behold. Then said the Lord to him, Put off thy shoes from thy feet: for the place where thou standest is holy ground.

Moses, after all, was merely a sinful man. There were lessons he had to learn that Jesus never had to learn. Moses had to learn what it meant to stand as a sinner in the presence of a thrice-holy God, a God who was, indeed, a flaming fire. The holiness of God was the basis of the judgment about to be unleashed on Egypt. Moses was to be the minister of that holiness. He first had to learn his personal unfitness for the task.

Moreover, the God whose mediator he had now become was a living God. Time had no mark on Him. He was the God of Abraham, Isaac, and Jacob. He was eternal, self-existing, uncreated; the great I AM dwelling in the timeless present, not moving from past to future but gathering all the tenses of time into one embracing present.

Jesus did not need to learn such lessons. The parallel now becomes a study in contrast. He was the eternal Son. He could say, "Before Abraham was, I AM" (John 8:58). What did the onward march of time mean to Him? A thousand ages in His sight were:

> Like an evening gone;
> Short as the watch that ends the night,
> Before the rising sun.
>   (Isaac Watts, "O God, Our Help in Ages Past")

Nor did He need to learn what it meant to stand on holy ground. He was "holy, harmless, undefiled, separate from sinners" (Heb. 7:26). He entered the holy of holies in heaven with His own blood. He passed inside the veil in His own right and sat down between the cherubim at God's right hand as the holy One of Israel.

At His second coming He will act in holiness. But that holiness is not something foreign to Him; it is inherent holiness, the holiness of God. It is the holiness acclaimed by the chanting cherubim: "Holy, Holy, Holy" (Isa. 6:3). That flaming holiness will be the basis of the judgment that will be manifested at His second coming as Israel's returning Kinsman. "Then shall that Wicked [one] be revealed, whom the Lord shall consume with the spirit of his mouth, and shall destroy with the brightness of his coming" (2 Thess. 2:8).

2. TO A LOVING GOD (7:34)

I have seen, I have seen the affliction of my people which is in Egypt, and I have heard their groaning, and am come down to deliver them. And now come, I will send thee into Egypt.

It was not merely that God's wrath was to be poured out on Egypt; His love was to be revealed to His people. The initiative was all with God. Love was what moved Him to act, at last, in the fullness of time. Moses was to be sent back now to redeem by power the children of Israel, whose groanings God had heard and whose long and now-climaxing suffering He had seen. God had now taken His stand upon the earth.

Thus, too, at the final return of Christ, love will be the supreme motive. God's great heart will be moved by Israel's sufferings, and He will take up His stand upon the earth. The time for Christ's second coming will have arrived. The Father will send Him back to rescue His kinsmen according to the flesh in the battle of Armageddon. The type holds true to the end.

And at this point Stephen skillfully dropped his brush and palette and picked up his sword. He had drawn a breath-taking parallel between Joseph and Jesus and Moses and Jesus. Now came the sword-thrust application.

iv. THE FATAL BLINDNESS OF ISRAEL (7:35–36)

a. MOSES HAD BEEN SENT TO SAVE THEM (7:35)

This Moses whom they refused, saying, Who made thee a ruler and a judge? the same did God send to be a ruler and a deliverer by the hand of the angel which appeared to him in the bush.

Such was Israel's blindness. They had rejected the savior sent to them by God, but God had no other savior. All they had gained by their blind and wicked rejection of Moses was further bondage. In the end the very savior they had spurned was sent back by God to be ruler and deliverer.

Encompassed in this forceful summary of the type are the two comings of Christ with Israel's age-long rejection sandwiched in between. The Sanhedrin could hardly miss the point Stephen was driving home.

b. MOSES HAD BEEN SENT TO SEPARATE THEM (7:36)

He brought them out, after that he had shewed wonders and signs in the land of Egypt, and in the Red sea, and in the wilderness forty years.

Israel, redeemed by power, was set free from centuries of discrimination and bondage. Egypt was judged, and Israel was set apart by God to begin a new life under the personal direction of Moses, a life of miracle after miracle, a life of divine love and leading, a life of victory and daily, multiplied tokens of God's presence, government, and supply. Stephen dropped the story there, at the point where Israel, emancipated by Moses, marched triumphantly forward in the power of a new life.

There is a hint here of Israel's future emancipation, regeneration, and victory at the second coming of Christ, but it was not Stephen's purpose to labor this point. His main goal was to show how Israel had rejected the saviors God had sent. Now to Joseph and Moses had to be added the name of Jesus. It was all of the same pattern, only now the rejection was serious beyond all measure.

(2) HOW ISRAEL HAD TREATED THEIR SCRIPTURES (7:37–43)

(a) THE SCRIPTURES DELIVERED TO ISRAEL (7:37–38)

i. A WORD ABOUT THEIR MESSIAH (7:37)

This is that Moses, which said unto the children of Israel, A prophet shall the Lord your God raise up unto you of your brethren, like unto me; him shall ye hear.

The studied parallel between Moses and Jesus was now brought into sharp focus by Stephen. Moses had prophesied that there would be just such a parallel (Deut. 18:15). In their own beloved law, in the Torah, Moses and the Messiah were brought together, the one to be a type of the other. "Him shall ye hear," Moses had said. Well, they had heard Him and had deliberately turned a deaf ear to Him. But they had not heard the last of Him by any means.

"Unto him ye shall hearken," (Deut. 18:15), said Moses. "Him shall ye hear," echoed Stephen. And one can well imagine that his voice rang out in that chamber with triumph. Israel has not heard Him yet, but the day is coming when she will.

ii. WORD ABOUT THEIR MANDATE (7:38)

a. THEIR GATHERING (THE CHURCH) (7:38a)

This is he, that was in the church in the wilderness.

In the wilderness, Israel was "the church," the *ecclesia* of God, the company of called-out ones. In no way were they *the* church as we have the concept in the New Testament. That church was as yet unborn when Jesus said to Peter, "Upon this rock I will build my church" (Matt. 16:18). It was supernaturally injected into history at Pentecost, and it will be supernaturally removed at the rapture. The church as such is a separate entity in God's eternal purpose, something distinct and different from the nation of Israel.

However, in the wilderness, Israel too had her called-out character. Israel, too, was supernaturally gathered around the Lord, who took His place in their midst. The threefold movement in Israel's redemption was similar to ours. God put His people under the blood, brought them through the water, baptized them in the cloud and in the sea, and gathered them around the table.

And for all those significant moves they had God's Word to lead them. Those were not things they decided to do of themselves. They would never have thought of such things. God's Word, spoken to Moses, led them.

b. THEIR GUIDE (THE ANGEL) (7:38b)

. . . with the angel which spake to him in the mount Sina, and with our fathers: who received the lively oracles to give unto us.

They had the Scriptures, written with the finger of God, written on the tables of stone, given to them by "the angel," often called the Angel of the Lord. This was no ordinary angel, but the Lord Jesus Himself in one of His preincarnate forms. He it was who gave the law to Moses. Thus the Scriptures were delivered to Israel. The inspired Word was conveyed by the One who now had become the incarnate Word.

(b) THE SCRIPTURES DISOBEYED BY ISRAEL (7:39–43)

i. THEIR REBELLION AGAINST THE LEADERSHIP GOD GAVE (7:39–40)

To whom our fathers would not obey, but thrust him from them, and in their hearts turned back again into Egypt, saying unto Aaron, Make us gods to go before us: for as for this Moses, which brought us out of the land of Egypt, we wot not what is become of him.

At the very moment Moses had ascended the mount to be seated with God in heavenly places and to receive a fresh word from God with which to bless and guide the people, they were rejecting him afresh and going back to a dead religion, utterly scornful of the one who had brought salvation to them.

That, of course, was the very thing the leaders of Israel were doing. The

Lord Jesus had ascended far higher than Moses ever did and was set down at God's right hand. He was, through His Spirit, revealing a whole New Testament to His new ecclesia, the church. The leaders of Israel, however, were clinging to Aaron, to the Levitical priestly system, to a dead religion. They were utterly scornful of the One who had wrought so great salvation for them. It would be hard to say which was worse, Israel's rejection of the saviors God sent them or their rejection of the Scriptures God sent them. In their rebellion against the leaders God gave them, Israel of old disobeyed the Scriptures. The same was true of the Jews of Stephen's day. And the same is true of those who reject Christ today. "Search the scriptures," Jesus said, "they are they which testify of me" (John 5:39).

ii. THEIR REBELLION AGAINST THE LAWS OF GOD GAVE (7:41–43)

a. THEIR INITIAL APOSTASY (7:41)

And they made a calf in those days, and offered sacrifice unto the idol, and rejoiced in the works of their own hands.

The sacred bull was one of the countless gods of Egypt. At the very moment the written Scriptures were being entrusted to Moses, the Israelites were making a golden calf and were apostatizing from the true and living God. They already had the oral Scriptures in the stories of God's dealings with the patriarchs. They knew that Jehovah was the true and living God, the God of Abraham, Isaac, and Jacob. No insult offered to God could have been greater than to make an Egyptian idol and worship it as the author of their salvation. Such was Israel's initial apostasy. It was deep and dreadful, made all the worse by Aaron's craven compromise and cooperation.

b. THEIR INCREASING APOSTASY (7:42–43)

Then God turned, and gave them up to worship the host of heaven; as it is written in the book of the prophets, O ye house of Israel, have ye offered to me slain beasts and sacrifices by the space of forty years in the wilderness? Yea, ye took up the tabernacles of Moloch, and the star of your god Remphan, figures which ye made to worship them: and I will carry you away beyond Babylon.

Stephen showed further that Israel's idolatries began in the wilderness and continued right on down to the Babylonian Exile. It was deep-seated, deliberate, and persistent. He appealed to Amos 5:25–27 as summing up the whole story of Israel's rejection of the Scriptures God gave them. The Scriptures were clear: "Thou shalt have no other gods . . . Thou shalt not make unto thee any graven image . . ." (Ex. 20:3–4). God "gave them up," said Stephen. And to what dreadful idolatries! The worship of the golden calf was formally adopted by Jereboam as the official religion of the Northern Kingdom. It was soon supplemented by the worship of all the false gods of the

Canaanites and their neighbors. The worship of Moloch, mentioned by Stephen, was a terrible thing, accompanied by the most horrible form of child sacrifice. The worship of Remphan points to the worship of the planets, a form of idolatry that grew in Israel as the country came under the growing influence of Assyria.

Thus Stephen showed how Israel treated the Scriptures God gave them. They treated them with ineffable contempt. In Stephen's day, lip service was paid to those Scriptures. Schools and synagogues were dedicated to their reading and study, but rabbinical tradition had long since taken the place of truth. The worthless traditions of the elders had so encrusted the Word of God that it had been made of no effect—a charge commonly brought against the nation by the Lord Himself. And now their rejection of the Scriptures had led the nation to its most serious crime, the murder of the incarnate Son of God, to whom all the Scriptures pointed.

Stephen now began the third and final thrust of his extensive appeal. He had been accused of attacking the temple. He now showed:

(3) HOW ISRAEL TREATED THEIR SANCTUARIES (7:44–50)

(a) THE TABERNACLE (7:44–45)

i. ITS HEAVENLY SIGNIFICANCE (7:44)

Our fathers had the tabernacle of witness in the wilderness, as he had appointed, speaking unto Moses, that he should make it according to the fashion that he had seen.

The Tabernacle was an object of great beauty and cost. Built to divine specification, it was God's tent in the midst of His people. In that tent He took up His abode, sitting between the cherubim upon the mercy seat upon the sacred Ark inside the veil. The Tabernacle was a model, made after a heavenly pattern revealed to Moses in the mount. Every peg and pin, every curtain and color, every board and bar spoke of Christ.

Stephen's point was that the Tabernacle, for all its divine origin, appointments, and purpose, was after all only a temporary structure. Built-in obsolescence was part of the plan. Even though it was made of incorruptible acacia wood and overlaid with gold, it was to be replaced by something better. Not a Jew present in the courtroom could deny that.

ii. ITS HOLY SOJOURNINGS (7:45)

Which also our fathers that came after brought in with Jesus [Joshua] into the possession of the Gentiles, whom God drave out before the face of our fathers, unto the days of David.

The history of that first sanctuary was one of impermanence and transcience. It was forever on the move. It was put up and taken down, carried and carted from place to place. In all the wanderings of the Hebrews

in the wilderness, in their crossing of the Jordan and their conquest of
Canaan, the Tabernacle moved when they moved. Even in the Promised Land
it had no fixed abode until David finally installed it in Jerusalem. But by then
its temporary nature was even more evident. It was to be replaced.

(b) THE TEMPLE (7:46–50)

i. THE BUILDER (7:46–47)

*Who found favour before God, and desired to find a tabernacle for the
God of Jacob. But Solomon built him an house.*

David, contrasting God's dwelling place on earth with his own palatial
residence, made up his mind that he would build a permanent Temple for
God. Nathan the prophet at first endorsed the scheme enthusiastically. The
very thing! Let God now permanently locate Himself in Jerusalem! But
shortly he was back with a message for David from God: God had no need of a
house of cedar. Nevertheless, because of the nobleness of David's thought,
God would establish David's house forever—an unequivocal prophecy concerning Christ. At the same time, David was told that a Son of his would arise
and build a house for God (2 Sam. 7:12–13), an obscure but equally pointed
reference to Christ and to the spiritual house He would build.

In due time, David's son Solomon did build a Temple in Jerusalem,
using the materials David had collected, urging the Hebrew people to join in
the vast work and calling on the skills of a foreign people to do some of the
more difficult tasks.

Stephen, however, now made short work of the notion that Solomon's
Temple was in any way intended to tie God down.

ii. THE BUILDING (7:48–50)

a. A CRAMPED CONCEPT OF GOD (7:48)

*Howbeit the most High dwelleth not in temples made with hands; as
saith the prophet.*

Solomon himself recognized this in his dedicatory prayer when the
Temple was finished (1 Kings 8:23–53). The idea that God could be confined
to a temple was a heathen idea, fitting for those whose god was a mere idol of
stone. Although God graciously placed the Shekinah glory cloud in Solomon's
Temple, a visible token of His presence (as the royal standard flying over
Buckingham Palace signals the presence of Britain's sovereign), He Himself
was not to be so confined. To think that the eternal, uncreated, self-existing
God could be limited to one location was ludicrous. Solomon had no such
cramped concept of God. Nor did the prophets.

b. A CORRECT CONCEPT OF GOD (7:49–50)

*Heaven is my throne, and earth is my footstool: what house will ye
build me? saith the Lord: or what is the place of my rest? Hath not my hand
made all these things?*

Stephen now turned to Isaiah 66:1–2 for his final word about the inadequacy of the Temple. What need did God have of a temple—God, who was able to create suns and stars, able to make a planet such as Earth and fill it to overflowing with all things man could ever need? What need did such a vast, infinite, eternal God have of a temple, however magnificent? Man might need a temple in the ritual and symbolic picturebook stage of his spiritual development, but God certainly had no need of a temple. The very Temple, indeed, of which the Jews were so inordinately proud in Stephen's day was not Solomon's Temple. God had allowed that one to go up in flames. Moreover, within a few decades, the present Temple would be destroyed. It made no difference. The Temple was not necessary to true spiritual faith. Like the Tabernacle before it, it was never intended to be more than a temporary phase in their spiritual education.

Their charge that he had blasphemed God by proclaiming Jesus to be greater than the Temple and to have declared the Temple redundant was answered. The transcendent church was greater far than the perishable Temple. Stephen might have added that Jesus, referring to Himself, proclaimed, "In this place is one greater than the temple" (Matt. 12:6). As for the Jews, they were turning the Temple into an idol.

C. HIS EXPLOSIVE APPLICATION (7:51–53)

(1) THEY HAD ACCUSED HIM OF REVILING THE HOLY PLACE—HE ACCUSED THEM OF RESISTING THE HOLY GHOST (7:51)

Ye stiffnecked and uncircumcised in heart and ears, ye do always resist the Holy Ghost: as your fathers did, so do ye.

There are three ways in which the Holy Spirit can be opposed. He can be grieved, He can be quenched, and He can be resisted. Only a Spirit-indwelt believer can *grieve* the Holy Spirit. The word *grieve* is a love-word. We can grieve only someone who loves us and who stands in a special relationship to us. A church can *quench* the Holy Spirit by allowing men to usurp His authority, by refusing to follow His leading, or by permitting false doctrine or moral evil to take root. Sinners *resist* the Holy Spirit.

Stephen now dropped his defense and went boldly to the attack, vilifying his listeners for their persistent and continuing opposition to God. Their chief sin was that of resisting the Holy Spirit. Their treatment of the saviors, the Scriptures, and the sanctuaries God had given them, and, above all, their treatment of the Son of God, constituted a persistent sin against the Holy Ghost.

(2) THEY HAD ACCUSED HIM OF SLIGHTING MOSES, THE MAN OF GOD—HE ACCUSED THEM OF SLAYING JESUS, THE MESSIAH OF GOD (7:52)

Which of the prophets have not your fathers persecuted? And they have slain them which shewed before of the coming of the Just One; of whom ye have been now the betrayers and murderers.

Old Testament prophets expected persecution. Much of their ministry involved denouncing people for their sins and for their false religion—not a ministry calculated to endear them to their audience. Nor did they worry too much about putting things diplomatically. They spoke boldly and bluntly to the issues.

Martyrdom and persecution was their expected lot. Moses was once threatened with stoning by the people. Elijah would have been executed if Jezebel could have laid hands on him. Isaiah is said to have been put into a hollow tree and sawn asunder in the days of Manasseh. Jeremiah was told by God not to marry, because no woman ought to share sufferings such as his, and after being forcibly abducted to Egypt by apostate Jews he was stoned to death. Zechariah was martyred between the Temple and the altar.

All those crimes against God's messengers were nothing compared with the crime Stephen's accusers had committed. They had murdered God's Son, "the Just One" (or "the Righteous One"). No crime could be greater, no murder more dreadful. Stephen called the crime of Calvary what it was—murder.

(3) THEY HAD ACCUSED HIM OF BLASPHEMING THE LAW—HE ACCUSED THEM OF
BREAKING THE LAW (7:53)

Who have received the law by the disposition of angels, and have not kept it.

Moses, in his account of the giving of the law, says, "The LORD came from Sinai, and rose up from Seir unto them; he shined forth from Mount Paran, and he came with ten thousands of saints: from his right hand went a fiery law for them" (Deut. 33:2). The Septuagint renders that last clause: "with the myriads of Kadesh were angels with him at his right hand." The clear inference is that God brought the law down to Moses, but it was given to him by the hand of a mediating angel. We gather the same facts from Galatians 3:19 and Hebrews 2:2.

Had Stephen blasphemed the law? Not a bit of it! But they had broken the Law. If any charge was to be made in respect of the law, the charge was against Israel. From the very beginning they had broken the law, broken it so badly that Moses had taken the tables of stone, upon which the law had been written with the finger of God, and dashed them to pieces. Israel's whole history had been such—one long record of law-breaking.

Now, in addition to all their other crimes, they had taken the Son of God, one far superior to the angel mediators of the Old Convenant, He who was the Mediator of a New Covenant, and they had murdered Him.

They had accused Stephen of three things. He answered their charges and hurled a counter charge in their faces. Such was the explosive application of his long but masterly defense.

3. STEPHEN, THE TRIUMPHANT WARRIOR (7:54–60)

a. HIS CONVICTING VOICE (7:54)

When they heard these things, they were cut to the heart, and they gnashed on him with their teeth.

They had heard Stephen with patience, interest, and even some agreement at first, but as soon as it became obvious what he was driving at, their outrage increased until at last it burst forth in fury. One can picture them standing, waving clenched fists at him, gnashing their teeth at him, yelling and shouting at him. It was like a scene out of hell.

"They were cut to the heart," the Holy Spirit says. The verb means "they were sawn asunder." They were infuriated. They were like a pack of wild animals—these, the supposed spiritual leaders of Israel.

b. HIS COMPLETE VINDICATION (7:55)

But he, being full of the Holy Ghost, looked up stedfastly into heaven, and saw the glory of God, and Jesus standing on the right hand of God.

The Holy Spirit now graciously directed Stephen's gaze away from that clamoring mob towards heaven. The glory of God burst upon his enraptured sight. The true sanctuary in heaven was opened to his view. And in the same instant he saw Jesus, saw Him standing, saw Him standing at God's right hand, saw Him standing to register His applause, His approval, His "Well done, Stephen!" In a few more minutes Stephen would be there, absent from the body, present with the Lord. But first he must bear one final witness to the nation and its leaders now set irrevocably on a collision course with judgment.

c. HIS CONTINUING VALOR (7:56–59)

(1) HIS FINAL TESTIMONY (7:56)

And said, Behold, I see the heavens opened, and the Son of man standing at the right hand of God.

Many in the court that day had been present a few years before when the Lord Himself, put under oath by the same high priest Caiaphas, had unequivocally proclaimed His absolute deity. Asked if He was the Son of God, He had said He was indeed. Then He added, "And ye shall see the Son of man sitting on the right hand of power" (Mark 14:62).

"I see Him!" cried Stephen. "He is indeed at the right hand of God. I see Him standing there. I see Him, the Son of Man, in heaven." The title Son of Man was the Lord's own usual title for Himself. It was a messianic title, full of prophetic significance for Israel.

Stephen voiced what the Sanhedrin considered the ultimate blasphemy. Not only was he upholding the claim of the Lord Jesus to be co-equal with God, but he was putting Him on the throne of the universe. Jesus was no mere Jewish messiah. He was God, over all, blessed for evermore. All the institutions of the past were obsolete. Access to the immediate presence of God was available to all through the Lord Jesus Christ.

  (2) HIS FINAL TRIAL (7:57–58)

   (a) HOW THEY STOPPED HIM (7:57)

  Then they cried out with a loud voice, and stopped their ears, and ran upon him with one accord.

  They had heard enough. As the thunder of Niagara drowns out a lone human voice, so their mob-cry of rage now drowned out Stephen's voice. They put their fingers in their ears. They had heard enough blasphemy for one day. Then, with mob violence, they burst from their seats and surged forward to lay their hands upon God's fearless witness.

  It is doubtful whether Stephen heard or saw them. His soul was still enraptured in his vision of Jesus.

   (b) HOW THEY STONED HIM (7:58)

  And cast him out of the city, and stoned him: and the witnesses laid down their clothes at a young man's feet, whose name was Saul.

  The Mosaic law required that the first stones thrown in the execution of a condemned criminal be cast by the very witness who threw verbal stones at him during his trial (Deut. 17:17). That in itself would make any but a wicked person doubly careful to examine both his motives and his honesty at the time of the trial.

  Jewish custom had established a formality about the execution designed to diminish passion. Just before arriving at the site, the condemned was given a chance to confess and make his peace with God. The site being reached, which was some ten to twelve feet above the actual place of death, one of the witnesses came up behind the victim and pushed him over the edge so that he fell face downward on the ground below. It was hoped that the fall itself would kill him, but if not he was turned over on his back and another of the witnesses threw a stone at him. If he survived that operation, all the congregation joined in the stoning.

  All such cold and deliberate formality was not likely to be observed by the mob now set on lynching Stephen. They "cast him out of the city." We can picture his being hurried along to the place of execution surrounded by a howling mob. At the fatal spot there was a momentary pause while the witnesses flung off their hampering outer garments. Stephen was pushed over the edge, and eager hands were ready to turn him on his back to receive the full discharge of the stones they were now eagerly collecting.

  The Holy Spirit pauses here for a moment. There was in that mob a man who was to be Stephen's spiritual heir. He did not know it, nobody knew it, but it was at his feet that the witnesses put their coats. His name was Saul.

We learn later that Saul came from Tarsus in Cilicia. It was more than likely that this brilliant young rabbi attended the very synagogue in Jerusalem where Stephen had so zealously defended the cause of Christ (6:9). Likely enough he himself had been silenced by the power of Stephen's arguments. Not for the hot-headed young Saul was the moderation and compromise recommended by Gamaliel, whose school he had attended. Young Saul clearly saw the threat Christianity posed for Judaism. The two systems were mutually exclusive. Christianity, if true, abolished Judaism. He took the same stand later when, as the apostle of Christ, he proclaimed the Christian cause.

So Stephen was stoned, but not before making his indelible mark on the soul of Saul. Stephen's martyrdom must have looked to the early church as a waste. Little did his fellow believers know that Stephen was another corn of wheat falling into the ground to die so that it might not abide alone. Little did they know, either, that it had fallen into soil that would provide a marvelous harvest for Christ in the conversion and ministry of Saul of Tarsus.

(3) HIS FINAL TRIUMPH (7:59)

And they stoned Stephen, calling upon God, and saying, Lord Jesus, receive my spirit.

Stephen's last words proclaimed still the deity of the Lord Jesus. When Jesus died He said, "Father, into thy hands I commend my spirit" (Luke 23:46). When Stephen died he said, "Lord Jesus, receive my spirit," thus confessing the fact that Jesus was co-equal with the Father, the Author of life and the Victor over death. Stephen was on the verge of departing this life. He spoke words that Saul never forgot. Later Paul took them up and formalized them into one of the great doctrines of the faith. Death for a Christian involved much more than a departure of the soul to Abraham's bosom in some gloomy underworld. Death for a Christian meant "to be absent from the body, and to be present with the Lord" (2 Cor. 5:8).

d. HIS CROWNING VICTORY (7:60)

And he kneeled down, and cried with a loud voice, Lord, lay not this sin to their charge. And when he had said this, he fell asleep.

Stephen's last words were not only a mark of Christian grace, an echo of the Lord's words on the cross, and a triumphant demonstration of the Sermon on the Mount in action ("pray for them which despitefully use you" [Matt. 5:44]), they were a final proclamation of the deity of the Lord Jesus. For "who can forgive sins but God only?" (Mark 2:7).

Thus he "fell asleep." With force and fury the missiles fell about him, striking him with stunning violence. But amid them all is a scene of peace.

We see Stephen of the shining angel face, on his knees, heedless of the stones, talking with the standing Savior at God's right hand. Presently one stone more violent than the rest ended his life, and Stephen was—asleep! Dead? No! Very much alive on the other shore. But his battered body was now asleep.

C. THE FIRST MISSIONARY (8:1–40)

    1. *A NEW FOE: EMPHASIS—PERSECUTED CHRISTIANS (8:1–4)*

        a. THE MAGNITUDE OF THE PERSECUTION (8:1–4)

            (1) ITS FOCUS (8:1–2)

                (a) AN EXPLOSION (8:1*a*)

And Saul was consenting unto his death. And at that time there was a great persecution against the church which was at Jerusalem; and they were all scattered abroad throughout the regions of Judea and Samaria . . .

Saul looked with approval on the murder of Stephen. He did not see it as murder. Religion blinded his eyes. "I obtained mercy," he wrote in later years, "because I did it ignorantly," (1 Tim. 1:13). Consenting to evil is as bad as committing evil. Saul was too refined to stand there throwing stones, but not too refined to hold the coats of those who did. His religion was of the same brand as Cain's, whose convictions were too refined to slay a lamb but not too refined to assassinate Abel. Religion without the Holy Spirit is the cruelest force in the world. It bears the imprimatur of its father, the Devil, the old serpent, he who was a liar and a murderer from the beginning.

The death of Stephen signaled a fierce outbreak of persecution against the Jerusalem church. Nearly all the opposition against Christianity in Acts came from the Jews. It was to be another in that series of nails driven into the coffin of Jewish national life by the Christ-rejecting undertakers of Judaism.

The Holy Spirit describes this outbreak of persecution as "a great persecution." No details are given except the note that it resulted in the scattering of the believers throughout Judea and Samaria. All Satan accomplished by this violence was to scatter the glowing embers of the church's fire far and wide, so that wherever they settled new fires might spring up.

"Ye shall be witnesses unto me both in Jerusalem, and in all Judea, and in Samaria" (1:8), said the Lord Jesus. Because the Jerusalem church had little vision beyond its own narrow borders, the persecution by Satan simply accomplished the Holy Spirit's purpose. God makes the wrath of man to praise Him.

                (b) AN EXCEPTION (8:1*b*)

Except the apostles.

The apostles remained in Jerusalem. Perhaps they felt the post of danger was the post of duty. Perhaps the organizers of the persecution, having made a martyr out of Stephen, left the apostles alone lest they make martyrs out of them. Perhaps the apostles still thought of the Jerusalem church as the mother church, and thought they should remain with her no matter what. They certainly do not seem to have taken seriously, as yet, the great world commission of Acts 1:8.

(c) AN EXAMPLE (8:2)

And devout men carried Stephen to his burial, and made great lamentation over him.

Of course they did. The church on earth had lost a champion. Where, even among the apostles, could be found so able a polemicist, so eloquent an expositor, so fearless a fighter? There can be little doubt that, had he lived, Stephen would have done the work later done by Paul. He had a clear enough vision of the true nature of the church and its distinctives, and of its world mission and its uniqueness, its spirituality, eternity, and essential difference from Israel. The devout men of the Jerusalem church buried Stephen with full honor and lamented his death.

Stephen would not have wanted that. He was now with the church invisible in heaven. Moreover, he could have echoed Paul's noble words when, years later, he was facing his martyrdom: "I have fought a good fight, I have finished my course, I have kept the faith: henceforth there is laid up for a me a crown of righteousness" (2 Tim. 4:7–8). Stephen had left an example that has been followed by a countless host of noble martyrs.

(2) ITS FURY (8:3–4)

(a) THE MANNER OF THE PERSECUTION (8:3)

As for Saul, he made havock of the church, entering into every house, and haling men and women committed them to prison.

Saul now went mad. He tells us so himself in later years. He "made havoc of the church." The expression is used of the ravages of a wild boar. He had his hit list. He entered every house where a believer lived. There was hardly a home where his cruelty was not felt. The prisons overflowed. In later years we find Paul, wherever his gospel travels took him, zealously taking up collections for "the poor saints which are at Jerusalem" (Rom. 15:26). Many of them he had made poor. Their faces haunted him. Whenever he met with the Jerusalem church he would see bereaved saints, a husband missing here, a brother, a father missing there—the fruits of his furious persecution of the church in his unregenerate days.

(b) THE MINISTRY OF THE PERSECUTION (8:4)

Therefore they that were scattered abroad went every where preaching the word.

Thus began the worldwide witness of the church. True, on the day of

Pentecost there were in Jerusalem "Jews, devout men, out of every nation under heaven" (2:5) who witnessed the birthday of the church, who saw the signs, who heard the preaching of Peter, and who doubtless carried back with them the good news. Doubtless many of the 3,000 who were saved were from the Dispersion. Their knowledge of Christianity would have been rudimentary in the extreme, however. Their spiritual horizons would still be bounded by Judaism. Stephen's preaching was a great advance on Simon's. Those now leaving Jerusalem had the certain knowledge that the official leaders of Judaism had turned against the Christ and the church. Although many of the tattered rags of an outworn Judaism might be kept in the religious wardrobe of those scattered Jewish Christians, they would soon be consciously replaced by the robes of that righteousness that is to be found in Christ alone.

So the great trek began. Far from being intimidated by the persecution, the believers, now scattering far and wide, went everywhere preaching the Word. Prudence might advise them to be scattered, but nothing could advise them to be silent.

    2. *A NEW FIELD EMPHASIS—PREACHING CHRIST (8:5–25)*

      a. PHILIP'S FRUIT IN THE GOSPEL (8:5–8)

        (1) REVIVAL (8:5–7)

          (a) HIS GOSPEL PREACHING (8:5)

Then Philip went down to the city of Samaria, and preached Christ unto them.

Like Stephen, Philip was one of the seven deacons chosen by the Jerusalem church to handle its more secular affairs. They had chosen their deacons well. One became the first great martyr of the faith; another became the first great missionary of the faith.

"Ye shall be witnesses unto me both in Jerusalem, and in all all Judea, and in Samaria" (1:8), the Lord had said. Philip, a Hellenist Jew, not so branded with narrow Palestinian prejudices as some of the others, took the call to Samaria seriously. It was not a popular mission field.

Samaria was a small province to the north of Judaea. The area had been settled with pagans by the Assyrians, who, having deported many thousands of Israelites from the city of Samaria and the Northern Kingdom, replaced them with heathen from elsewhere (2 Kings 17:24–26). The settlers adopted a bastard form of Judaism and built a rival temple on Mount Gerizim, which they regarded as equally sacred as the Jewish Temple in Jerusalem. Ill-feeling between the Jews and the Samaritans had deep roots. The Jews never accepted them. They spurned their offer of help when, their captivity ended, they returned to Jerusalem. They considered them religious and racial mongrels and refused to have anything to do with them. The Hasmonean ruler

John Hyrcanus I conquered Samaria and destroyed their temple a century before the coming of Christ. The Romans treated Samaria as an independent area, separate from Judea and Galilee. No self-respecting Jew would, of his own preference, go to Samaria.

Jesus did. Now Philip did. The "city of Samaria" to which he now went may well have been Samaria itself. The original city had been rebuilt by Herod the Great and dedicated to Caesar. Or, as some have suggested, the city to which Philip went might have been Gitta, the birthplace of Simon the Sorcerer.

Philip wasted no time. He preached Christ to the Samaritans. Not Judaism, but Christ! Not religion, but Christ! One wonders if in his audience there might not have been the woman who once had met that very Christ at the well of Sychar. She, at least, would instantly recognize the validity of the message. The preaching of Christ to needy hearts cannot help but win a response. And so it was.

(b) HIS GREAT POWER (8:6–7)

i. THEY WERE CONVICTED BY WHAT HE SAID (8:6a)

And the people with one accord gave heed unto those things which Philip spake . . .

That would not have happened if he had attempted to preach a form of reformed Judaism or some other religious system. They already had religion. What they needed was Christ. The name of Jesus warmed their hearts. Maybe Philip reminded them of the story of the woman at the well; how she came to the well, weary, unsatisfied, full of restless longings, and how she went away with the joybells ringing in her heart; how she had brought Samaritans to Jesus and how He had stayed among them as their guest (John 4:7–42). Maybe he told them of the time James and John wanted to call down fire on Samaria and how Jesus had rebuked them for their ignorance of the true nature of the Holy Spirit (Luke 9:54–55). Those would certainly have been attention-getting starters!

Then, of course, he would tell the whole wonderful story of the Lord who came from glory, who died upon the cruel tree that we might have redemption through His blood. There was one sure thing: he had their undivided attention. With one accord the people heeded the things that Philip spoke.

ii. THEY WERE CONVINCED BY WHAT THEY SAW (8:6b–7)

. . . hearing and seeing the miracles which he did. For unclean spirits, crying with loud voice, came out of many that were possessed with them: and many taken with palsies, and that were lame, were healed.

Demons and disease fled before the power of God in Philip. As we read the narratives of the gospels and the Acts, we cannot fail to notice the prevalence of both demon possession and disease in those days. We cannot help but believe that both those afflictions are common in all ages. We easily enough diagnose the bodily afflictions for what they are, but we tend to ignore the parallel affliction of the soul. We tend not to believe in demons any more, and even if we give intellectual assent to their existence, we discount their activity. Modern psychology has done much to turn our attention away from demon activity. We have so many other, more plausible explanations today for abnormal and aberrant human behavior. We have phobias, psychoses, and syndromes; we find causes for our depressions and distortions in childhood experience, in sex, and in heredity. Much of that may be true enough, but none of it gives credibility to what the Bible says about demon possession and oppression. We might be very much surprised, if the truth were really told, to discover that demons are as active in the twentieth century as they were in the first.

Philip's evident power gave tremendous weight to his preaching.

(2) REJOICING (8:8)

And there was great joy in that city.

Of course there was! Revival always produces rejoicing. When people get right with God and consequently get right with each other, heaven comes down and glory fills the soul. The firstfruits of the Spirit, after all, are love, joy, and peace. Turn those things loose in a community, and great will be the happiness that follows. As the psalmist said, "Happy is that people, whose God is the Lord" (Ps. 144:15). There is nothing more welcome in this dark, dreary world than a man, a woman, a boy, or a girl filled with the sunshine of heaven.

b. PHILIP'S FAME IN THE GOSPEL (8:9–14)

(1) SIMON MAGUS HEARS THE NEWS (8:9–13)

(a) HIS DECEPTIONS (8:9)

i. HIS METHOD (8:9a)

But there was a certain man, called Simon, which beforetime in the same city used sorcery, and bewitched the people of Samaria . . .

"But." That spoils the picture. Everywhere there was love, joy, peace, repentance, revival, rebirth; everywhere except in the life of one individual. In the soul of a certain Simon the sorcerer Satan still reigned supreme. This man had met his match. He had power, the kind of power Satan can give. But he knew that what he had was poor and shoddy stuff indeed compared with the mighty power of Philip.

We must pause and look at Simon Magus, because the Holy Spirit tells his tale at some length. Satan had tried *money* as a means of stopping the church in the case of Ananias and Sapphira, and he had tried *murder* as a means in the case of Stephen. Now he was to try *mimicry*. He had a man ready, a willing agent. He would have this man go through a form of conversion and insinuate him into the church so that he would have one of his men in a position to do mischief.

A considerable literature eventually grew up around Simon Magus. He was credited with being the founder of Gnosticism, one of the most persistent and pernicious heresies with which the church has ever had to cope. He was supposed to have performed miracles in Samaria and later in Rome, where he went in the reign of Claudius. It is said that in Rome he subverted the church by false teaching and that he incited the authorities against the Christians. He was accompanied in his travels by a slave woman named Helen, whom he had purchased at Tyre and whom he declared to be an incarnation of "the Divine mind." He is said to have had a magical confrontation with Peter during which he practiced levitation and flew up into the air, only to be brought crashing to the ground by Peter's superior spiritual power. In the end he is supposed to have tried to emulate the resurrection of Christ by having himself buried alive in Rome, promising to rise on the third day. That seems to have been the end of him.

Much of the Simon Magus myth can be discounted. Just the same, he did have psychic power, and he used his satanic gifts to dazzle and mesmerize the people of Samaria.

ii. HIS MOTIVE (8:9*b*)

. . . giving out that himself was some great one.

Simon Magus enjoyed the reputation he had established for himself. People spoke of him with awe and were impressed with his mysterious, magical powers. He cultivated their adulation; he announced that he was indeed a great person. He was inflated with pride. He had fallen not only into the clutches of the devil but into the condemnation of the devil. Whenever God is at work in revival, watch out for Simon Magus. Satan will always have one of his agents ready.

(b) HIS DISCIPLES (8:10–12)

i. WHY THEY FOLLOWED HIM (8:10–11)

To whom they all gave heed, from the least to the greatest, saying, This man is the great power of God. And to him they had regard, because [for a] long time he had bewitched them with sorceries.

Evidently Simon Magus was no quack. He had real satanic power to do supernatural things. He had a wide following from all ranks of society. He had been practicing his sorceries for a long time and was a well established power in Samaria. He claimed the title "the great power of God." He claimed to be the Grand Vicar of God, the one through whom God spoke to men and through whom He released His power.

Philip was not intimidated by this man. Doubtless he expected opposition. Strangely enough, that opposition did not develop. The evil spirit that energized Simon Magus recognized the superior power of the Spirit of God in Philip and was not anxious for a confrontation. Satan had deeper plans. Simon Magus bided his time.

ii. WHY THEY FORSOOK HIM (8:12)

But when they believed Philip preaching the things concerning the kingdom of God, and the name of Jesus Christ, they were baptized, both men and women.

Philip's Spirit-anointed preaching produced immediate results. The people believed and were baptized. It is important to note that their faith rested solidly on the preaching of the Word of God, not on the miracles Philip performed. The faith that rests on miracles is not worth much. If we win people with sensationlism we will need sensationalism to keep them. People who come for loaves and fishes will have to be kept with loaves and fishes.

Philip preached "the things concerning the kingdom of God." Whatever else may or may not have been included in that, we can be sure he preached what Jesus preached to Nicodemus: "Except a man be born again, he cannot see the kingdom of God" (John 3:3).

He preached the name of Jesus Christ, the sovereign, saving, sanctifying name, the name all hell fears and all heaven hails, the name in which alone salvation is to be found.

No wonder Simon Magus held his peace.

The people responded at once to the preaching. This was the real thing. It made Simon Magus and his bag of magic tricks look cheap and tawdry. If "the great power of God" (8:10) was to be found anywhere, it was in Philip's preaching. If anyone could speak to men in the name of God, it was Philip. If anyone had the power of God, it was Philip. Philip did not waste his time refuting Simon Magus. He preached Christ.

So Simon Magus lost his disciples. His cunning mind, however, was hard at work: "If you cannot beat them, join them" seems to have been his idea.

(c) HIS DECISION (8:13)

Then Simon himself believed also: and when he was baptized, he continued with Philip, and wondered, beholding the miracles and signs which were done.

Simon's faith was spurious from the start. He was not won by Philip's message but by Philip's miracles. He "believed," it says. But *what* did he believe? Whatever it was he believed, it did not regenerate his soul. He was as lost after he "believed" as he was before he "believed," as the sequel of the story makes clear.

He deceived Philip, however. Perhaps he even deceived himself. What Simon Magus coveted was not the Master but the miracles, not the Savior but the signs.

How careful we need to be in preaching the gospel and in personal witnessing to distinguish between those who "believe" and those who *believe*. Simon Magus went so far as to be baptized. Certainly Philip seemed to have made a very notable convert.

(2) SIMON PETER HEARS THE NEWS (8:14)

Now when the apostles which were at Jerusalem heard that Samaria had received the word of God, they sent unto them Peter and John.

About five or six years had elapsed since the resurrection of Christ, the giving of the Great Commission, and the birthday of the church. As yet the apostles had made little enough effort to evangelize Judaea; and as for Samaria, that was certainly not likely to be high on their agenda. It must have come as a shock to them to discover that the Lord was serious about Samaria and that the evangelization of that area had now taken place without them. God will never leave Himself without a man to do His will. If those who are called will not do it, He will choose someone else.

Belatedly they began to think about Samaria. The news of the revival there convinced them to send a delegation to see what was going on. That "mother church" attitude of the Jerusalem hierarchy is understandable, given the presence of the apostles in the city. The evangelization of Samaria, however, was the first tolling of the bell of doom for the idea that one church can be the headquarters for running all church affairs. Soon the tidal waters of church expansion would sweep all such notions into oblivion. The church is not an organization but an organism. It is not "spiritual Israel" to be run along imperial lines by man, but the mystical body of Christ to be directed from heaven and energized by the Holy Spirit.

However, at this stage, the apostles still felt it their right and responsibility to investigate new movements within the church. And in this case, given the age-old Jewish suspicion and prejudice against Samaritans, it was a sensible move. So Peter and John went to Samaria.

c. PHILIP'S FELLOWSHIP IN THE GOSPEL (8:15–25)

(1) DISPENSING THE GIFT OF THE HOLY SPIRIT (8:15–17)

(a) ENDING THE HISTORIC ISOLATION OF THE SAMARITANS BY THE JEWISH COMMUNITY (8:15–16)

Who, when they were come down, prayed for them, that they might receive the Holy Ghost: (for as yet he was fallen upon none of them: only they were baptized in the name of the Lord Jesus).

Philip now faded into the background. He does not seem to have been resentful. There was no partisan spirit in the early church. He was doubtless glad that the leading apostles themselves had come to Samaria to officially welcome the new Samaritan believers into the Body of Christ. It must have warmed the hearts of the Samaritans also to know that their age-old historic isolation by the Jews was now abolished. They were not to be second-class members of the Body. Peter and John wasted no time. As soon as they saw that the revival was genuine they prayed that the new Samaritan brethren might receive the gift of the Holy Spirit.

Nowadays we receive the Holy Spirit the moment we are saved (Rom. 8), but in the transition stage, as here in Samaria, formal identification of the Samaritans was necessary. This prayer cemented the fellowship between people long separated by racial and religious prejudice. The apostles abolished their prejudice by praying for their newfound brethren that they might be equal members of the mystical body; the Samaritans abolished prejudice by accepting the blessing from Jewish brethren.

(b) ENSURING THE HAPPY IDENTIFICATION OF THE SAMARITANS IN THE CHRIS-
TIAN COMMUNITY (8:17)

Then laid they their hands on them, and they received the Holy Ghost.

In the Bible the laying on of hands is always a symbol of identification. In the Old Testament the sinner identified himself with his offering by laying his hands upon it. Then, when it was slain, it was as though he had been slain. By laying their hands on the Samaritans, Peter and John formally identified themselves, the rest of the apostles, and all the Jewish church with the new believers. Henceforth they would be one church. There would be one Lord, one faith, one baptism. What a happy ending to centuries of strife and ill will!

The Holy Spirit responded at once, and all the Samaritan believers received the Holy Spirit. Thus He endorsed the fact of their spiritual oneness in Christ. This laying on of hands was a once-for-all act. The word "received" here means "were receiving" (were continuing to receive). There was no need for a repetition of this extraordinary measure. It was necessary in the case of the Samaritans because of the special situation existing between Samaria and the Jewish world. It is not necessary today.

No mention is made of tongues or other spectacular sign gifts of the Spirit. If they were in evidence, the Holy Spirit does not say so. His silence on the matter depreciates the importance of those things on this occasion. The important thing was that Samaritans and Jews were now one in Christ, sharing in the person and work of the Holy Spirit.

(2) DETECTING THE GUILT OF SIMON MAGUS (8:18–24)
    (a) SIMON'S CONCLUSIONS (8:18–19)
        i. WHAT HE DISCERNED (8:18a)

And when Simon saw that through laying on of the apostles' hands the Holy Ghost was given . . .

Watching all that was going on with an avid and avaricious interest was the sorcerer. All his life he had dabbled with forbidden mysteries, seeking the deep things of Satan, hankering after power conferred by the spirits. Now he was confronted by the power conferred by the Holy Spirit. His eyes gleamed. Here was power indeed! If only he had the kind of power possessed by Peter and John: what prestige it would give him to be able to convey spiritual power by a touch of his hand. People would flock to him; he could name his own price. He saw at once the immense opportunities open to a man with such power.

        ii. WHAT HE DECIDED (8:18b)

. . . he offered them money.

In Simon's world everything had a price, just as it had in Judas's world. Judas could express the worship of Mary of Bethany in terms of cold cash— "three hundred pence" (a year's salary) was his estimate of its worth (Mark 4:4). Judas would sell his Savior for thirty silver coins. Simon Magus did the same. He set a cash value on spiritual things and offered the apostles money. Judas decided the Savior had a market value; Simon Magus decided the Spirit had a market value.

It is from this incident that the word *simony* comes, referring to the purchase and sale of spiritual office and benefits. The purchase and sale of bishoprics and cardinalates by the Roman Catholic church reached its height in the days of the Borgias; the purchase and sale of indulgences reached its height in the days of Martin Luther. Not that Rome has been alone. Well-paying "livings" (as they have been called) have often been dispensed by squires and landowners in other communions.

"He offered them money," and in that one act betrayed himself.

        iii. WHAT HE DESIRED (8:19)

Saying, Give me also this power, that on whomsoever I lay hands, he may receive the Holy Ghost.

He put his covetousness into words. He wanted to be able to buy and sell, to market as a mere commodity, the Holy Spirit of God. Sins against the Son of God are always terrible, and in due time they reap their due reward of judgment, but in this age of grace the penalty is often withheld. Sins against the Spirit of God, even in an age of grace, are treated with more immediate severity. In this age the Holy Spirit is the resident member of the triune

Godhead on earth. Sins against him are treated with the utmost gravity. Ananias and Sapphira had sinned against the Holy Spirit and were instantly executed as a warning. Now Simon Magus sinned against the Holy Spirit and was instantly excommunicated.

(b) SIMON'S CONDEMNATION (8:20–23)

i. PETER'S GODLY INDIGNATION (8:20)

But Peter said unto him, Thy money perish with thee, because thou hast thought that the gift of God may be purchased with money.

The gift of the Holy Spirit is the greatest gift God can give to man, for the Holy Spirit is a member of the triune Godhead. He brings with Him into human life all that is purely spiritual. When Adam sinned, the spirit part of man was extinguished. The human spirit had been indwelt by the Holy Spirit. But when Adam sinned the Holy Spirit departed, and the lamp went out. At the time of our conversion the Holy Spirit comes back to indwell the human spirit, and He relights the lamp. He Himself is the holy, fragrant oil that makes possible spiritual life for man.

Money is exactly the opposite. Money represents human labor, effort, wealth, position, power. "The love of money is the root of all evil" says the apostle (1. Tim. 6:10). Money is the medium of exchange by which we convert our talents, time, and effort into material possessions, position, and power on earth.

Simon Magus betrayed his utter spiritual ignorance by thinking that man's money could buy God's gift.

"You and your money can go to destruction," Peter said. The spirit of discernment in Peter enabled him to recognize the man for a fraud. His profession of faith was utterly worthless, his baptism meaningless. He was as lost as he had ever been.

ii. PETER'S GODLY INTUITION (8:21)

Thou hast neither part nor lot in this matter: for thy heart is not right in the sight of God.

Jesus said "of the abundance of the heart [a man's] mouth speaketh" (Luke 6:45). What came out of the mouth of Simon Magus indicated the unregenerate state of his heart. No truly Spirit-regenerated, Spirit-indwelt believer could have made such an offer as Simon Magus made. We may say false things and foolish things even after we are saved, but there are some things we cannot possibly say. The Holy Spirit within us will not permit the words to rise within us or to pass our lips. The moment Simon Magus opened his mouth, Simon Peter saw into his soul. "You are not right with God," he said. "You have nothing to do with spiritual things at all."

iii. PETER'S GODLY INJUNCTION (8:22)

Repent therefore of this thy wickedness, and pray God, if perhaps the thought of thine heart may be forgiven thee.

Peter now treated Simon Magus as an unsaved man. Peter had the heart of a soul-winner, and he urged Simon Magus to repent. It was not too late for him to be saved. His false profession could be replaced by genuine conversion. The essential prerequisite to regeneration is repentance, and there had been no repentance in Simon Magus's life. He was in a desperate spiritual condition. His false profession of faith had put him in great spiritual danger.

That, of course, is what is wrong with the "easy believism" characteristic of much preaching today. There is no conviction of sin and no repentance. The first work of the Holy Spirit in a human heart is to convince of sin, of righteousness, and of judgment to come—of the *nature* of sin, of the *need* for righteousness, and of the *nearness* of judgment. What we have today is profession without possession, conversion without repentance, and religion without the Holy Spirit or riddled with misconceptions about the Holy Spirit.

They had it back in Peter's day, too. So Peter preached repentance to this poor, lost, Satan-blinded, money-loving, power-hungry sinner, whom everyone else had thought to be a believer.

iv. PETER'S GODLY INSIGHT (8:23)

For I perceive that thou art in the gall of bitterness, and in the bond of iniquity.

He had disguised it very well. He had pretended to be a believer. He had deceived the saints, but he had not deceived the Holy Spirit. This man's heart was a seething cauldron of gall, and he was in bondage to bitterness. He had deeply resented his loss of influence and power and was bitterly jealous of the evangelist and the apostles. He envied them their power. His crafty mind had seen a way to recoup his own waning influence if only he could get his hands on the power they had. He had hidden his secret rage and resentment, biding his time. He was Satan's tool and Satan's fool.

With spiritual, godly insight Peter saw through him and gave him a picture of his soul.

(c) SIMON'S CONCERN (8:24)

Then answered Simon, and said, Pray ye to the Lord for me, that none of these things which ye have spoken come upon me.

Simon Magus was frightened. He was suddenly afraid of Simon Peter and afraid of the consequences of his own behavior. But it was not the godly fear that leads to repentance, the fear of the Lord that is the beginning of wisdom. Had he been under such genuine conviction he would not have asked Peter to pray for him; he would have prayed for himself. He would have prayed the publican's prayer: "God, be merciful to me a sinner" (Luke 8:13). Many, like Simon Magus, would like to avoid the consequences of their sin but are not willing to give up the sin itself.

There the Holy Spirit leaves Simon Magus. He is still outside the fold, still in his sins, still Satan's slave. Like king Agrippa (26:28) we leave him almost persuaded. Almost—but lost.

(3) DECLARING THE GOSPEL OF JESUS CHRIST (8:25)

And they, when they had testified and preached the word of the Lord, returned to Jerusalem, and preached the gospel in many villages of the Samaritans.

It would seem from the wording of the next verse that Philip accompanied Peter and John back to Jerusalem once the apostles had confirmed the faith of the Samaritan believers and had imparted to them the basic truths of the gospel.

On the way back, they stopped here and there, thoroughly evangelizing the province of Samaria. Thus the third phase of world evangelism was accomplished. Jerusalem, Judaea, and Samaria had heard the Gospel. The stage has now to be set to evangelize "the uttermost parts of the earth."

3. A NEW FOLLOWER: EMPHASIS—PERSONAL CONTACT *(8:26–40)*

a. FOREKNOWLEDGE (8:26–31)

(1) THE STRANGE COMMAND (8:26)

And the angel of the Lord spake unto Philip, saying, Arise, and go toward the south unto the way that goeth down from Jerusalem unto Gaza, which is desert.

This was indeed a strange command. Again it was Philip the evangelist, not one of the apostles, who was called to make the move. The great pagan Gentile world was now to be contacted through an Ethiopian proselyte to Judaism. Philip was alerted by the Holy Spirit to again leave his ministry of waiting on tables in order to make contact with this man.

The command to head for the desert country near Gaza must have astonished Philip, but he had no hesitation in going. An angel of the Lord left him in no doubt as to his leading. Behind this abrupt command was the foreknowledge of God, who knew all about the Ethiopian, knew the position he held in his native land, knew why he had come to Jerusalem, knew the deep, unsatisfied hunger of his heart, knew he was on the way home, knew all about his chariot, knew exactly where he was on the road, knew what book he was reading, knew his perplexity and his dogged persistence. We are now about to witness one of those amazing meetings that take place from time to time on earth, the details of which are all determined in heaven and directed by the Spirit of God.

The call of God to Philip was given in an extraordinary way. "The angel of the Lord" appeared to him. Some versions give the translation as "an angel of the Lord." In the Old Testament "the angel of the Lord" is a title for the second person of the Godhead when He appeared to men in visible angelic form. Here the indefinite article is better perhaps. The Lord sent one of His angels on this unexpected mission. Angels appear on several important occasions in the book of Acts.

(2) THE SACRED CAUSE (8:27–28)

(a) THE EUNUCH'S SOCIAL STATUS (8:27)

And he arose and went: and, behold, a man of Ethiopia, an eunuch of great authority under Candace queen of the Ethiopians, who had the charge of all her treasure, and had come to Jerusalem for to worship . . .

We are now to witness the first of three remarkable conversions. In chapter 8 we have the conversion of an Ethiopian, a black, a representative of the racial family of *Ham*; in chapter 9 we have the conversion of Saul of Tarsus, a Jew, a representative of the racial family of *Shem*; in chapter 10 we have the conversion of Cornelius, a Roman centurion, a representative of the racial family of *Japheth*. The three great racial families are now made one in the family of God. The curse of Babel, which enforced God's deliberate division of mankind, is reversed in the church.

The Ethiopian here may possibly have come from the area of Africa we now call the Sudan, near present-day Khartoum, where the White and Blue Niles join, an area adjoining the modern country of Ethiopia. Christianity came to Ethiopia at a very early date, probably introduced into the country by this eunuch.

The Ethiopian king was "a child of the sun," far above such mundane matters as running the secular affairs of a kingdom. Such menial duties were the responsibility of the Queen Mother, who bore the title of Candace.

The Ethiopian in the story was a eunuch. In the East, eunuchs often attained positions of great power and trust. The phrase rendered "of great authority" comes from the word *dunastēs* and suggests our English word *potentate*. This man held high office in his native land. He was in effect the Secretary of the Treasury.

He seems to have been a Gentile God-fearer. As a eunuch he was not likely to have been a full proselyte of the Jewish religion because of a restriction of the Mosaic law (Deut. 23:1). However, contact with Judaism had convinced him that truth concerning God was to be found only among the Hebrew people. Jerusalem would draw him as a magnet draws a needle.

One can well imagine with what eager anticipation he planned for his pilgrimage to the Holy City. There he would learn the truth, he would be among God's people. He could visit the Temple, make his offerings, walk in the Court of the Gentiles, converse with the rabbis, talk to the priests and the Levites. His position and authority would give him access to members of the Sanhedrin, even to Annas and Caiaphas the high priests, just as Naaman's contacts opened doors for him into the presence of Israel's king.

One can imagine with what high hopes he set off on his expedition, coming all the long way up the Nile, across the sands of Sinai and on up into the hill country of Judea. At last the mighty walls and battlements of Jerusalem would break upon his sight. He would see the Temple in all its golden splendor bathed in the fires of the setting sun like some burning beacon on Mount Moriah.

But, oh, the bitter disappointment! Like Martin Luther when he first came to Rome, the eternal city of his dreams, how bitterly disappointed this eunuch must have been. The materialism, the hypocrisy, the intolerance, the narrow exclusivism, the squabbles and sectarianism, and, above all, the deadness of Judaism. How long was he there? Had he come across Christians in the Court of the Gentiles? Had he heard Stephen? Had he heard the views of Gamaliel? Had he run into the radical Saul of Tarsus?

We do not know. All we know is he had come up to Jerusalem to worship and was now returning home. Jerusalem had left him disappointed and disillusioned, but his search, it seemed, was not yet over.

(b) THE EUNUCH'S SPIRITUAL STATE (8:28)

Was returning, and sitting in his chariot read Esaias the prophet.

Had he bought a copy of this Old Testament book of Isaiah while in Jerusalem? He could not have made a wiser purchase. If he was to find the truth about the Christ anywhere in the Hebrew Bible it would be in the writing of Isaiah, the great evangelical prophet.

He had not found what he wanted in rabbinic Judaism. Maybe he would find it in Scripture. So he was reading his Bible, diligently plowing his way through, longing for some phrase, some key, that would unlock the truth to his hungry heart.

(3) THE STRATEGIC CONTACT (8:29–31)

(a) THE COMMAND (8:29)

Then the Spirit said unto Philip, Go near, and join thyself to this chariot.

Philip had no doubt he was to minister to this wayfaring man whose chariot was thundering towards him. He might well have been hesitant, for the traveler was obviously a person of considerable importance. Ordinary people did not travel in such style with such impressive retinues. Philip could well have feared a snub. However, he was so sensitive to the Spirit's leading that he really had no doubt that here was a soul whose heart was ready to hear of Jesus.

We are not called upon to witness to everyone we meet, but we are called upon to speak to those who have been prepared by the Holy Spirit.

Some years ago one of Scotland's great saints was walking across the Highlands with a young friend. They passed a shepherd. The younger man, perhaps to impress his colleague, accosted the shepherd, asked him if he was saved and gave him a tract. Expecting, perhaps, a word of commendation, he was surprised and rebuked when the old believer said,"Did you have the Holy Spirit's permission to speak to that man about his soul?"

"Go near, and join thyself to this chariot." The Holy Spirit, after all, is the Lord of the Harvest. It is a great thing to be so in touch with heaven that our witness and our attempts at soul-winning are directed by the Lord.

(b) THE COMPULSION (8:30)

And Philip ran hither to him, and heard him read the prophet Esaias, and said, Understandest thou what thou readest?

"Run, Philip, run!" The compulsion of the Holy Spirit was unmistakable. It was not just that he might miss the traveler, he might miss the *text*. The Holy Spirit knew just how far the eunuch had read in his perusal of the prophet Isaiah. He knew he had come to chapter 53, knew just how far down that strategic chapter he had progressed, knew just what soul-searching questions were welling up in that Ethiopian's heart.

"Run, Philip, run!" There are times when the King's business calls for haste. This particular incident illustrates the magnificent timing of God.

(c) THE COMPLAINT (8:31)

And he said, How can I, except some man should guide me? And he desired Philip that he would come up and sit with him.

"Do you understand what you are reading?" Philip had asked. At once this educated, cultured man confessed his perplexity. He had no trouble understanding the manuscript, but he had considerable trouble understanding the message.

We have trouble ourselves understanding some of the Old Testament prophets, even when we know that Christ is the key. That is why one of God's gifts to His church is the teacher. We should be grateful for the vast amount of work done through the centuries by devoted and diligent students of the Scriptures.

b. FACT (8:32–35)

(1) THE TEXT THAT ENGAGED THE EUNUCH (8:32–33)

(a) THE SILENCE OF THE LAMB (8:32)

The place of the scripture which he read was this, He was led as a sheep to the slaughter; and like a lamb dumb before his shearer, so opened he not his mouth.

What greater gospel text, and what greater opening for Philip, could be found in all the Old Testament? Here was a seeking sinner reading in the Scripture all about the Savior! He had come to the great passage in Isaiah that described Christ on the cross, and he asked the question that enabled Philip to lead him by the hand to Calvary and introduce him to Jesus.

The text tells of the Messiah silent before His shearers. We see Jesus abused by the Sanhedrin, ridiculed by Herod, scourged by Pilate, scoffed at by the soldiers. We see Him stripped, seemingly as helpless in their hands as a sheep in the hand of its shearer. All the dignity that comes from dress was stripped away. But His silence clothed Him with a dignity no insult or injury of man could ever take away. How Philip must have seized upon the silence of Jesus! Yonder in the glory were twelve legions of angels, straining over the battlements of heaven with drawn swords, waiting for a word. One word, and they would have flashed down the skyways of the stars, burst upon our planet, stamped flat the high hills of Judaea, turned to blood the waters of the seven seas, and ushered in Armageddon then and there. But that word never came. He was silent before His shearers.

(b) THE SLAUGHTER OF THE LAMB (8:33)

In his humiliation his judgment was taken away: and who shall declare his generation? for his life is taken from the earth.

The word for "judgment" here is an interesting one. It is *krisis*, from which we derive our English word *crisis*. It indicates a turning point. The word occurs forty-eight times in the New Testament. It is rendered "damnation," "condemnation," "accusation," but mostly "judgment." It has to do with a judicial proceeding.

The murder of Jesus was given legal sanction by Jews and Gentiles alike. The Sanhedrin found Him guilty of blasphemy; and Pilate, finding Him guilty of nothing, condemned Him on a trumped-up charge of treason.

"Who shall declare his generation?" demanded the prophet. The word used here is *genea* ("posterity"). The Jewish authorities certainly did not want Jesus' generations declared. The Temple records proved only too clearly His link with David both through Joseph His foster father and through Mary His mother.

All these statements greatly perplexed the eunuch. He gathered clearly enough from the text that the violent death of someone was described. But he did not have the key to unlock that door and enter into all truth.

(2) THE TRUTH THAT ELUDED THE EUNUCH (8:34–35)

(a) THE QUESTION ASKED (8:34)

And the eunuch answered Philip, and said, I pray thee, of whom speaketh the prophet this? of himself, or of some other man?

What a leading question to ask a preacher of the gospel! It was only a step from the Scripture portion to the Savior's person. The question was like that which Nicodemus asked Jesus: "How can a man be born when he is old?" (John 3:4); or like the question the Philippian jailer asked Paul and Silas: "What must I do to be saved?" (Acts 16:30); or like the question the Jerusalem crowd asked Peter on the Day of Pentecost: "Men and brethren, what shall we do?" (2:37).

Such leading questions are certain evidence that the Holy Spirit is at work and has brought a person to the point of salvation.

(b) THE QUESTION ANSWERED (8:35)

Then Philip opened his mouth, and began at the same scripture, and preached unto him Jesus.

How Philip would have delighted to relate that great Isaiah passage to the Christ of Calvary!

"Why, sir," he would say, "the prophet speaks of some other Man! And what a Man! He is the Man Christ Jesus, the promised Messiah of the Jewish people, born as Isaiah said, of a virgin. He came, as Isaiah said, as the child born and the son given, as the wonderful counselor, the mighty God, the everlasting Father, the Prince of Peace, and upon whose shoulder the government is yet to be set. This is the One who was taken from prison and from judgment, who was led as a sheep to the slaughter." And Philip would retrace the tragedy of Calvary. He would speak of the resurrection and the ascension. He would tell of the coming of the Spirit at Pentecost, of the birthday of the church, of the Great Commission to go into all the world to preach the gospel, baptizing believers in the name of the Father, the Son, and the Holy Spirit.

c. FAITH (8:36–38)

(1) FAITH EXERCISED (8:36)

And as they went on their way, they came unto a certain water: and the eunuch said, See, here is water; What doth hinder me to be baptized?

Obviously, Philip had made clear to the eunuch that faith in Christ called for public confession of Him in baptism. The Ethiopian had found in Jesus what he had not found in Jerusalem. At last his search was over. All his life had been a preparation for this moment. His education enabled him to read; his scholarship enabled him to read the language of the Bible; his high position made it possible for him to travel to Jerusalem; his wealth made it possible for him to buy an Isaiah scroll; his interest in Judaism drew him from afar to the city where Christ was crucified; his deep disappointment in Judaism, the great hunger of his heart, all prepared him. Nothing was wasted. All that God allows to come into our lives is significant. From the cradle to the grave the goodness of God is at work in our lives to lead us to repentance and to a closer walk with Himself. All is grist to His mill. Sunshine and shadow, mountain top and the valley of the shadow, gain and loss, joy and sorrow, advancement and adversity, all things work together in the purposes and providence of God.

So faith was exercised. Pointing to the water, the eunuch asked for baptism.

(2) FAITH EXPRESSED (8:37)

And Philip said, If thou believest with all thine heart, thou mayest. And he answered and said, I believe that Jesus Christ is the Son of God.

Scholars say that most of the texts from which our New Testament is derived omit this verse. At a very early date, however, it was included. Philip must have said something to make sure the eunuch was genuinely saved. There can be little doubt, too, that such questioning of a candidate for baptism was common practice in the early church.

It is still a good practice. If a person has genuinely accepted Christ he should not only be able but also willing to say so. "If thou shalt confess with thy mouth the Lord Jesus, and shalt believe in thine heart that God hath raised him from the dead, thou shalt be saved," Paul said (Rom. 10:9). That is not a condition of salvation but a confession of salvation; if a person believes in his heart, confession will come out of his mouth.

(3) FAITH EXHIBITED (8:38)

And he commanded the chariot to stand still: and they went down both into the water, both Philip and the eunuch; and he baptized him.

Baptism is the outward expression of an inward experience. As one of the two ordinances Christ left with His church, it is of great significance. For the believer it is a time of *triumph*. He takes his stand in an element that spells death to all that he is by natural birth—water; he is immersed to symbolize his burial; then he is raised by the power of another's arm to stand on the resurrection side of death in newness of life. The act of baptism symbolizes in a graphic and memorable form the great thing that has already happened in his heart. By virtue of Calvary and his faith in Christ he has been identified with Christ in His death, His burial, His resurrection. He has passed from death unto life. Baptism proclaims that.

For the onlooker it is a time of *testimony*. The believer witnesses to the world that he is now to be identified with Christ, the One the world has rejected.

d. FEELING (8:39)

(1) THE MESSENGER WAS REMOVED FROM HIS SIGHT (8:39a)

And when they were come up out of the water, the Spirit of the Lord caught away Philip, that the eunuch saw him no more.

Still dripping wet, the eunuch turned, one can well imagine, to say a word to Philip, but—he was gone! He had vanished. The text says that the Spirit of the Lord had "caught" him away, or snatched him away, as some render it. One moment he was there; the next moment he was gone. The eunuch must have been stunned. He saw him no more.

This sudden disappearance of Philip must have left an indelible impression on the eunuch's mind. Already convinced that he had heard and believed the truth, the mysterious vanishing of the messenger would surely underline indelibly on his soul the fact that he had been brought in touch with the supernatural. What a story he would have to tell to his wife (if he had one), to Candace, queen of the Ethiopians, to his colleagues at court, to his servants, and to his fellow countrymen! And it was a story fully corroborated by his retinue.

The snatching away of Philip was necessary for Philip, too. He might have decided that he had received God's call to Ethiopia as he had received it to Samaria. But the formal opening of the door of the church to the Gentiles was not his calling. That was the work of an apostle, not an evangelist, and Peter, not Philip, had been given the key to that door. Moreover, a Roman, not an Ethiopian, was to be at the heart of that significant step. Japheth was to be formally invited to come and dwell in the tents of Shem. The *formal* opening of the church's door to the Gentiles would not be to a Jewish proselyte, the representative of a remote African country on the edge of the civilized world, but to the representative of a super-power, whose imperial arm reached across the civilized world.

(2) THE MESSAGE WAS RINGING IN HIS SOUL (8:39*b*)

And he went on his way rejoicing.

Joy is the outcome of genuine conversion. We think of Bunyan's Pilgrim, bowed beneath his load of sin, reading in his Book, finding his burden getting heavier all the time. We think of his falling into the Slough of Despond but struggling out on the side farthest from the City of Destruction, still longing to find relief from his load. We see him at last, arriving at the foot of the cross where his burden rolls away. We watch him as he sees it roll down a steep place until it vanishes into an open tomb. We think of the joy that wells up in his heart as, like the eunuch, he goes on his way rejoicing. For as he goes he sings.

> Blessed cross! Blessed sepulchre!
> Blessed rather be
> The One Who there was put to shame for me.

And so the Ethiopian went singing all the long way home.

e. FAITHFULNESS (8:40)

But Philip was found at Azotus: and passing through he preached in all the cities, till he came to Caesarea.

Azotus was the name of the old Philistine city Ashod, about twenty miles north of Gaza. Faithful Philip preached there. He continued on up the coastal road preaching here and there until he reached Caesarea. Caesarea had been built by Herod the Great in honor of Caesar Augustus. He called it Caesar Sabaste (literally, Caesar Augustus). It was the capital of all Roman administration for Palestine, and a thoroughly Gentile city. Here was stationed Cornelius, the Roman centurion Peter was soon to lead to Christ and in whose home the Gentile church was to be born. So Philip, although not chosen for that significant step, was there when it happened, a key man in a key place to follow up the new moving of the Spirit of God.

Philip seems to have settled down at Caesarea. The next time we meet him (21:8-9), twenty years later, he is still there, a family man with four grown daughters following zealously in the footsteps of their faithful dad.

Part Three: (Continued):

The Forward Emphasis: Stephen (6:1–12:25)

II. NEW VICTORIES (9:1—11:30)

A. A Messenger for the Gentiles Is Saved (9:1–31)
  1. The Miracle of Saul's Conversion (9:1–3*a*)
    a. His Deadly Enmity (9:1*a*)
    b. His Driving Energy (9:1*b*– 3*a*)
      (1) His Marked Initiative (9:1*b*–2)
      (2) His Maintained Intention (9:3*a*)
  2. The Manner of Saul's Conversion (9:3*b*–9)
    a. The Tremendous Revelation to Him (9:3*b*–5)
      (1) The Light from Heaven (9:3*b*)
      (2) The Lord from Heaven (9:4–5)
    b. The Total Revolution in Him (9:6–9)
      (1) The Sovereignty of Jesus Established in His Life (9:6–7)
        (a) How the Lord Changed Him (9:6)
        (b) How the Lord Chose Him (9:7)
      (2) The Sufficiency of Jesus Is Established in His Life (9:8–9)
        (a) Walking in the Light (9:8)
        (b) Waiting in the Dark (9:9)
  3. The Meaning of Saul's Conversion (9:10–16)
    a. How God Called Ananias (9:10)
    b. How God Commissioned Ananias (9:11–12)
      (1) Where He Was to Go (9:11)
      (2) What He Was to Do (9:12)
    c. How God Convinced Ananias (9:13–16)
      (1) How His Objection Was Raised (9:13–14)
        (a) He Had Heard of Saul's Malignity (9:13)
        (b) He Had Heard of Saul's Mission (9:14)

(b) The Spiritual Awakening of Joppa (9:42–43)
3. Peter's Ministry (10:1—11:18)
  a. How This Ministry Was Commanded (10:1–23)
    (1) The Heavenly Visitor Who Aroused Cornelius (10:1–8)
      (a) The Actions of Cornelius Toward God (10:1–2)
      (b) The Acceptance of Cornelius by God (10:3–4)
      (c) The Advice to Cornelius from God (10:5–8)
        i. How Precisely It Was Heralded (10:5–6)
        ii. How Promptly It Was Heeded (10:7–8)
    (2) The Heavenly Vision That Arrested Peter (10:9–23)
      (a) How Peter Was Prepared by God (10:9–16)
        i. A Very Human Kind of Dichotomy (10:9–10)
        ii. A Very Hebrew Kind of Difficulty (10:11–16)
          a. The Command (10:11–13)
          b. the Conflict (10:14–15)
          c. The Confirmation (10:16)
      (b) How Peter Was Prompted by God (10:17–23)
        i. His Doubts (10:17–20)
          a. His Secret Perplexity (10:17*a*)
          b. His Sudden Perception (10:17*b*–20)
        ii. His Decision (10:21–23)
          a. His Courtesy (10:21–23*a*)
          b. His Caution (10:23*b*)
  b. How This Ministry Was Confirmed (10:24–48)
    (1) The Meeting That Was Convened for Peter by Cornelius (10:24–33)
      (a) The Gathering (10:24)
      (b) The Greeting (10:25–27)
        i. How Peter Was Worshiped (10:26–26)
        ii. How Peter Was Welcomed (10:27)
      (c) The Guidance (10:28–33)
        i. How God Overruled Peter's National Intolerance (10:28–29)
        ii. How God Overruled Cornelius's Natural Ignorance (10:30–33)
          a. His Exemplary Conduct (10:30*a*)
          b. His Exciting Confirmation (10:30*b*–32)
          c. His Expectant Condition (10:33)
    (2) The Message That Was Conveyed by Peter to Cornelius (10:34–43)
      (a) What Peter Perceived (10:34–35)

   (b) What Peter Proclaimed (10:36–43)
    i. He Talked About the Living Word (10:36–38)
     a. The Point of the Message (10:36)
     b. The Preaching of the Message (10:37)
     c. The Proof of the Message (10:38)
    ii. He Talked About the Living Witnesses (10:39–42)
     a. They Witnessed the Reality of Christ (10:39*a*)
     b. They Witnessed the Rejection of Christ (10:39*b*)
     c. They Witnessed the Resurrection of Christ (10:40–42)
      1. The Chosen Few (10:40–41)
      2. The Challenging Fact (10:42)
    iii. He Talked About the Living Way (10:43)
  (3) The Mystery That Was Consummated in Peter and Cornelius (10:44–48)
  (a) The Outpoured Spirit (10:44)
  (b) The Outward Sign (10:45–47)
  (c) The Outright Stand (10:48)
 c. How This Ministry Was Criticized (11:1–18)
  (1) The Accusation (11:1–17)
  (a) How the Accusation Was Made (11:1–3)
   i. How the Great News Was Received (11:1)
   ii. How the Great News Was Resented (11:2–3)
  (b) How the Accusation Was Met (11:4–17)
   i. Peter Recounts the Story of Divine Constraint (11:4–12)
    a. The Vision (11:4–10)
     1. Its Revolutionary Nature (11:4–9)
     2. Its Repetitive Nature (11:10)
    b. The Visitors (11:11)
    c. The Voice (11:12)
   ii. Peter Recounts the Story of Definite Conversion (11:13–17)
    a. How Cornelius Received the Guidance of God (11:13–14)
    b. How Cornelius Received the Gift of God (11:15–17)
     1. It Was an Identical Gift (11:15–16)
     2. It Was an Identifying Gift (11:17)
  (2) The Acceptance (11:18)
C. A Multitude of the Gentiles Saved (11:19—12:25)
 1. The Planting of the Church at Antioch (11:19–30)
 a. Two New Moves (11:19–26)

(1) A Move to Reach Hebrew People in Foreign Lands (11:19)
    (a) The Reason for the Move (11:19*a*)
    (b) The Result of the Move (11:19*b*)
(2) A Move to Reach Heathen People in Foreign Lands (11:20–21)
    (a) The Daring Venture (11:20)
    (b) The Divine Vindication (11:21)
  b. Two New Men (11:22–30)
    (1) The Man Chosen by the Brethren in the Mother Church in Jerusalem (11:22–24)
      (a) He Was a Sent Man (11:22)
      (b) He Was a Sensible Man (11:23)
      (c) He Was a Spiritual Man (11:24)
    (2) The Man Chosen by Barnabas for the Mission Church at Antioch (11:25–30)
      (a) How He Went for Saul (11:25)
      (b) How He Worked with Saul (11:26–30)
        i. Their Faithfulness (11:26*a*)
        ii. Their Fruitfulness (11:26*b*)
        iii. Their Fellowship (11:27–30)
          a. Help from Jerusalem (11:27–28)
          b. Help for Jerusalem (11:29–30)
2. The Persecution of the Church at Jerusalem (12:1–23)
  a. How It Was Organized (12:1–4)
    (1) The Death of James (12:1–2)
      (a) The Murderer (12:1)
      (b) The Martyr (12:2)
    (2) The Detention of Peter (12:3–4)
      (a) Why He Was Imprisoned (12:3*a*)
      (b) When He Was Imprisoned (12:3*b*)
      (c) Where He Was Imprisoned (12:4)
  b. How It Was Obstructed (12:5–19)
    (1) Human Intercession (12:5)
    (2) Heaven's Intervention (12:6–17)
      (a) Peter's Restfulness (12:6)
      (b) Peter's Rescuer (12:7–10)
        i. The Angel's Descent (12:7*a*)
        ii. The Angel's Demand (12:7*b*–9)
        iii. The Angel's Deeds (12:10*a*)
        iv. The Angel's Departure (12:10*b*)

Part Three (Continued):

The Forward Emphasis: Stephen (6:1—12:25)

II. NEW VICTORIES (9:1—11:30)

A. A MESSENGER FOR THE GENTILES IS SAVED (9:1–31)

1. THE MIRACLE OF SAUL'S CONVERSION (9:1–3a)

a. HIS DEADLY ENMITY (9:1a)

And Saul, yet breathing out threatenings and slaughter against the disciples of the Lord . . .

Our attention is now drawn back to Saul of Tarsus and his campaign of persecution against the church, instigated by the boldness and martyrdom of Stephen.

Saul was an intellectual giant, farsighted enough to see that there could be no peaceful coexistence between militant Judaism and militant Christianity. Whatever his teacher Gamaliel might have advised about moderation, Saul saw the incompatibility of the two faiths. Either Judaism was right and Christianity was apostasy, or Christianity was right and Judaism was obsolete. Saul's birth, beliefs, and background all drove him into a head-on confrontation with the Christians. He concluded, logically enough from his own biased point of view, that Christ was a blasphemer and Christianity a cult. Because Jesus of Nazareth was dead, nothing could be done about Him. Christianity, however, was something else; the sooner it was dead and buried too, the better for everyone.

We can see how Saul arrived at his conclusion. Jesus had not only claimed to be Israel's Messiah but had claimed to be the Son of God. Yet He had died on a Roman cross. The Jewish law said, "Cursed is every one that hangeth on a tree" (Gal. 3:13). Jesus had been hanged on a tree, and so He was accursed of God and could in no way have been the Son of God. He therefore was a blasphemer, and the sooner the semi-Judaistic cult devoted to

His worship was eradicated the sooner Judaism and the world would be purged of a terrible heresy. Such would have been Saul's reasoning. We catch a glimpse of that in his letter to the Philippians where, in awe and wonder, he writes of the Lord Jesus that He "became obedient unto death, *even the death of the cross*" (Phil. 2:8, emphasis added). That which in his unconverted days was the most *impossible* thing about the claims of Christ, in his converted days became the most *impressive* thing about those claims.

So we see Saul "breathing out threatenings and slaughter against the disciples of the Lord." The word for "slaughter" is the Greek word *phonos*, which occurs ten times in the New Testament and which is always translated "murder" except here and Hebrews 11:37. Saul now set himself to get rid of the church by means of intimidation and murder.

b. HIS DRIVING ENERGY (9:1*b*–3*a*)

(1) HIS MARKED INITIATIVE (9:1*b*–2)

. . . went unto the high priest, and desired of him letters to Damascus to the synagogues, that if he found any of this way, whether they were men or women, he might bring them bound unto Jerusalem.

The Sanhedrin wielded great power not only in Jerusalem but throughout the Jewish Diaspora. That wide authority had been upheld by Rome for well over a century. It had its roots in Rome's treaty with the Hasmoneans. It had been put to the test in an important case in 138 B.C. involving Egypt and other Near East countries. Julius Caesar seems to have included it in his negotiations with the high priest.

Saul of Tarsus, then, determined to destroy Christianity, root and branch, at home and abroad, applied to the high priest for written authority to extradite Jews who lived in the Diaspora and bring them to Jerusalem for trial. Damascus was to be the first target. No doubt many Palestinian Jews, fleeing his violent efforts at home, had taken up residence there, where was a very large Jewish community.

It is interesting to note how Christianity is described here. Saul wanted to go after those who were "of this way," a term that can be translated "the Way." It occurs a half dozen times in Acts and seems to have been one of the early descriptions for Christianity (cf. John 14:6).

The initiative against the believers was taken by Saul, not the Sanhedrin, though doubtless Caiaphas and his crowd were only too pleased to have such a willing, capable, and energetic agent to do their dirty work for them. The authority Saul requested was immediately forthcoming.

(2) HIS MAINTAINED INTENTION (9:3*a*)

And as he journeyed, he came near Damascus.

Damascus, considered to be the oldest city in the world, was already a city in the time of Abraham, whose steward came from there. It became capital of the powerful Aramaean kingdom. In the days of the Hebrew monarchy, the kings of Damascus were nearly always hostile to the Hebrews. Under the Romans Damascus continued to be an important city.

As soon as he was vested with the authority of the Sanhedrin, Saul, accompanied by a sufficient armed retinue to enforce his will, headed north. The Damascus road from Jerusalem stretched for about two hundred miles. Saul would have had plenty of time to nurse his hatred against the Christians. Yet one suspects that the angel face of Stephen haunted him at night and that Stephen's solid and unanswerable arguments raised themselves constantly in his mind, only to be vehemently struck down by the fierce Pharisee in his soul.

And so, at last, Saul "came near Damascus," and the walls and towers of the city raised their bold outlines across the distant skyline.

He was bitterly determined to wreak vengeance on the believers in that city, being exceeding enraged against them. Any doubts he had were ground under the iron heel of passionate resolve, so that Saul should be saved was indeed a miracle. His giant intellect, his fierce emotions fired to white-hot passion, and his iron will all fused together in a determined hatred of Jesus. No man could have reasoned with him in such a mood—no man on earth, that is. But there was a Man with nail prints in His hands about to stand astride Saul's path and bring about a miracle greater than raising Lazarus from the dead.

2. THE MANNER OF SAUL'S CONVERSION (9:3b–9)

a. THE TREMENDOUS REVELATION OF HIM (9:3b–5)

(1) THE LIGHT FROM HEAVEN (9:3b)

And suddenly there shined round about him a light from heaven.

In giving his testimony on later occasions, Paul tells us that it was high noon when the miracle took place (22:6; 26:13). As the candle pales before the rising sun so now the noonday sun paled before the glory light that burst upon the astonished Saul. The expression "shined round about" can be translated "flashed round about." It was a light from heaven. Saul had no doubt as to the place from whence it came; and light from heaven was about to break into his darkened soul.

(2) THE LORD FROM HEAVEN (9:4–5)

And he fell to the earth, and heard a voice saying unto him, Saul, Saul, why persecutest thou me? And he said, Who art thou, Lord? And the Lord said, I am Jesus whom thou persecutest: it is hard for thee to kick against the pricks.

The conversion of Saul of Tarsus was no case for a Philip, however faithful; Saul was made of different stuff than the Ethiopian. Nor was it a case for a Peter, however zealous; Saul was no Cornelius. The conversion of Saul was undertaken by the Lord Himself.

We do not know whether Paul ever met Jesus when He lived on earth. The possibility exists that he did, but if so Paul never mentions it. Paul's first encounter with Jesus seems to have been here and now. His view of Jesus was formed on the Damascus road. To Paul, the Savior was never "Jesus of Nazareth," but "the Lord from heaven" (1 Cor. 15:47). Saul's unique and remarkable view of the risen and ascended Christ colored all his thinking about Jesus. He never could forget what he calls "the heavenly vision." To Paul, the unique thing about Jesus was that He was God, over all, blessed for evermore; that though He was Man, real and human, He was seated by sovereign right as God at God's right hand.

Nor would Paul ever forget the truth about the mystical Body of Christ, the church, that he learned that day. When the Lord arrested him as the arch-persecutor of the saints of God, He did not say, "Why do you persecute *them?*" He said, "Why do you persecute *Me?*" In that moment Saul learned that there was a mysterious but real link between the Head of the church in heaven and the members of that church on earth—so much so that for Saul to put his hand upon a Christian was the equivalent of putting his hand upon the Christ. He never forgot that. He later developed the truth of the mystical Body in his epistles, especially Ephesians.

So then, one moment Saul of Tarsus was riding high, secure in the impenetrable armor of his iron-clad prejudices, breathing out threatenings and slaughter. The next moment he was prostrate on the ground, blinded by such a light as never shone on earth and listening to such a voice as charmed the very angels of God.

"Lord! The word sprang instinctively to his lips. "Who art thou, Lord?" Back came the soul-devastating reply, "I am Jesus Whom thou persecutest." *I am Jesus!* He was aghast! He had persecuted the Messiah of Israel, the Son of David, the Son of God. He had laid violent hands upon those beloved of heaven, the very members of the Body of Christ. It was all true! Jesus of Nazareth was God the Son, born of a virgin, unique in His person, marvelous in His life, falsely accused and callously rejected by the very Sanhedrin he served, and crucified (oh, crowning horror!) at the insistence of the Jews and at the hands of Rome. But now, He who had been buried was raised again in power was, in very truth, the ever-living One at God's right hand.

"It is hard for thee to kick against the pricks," Jesus said to him as he lay in the dust, filled with remorse, humbled beyond measure, contrite, repentant, and yet inspired with a strange mixture of wonder, hope, and fear.

b. THE TOTAL REVOLUTION IN HIM (9:6–9)

(1) THE SOVEREIGNTY OF JESUS ESTABLISHED IN HIS LIFE (9:6–7)

(a) HOW THE LORD CHANGED HIM (9:6)

And he trembling and astonished said, Lord, what wilt thou have me to do? And the Lord said unto him, Arise, and go into the city, and it shall be told thee what thou must do.

Paul used the word *Lord* again, but this time it was his confession of faith. God had put Jesus on the throne of the universe; Saul put Him on the throne of his heart. "Lord!" From henceforth He was to be:

> Lord of every thought and action,
> Lord to send and Lord to stay;
> Lord in speaking, writing, giving,
> Lord in all things to obey.
>
> (Source Unknown)

From henceforth Jesus was Lord in Saul's heart, mind, soul, and will. The old Saul died, crucified with Christ and buried with Him forever. The new Saul stood in Christ on resurrection ground. Jesus was Savior and Lord of his life from now on.

(b) HOW THE LORD CHOSE HIM (9:7)

And the men which journeyed with him stood speechless, hearing a voice, but seeing no man.

The Lord was not speaking to them; He was speaking to Saul. Whether or not they later came to Christ we do not know. But at that moment, God's choice was Saul of Tarsus.

It often happens that way. A meeting is attended by many. The message is given, a hundred walk out unmoved, but one person recognizes the voice of the Savior and passes from death unto life. It is a mysterious but evident fact, and characteristic of all evangelism. On this occasion, Paul's traveling companions were passed by. They were present, they knew something was going on, but they might as well have been in Babylon for all the effect it had on them.

(2) THE SUFFICIENCY OF JESUS ESTABLISHED IN HIS LIFE (9:8–9)

(a) WALKING IN THE LIGHT (9:8)

And Saul arose from the earth; and when his eyes were opened, he saw no man: but they led him by the hand, and brought him into Damascus.

Two interesting words for *sight* are used in these verses. Verse 7 says of Saul's traveling companions that they "stood speechless, hearing a voice, but seeing no man." The word used there is *theōreō*, which means to be a spectator, or to gaze upon, for instance, a spectacle. Our English word *theater* is from the same root and suggests the idea. The word implies bodily sight and takes for granted the actual presence of the object that rivets the gaze. The word is used to denote continued, prolonged gaze. They had their eyes open, in other words, and stared and stared but saw nothing.

The word used in this verse where we read that "when [Saul's] eyes were opened, he saw no man" is *blepō*, which means to have the power of seeing. It is used of the act of looking, even if nothing is seen, and it can be used of mental vision. The same word is used in the next verse.

We note the contrast between Saul and his fellow travelers. They gazed all about them and saw nothing. Saul was blinded and saw everything. They were as much in the dark for all their bodily sight as people could possibly be. Saul, though physically blinded, had his inner eyes opened to the light.

The last thing he saw before blindness fell upon his eyes was the glorious face of Jesus.

(b) WAITING IN THE DARK (9:9)

And he was three days without sight, and neither did eat nor drink.

His companions led him by the hand into Damascus, found him accommodations, and left him to his own devices. There, enrapt by the heavenly vision, he fasted and thought and prayed. His whole world had been turned upside down. He needed these days of absolute quiet and rest to reorient himself. His whole world, as a scholarly but fanatical rabbinical, Pharasaic Jew, had tumbled about his ears. How much could be salvaged from the rubble remained to be seen. Not very much. Paul later told the Philippians that all the things he had counted gain he now regarded as refuse (Phil. 3:4–9). A new world was opening up before him. He would have to rethink his Bible in the light of Calvary and in "the light of the knowledge of the glory of God in the face of Jesus Christ" (2 Cor. 4:6). He patiently waited in the dark, confident that God would soon speak, that his newfound Lord would, as He promised, tell him what he must do. How or when the word would come he did not know.

3. THE MEANING OF SAUL'S CONVERSION (9:10–16)

a. HOW GOD CALLED ANANAIAS (9:10)

And there was a certain disciple at Damascus, named Ananias; and to him said the Lord in a vision, Ananias. And he said, Behold, I am here, Lord.

God has His servants everywhere. Here at Damascus was a quiet, unsung believer of whom we would never have heard had it not been for this incident; he was to step on stage, say his few lines, do his tiny act in connection with the whole mighty drama, and go offstage never to be heard of again. But the Lord knew all about him: knew his name and address, knew his humble faith and secret fear. God knew how to speak to him. Here He used a common medium in Bible times—a vision.

Ananias knew instantly that God was speaking to him. He knew, too, that some demand was to be made upon him. "Behold, I am here, Lord," he said simply. May we ever be as ready.

b. HOW GOD COMMISSIONED ANANIAS (9:11–12)

(1) WHERE HE WAS TO GO (9:11)

And the Lord said unto him, Arise, and go into the street which is called Straight, and inquire in the house of Judas for one called Saul, of Tarsus; for, behold, he prayeth.

"The street which is called Straight" is still one of the principal thoroughfares of Damascus, running from the west gate to the east gate of the city. In Bible times such a street would be a busy bazaar. The house of Judas is traditionally believed to have been at the west end of the street.

The thing the Lord noted about Saul was "Behold, he prayeth." Saul had said his prayers since he was a little boy, but for the first time in his life he was genuinely praying.

(2) WHAT HE WAS TO DO (9:12)

And [he] hath seen in a vision a man named Ananias coming in, and putting his hand on him, that he might receive his sight.

As Saul was praying God spoke to him, told him that a man was coming to restore his sight, and told him the man's name was Ananias. All this was conveyed by a vision. Nowadays we tend to be skeptical of visions. Many false cults are founded on visions that, though genuine enough, do not come from heaven.

Normally God does not speak in visions when and where He can speak through His written word, but there are exceptions. Saul's case was an exception. God will not substitute a vision, however, when waiting upon Him and reading His Word will accomplish the same result.

Ananias was left in no doubt as to what he was to do.

c. HOW GOD CONVINCED ANANIAS (9:13–16)

(1) HOW HIS OBJECTION WAS RAISED (9:13–14)

(a) HE HAD HEARD OF SAUL'S MALIGNITY (9:13)

Then Ananias answered, Lord, I have heard by many of this man, how much evil he hath done to thy saints at Jerusalem.

Saul's reputation had preceded him. All Damascus was buzzing with the news that a grand inquisitor had been appointed by the Sanhedrin to root out heresy, particularly Christianity, from Judaism.

It is astonishing how patient God is with us. Here we have Ananias questioning his commission by telling God that he had heard terrible things about Saul—as though God did not know all about that! Often we argue with God as though we know better than He. And God patiently lets us do it!

(b) HE HAD HEARD OF SAUL'S MISSION (9:14)

And here he hath authority from the chief priests to bind all that call upon thy name.

Ananias had more to tell the Lord. All the Lord's people in Damascus knew that Saul was coming into the city to wreak havoc upon the church. "So there, Lord," he might just as well have added, "You can see why it would be very silly of me to go anywhere near the man. Besides, if he is blind, it will perhaps curtail his murderous activities. It's God's judgment on him. Let him remain blind, I say."

Evidently Ananias was so filled with alarm at the unexpected, unwanted, and unusual commission that he never grasped the meaning of those three words "Behold, he prayeth."

Ananias had no firsthand experience of Saul's persecutions, but he had evidently heard enough from those who had. In the circle of God's saints in Damascus were those who had suffered already in Jerusalem. Now the terror was to begin all over again. There must have been many an anxious thought, many a fearful discussion behind closed doors when the news arrived that Saul of Tarsus was in town. Should they stay and ride out the storm, daring deportation and death? Should they flee at once? That night many anxious mothers and fathers must have looked with aching hearts at sleeping little ones soon to know the terror and the heartache that ever marched in step with Saul.

(2) HOW HIS OBJECTION WAS REJECTED (9:15–16)

(a) SAUL HAD BEEN CHOSEN FOR SERVICE (9:15)

But the Lord said unto him, Go thy way: for he is a chosen vessel unto me, to bear my name before the Gentiles, and kings, and the children of Israel.

Saul was a chosen vessel. God had determined the course of his life. All Saul's previous life had been a preparation for this moment: his birth into a family enjoying Roman citizenship and in a city noted for its seafaring commerce and its schools of learning; his birth into a family of the Diaspora where he could grow up in familiar touch with the big, bustling world, in touch with Greek language, learning, and logic; his birth into a Hebrew home where he could be brought up in the synagogue, in a knowledge of the Scriptures, acquainted from childhood days with the knowledge of God, the Hebrew Bible, the truth about many things hidden to the Roman imperialists and the Greek intellectuals; his training as a rabbi and his induction into the fascinating but sterile and counterproductive traditions of the Mishna; even his hatred of Christ and the church and his savage persecutions would be turned to good account.

He was a chosen vessel. So are we all. Each of us has special training, talents, temperament, special background and upbringing, special culture and characteristics. God makes no two people alike.

Paul was chosen to carry the saving name of Jesus before Gentiles, kings, and the children of Israel, in that order. He was preeminently to be the apostle to the Gentiles. He was far better equipped for that than Peter, John, James, or even Philip the evangelist. Nobody in the apostolic circle or in the church at large had such intellectual gifts, such educational background, such strength of purpose, such breadth of vision, such tireless zeal, such a cultural blending of Roman, Greek, and Jew. Stephen perhaps came closest in his grasp of truth, and Philip came next in his evangelistic zeal. But Saul of Tarsus alone had all it took to take by storm the great Gentile world. Who else could have stormed Mars Hill or planted a church in Caesar's household? Who but Paul?

(b) SAUL HAD BEEN CHOSEN FOR SUFFERING (9:16)

For I will show him how great things he must suffer for my name's sake.

Years later Paul gave the Corinthians a partial catalog of his sufferings (2 Cor. 11:23–28). He had been beaten and bruised by Gentiles and by Jews. He had been in prison, and he had been stoned. He had been shipwrecked again and again. He had known peril and weariness, pain, hunger and thirst, nakedness, and cold. His body had been so ill-treated that he was a chronically ill man in constant need of a physician.

Ananias had no need to worry about Saul's making the saints to suffer. From now on Saul would do the suffering. He would take upon himself the care of all the churches and repay a thousand times in his own suffering all the pain and woe he had inflicted on the people of God. And to his dying day he could carry in his breast a great remorse for all he had done to the infant Jewish church.

4. THE MEASURE OF SAUL'S CONVERSION (9:17–31)

a. A NEW FAMILY (9:17–19)

(1) AN EXAMPLE OF FAMILY LOVE (9:17)

And Ananias went his way, and entered into the house; and putting his hands on him said, Brother Saul, the Lord, even Jesus, that appeared unto thee in the way as thou camest, hath sent me, that thou mightest receive thy sight, and be filled with the Holy Ghost.

Ananias had no more argument. He found the house on Straight Street where Saul was staying and went in. The first contact the saved terrorist had with the church was the kindly touch of a fellow believer's hand. The first

words he heard from another believer's lips was the lovely word "Brother."
"Brother Saul." It must have gone straight to his heart. The next words he
heard were the words "Lord Jesus." Well might we sing:

> Blest be the tie that binds
> Our hearts in Christian love;
> The fellowship of kindred minds
> Is like to that above.
>   (John Fawcett, "Blest Be the Tie That Binds")

This was Saul's introduction to his new family. Along with it came the
welcome news that he was to receive his sight at the hands of this heaven-
sent messenger. This confirmed the vision Saul himself had received. He
received the added word that he was now to be filled with the Holy Spirit.
Paul would later indicate that the filling of the Spirit is conditional, governed
by our own yieldedness (Eph. 5:18). No man was ever more open and yielded
than this penitent man. No man ever remained, as the fixed habit of life, so
open and yielded as this man whose mark on all history was to be as indelible
as it was remarkable.

(2) AN EXPRESSION OF FAMILY LOYALTY (9:18)

*And immediately there fell from his eyes as it had been scales; and he
received sight forthwith, and arose, and was baptized.*

The word translated "scales" is *lepis*. It occurs only here in the New
Testament. In the Septuagint version of the Old Testament it is the word used
for the scales of a fish (Lev. 11:9–10). It seems that some scaly substance had
covered Saul's eyes and that it now fell away. Saul's eyes were opened, and he
looked for the first time into the face of a Christian brother. He knew enough
of Christian life to know that he had an obligation to identify himself with
Christ and the family of God's people by being baptized.

Baptism, for a Jew, was and is a major step. Relatives may tolerate a
member of a Jewish family who professes to be a believer in Christ, but
baptism often severs all Jewish family ties. Often, too, it is followed by
ostracism from the family and by active persecution. The same, of course, is
true for many a Gentile believer.

There are reasons for supposing that Saul had to suffer the loss of his
family as part of the price of becoming a committed follower of the Lord
Jesus (Phil. 3:8). If so, Paul made up his mind that loyalty to the heavenly
family was far more important than loyalty to a human family. Baptism
publicly proclaimed him a member of the new and noble family of twice-born
children of the living God.

(3) AN EXPERIENCE OF FAMILY LIFE (9:19)

And when he had received meat, he was strengthened. Then was Saul certain days with the disciples which were at Damascus.

Paul broke his fast and tarried awhile in the fellowship of those he once had loathed but now loved. Luke does not mention Paul's retirement to Arabia, but Paul told the Galatians, "Immediately I conferred not with flesh and blood" (Gal. 1:16). There can be no doubt that Paul's visit to Arabia was in response to a powerful inner prompting of the Holy Spirit. Paul was to be given some of the greatest revelations of truth ever written down for man. His "gospel" was not of man and not received of man. He needed time to effect fully and systematically the change in his thinking initiated on the Damascus road, so he retired into Arabia with his copy of the Old Testament Scriptures in his bag. He returned some time later with the great truths of Romans, Ephesians, and Thessalonians in his heart. By the time he returned from the solitude of Sinai, his essential theology was formed. The great truths of Christ's cross (Romans), Christ's church (Ephesians), and Christ's coming (Thessalonians), which are at the heart of those pivotal epistles, were firmly fixed in his mind.

However, all of that could well have taken place after the brief period of fellowship and witnessing described here. Certainly Saul would know enough about the basic facts and features of the gospel, as it was taught by the Jewish church, to enable him to throw himself heart and soul into the new cause. His debates with Stephen would be sufficient for that. (Some think that Paul's self-imposed exile to Arabia must be inserted at this point in the narrative and that Luke picks up the story at the time of a second visit of Paul to Damascus.)

So Saul was "certain days with the disciples which were at Damascus." That is a wonderful evidence of genuine conversion. John says, "We know that we have passed from death unto life, because we love the brethren" (1 John 3:14). What a tremendous experience it must have been for this former predator of the wolf tribe of Benjamin to sit down with the sheep! And what an experience for them!

   b. A NEW FAITH (9:20–22)
      (1) PREACHING IT (9:20–21)
         (a) THE IMPORTANCE OF PAUL'S PREACHING (9:20)

And straightway he preached Christ in the synagogues, that he is the Son of God.

The use of "straightway" here lends credence to the idea that Paul's Arabian sojourn came after this brief period of witness. It is the same word in this same context as the word "immediately" (*eutheōs*) in verse 18: "And immediately [straightway] there fell from his eyes as it had been scales."

Saul was no man to sit still when there was work to be done. He seems to have wasted no time in making his way into the synagogues. We can well picture what happened. News of his arrival would cause an immediate stir. Here was the grand inquisitor of the Sanhedrin, armed with documents demanding full cooperation of the faithful in the task entrusted to him of rooting out heresy. The ruler of the synagogue would be deferential. It was not every day an accredited agent of the Sanhedrin crossed the threshold of his synagogue. Saul would be given the chief seat. Every eye would be on him. Some would gaze at him with approval, others with apprehension. In due course Saul would beckon for the Scriptures to be handed to him. He would stand and read a passage, hand back the scroll, and face the congregation. A hush would fall. Now it was coming—a denunciation of the new sect, reasons for regarding it as heresy, fierce invective against Jesus of Nazareth and of the common fisher-folk who headed the apostasy in Jerusalem, news of measures actively under way in the capital to put an end to the cult, and a demand that those knowing of any Christians in Damascus put their knowledge in Saul's hands on pain of sharing the fate of the Christians.

But instead, taking the reading of the day as his text, Paul preached Christ to the people, proving that Jesus is the Son of God. Their astonishment must have known no bounds. Incidentally, this is the only time the title "Son of God" occurs in Acts. It is typical of Paul's view of the Christ: He was the Lord from heaven, the Son of God. How the converted Saul would revel in proving from the Law, the Prophets, and the Psalms that Jesus was indeed the Son of God!

(b) THE IMPACT OF PAUL'S PREACHING (9:21)

But all that heard him were amazed, and said; Is not this he that destroyed them which call on this name in Jerusalem, and came hither for that intent, that he might bring them bound unto the chief priests?

Paul's preaching caused an uproar in the synagogues. Demands would be made for an explanation. So time and time again Saul would give his testimony, until soon the whole city was ablaze with the astounding news. Certainly someone would hurry off to Jerusalem to tell an outraged Caiaphas and court that their favorite son had become a Christian and was boldly preaching the new doctrines in all of Damascus.

(2) PROVING IT (9:22)

But Saul increased the more in strength, and confounded the Jews which dwelt at Damascus, proving that this is very Christ.

Saul made rapid strides in his newfound faith. He "increased the more in strength." The word for "strength" here is used elsewhere to describe the astonishing vitality of Abraham's faith (Rom. 4:20); it is used by Paul where he tells us to "be strong in the Lord, and in the power of His might," putting on the whole armor of God and waging war against the spirits of darkness (Eph. 6:10–11). The word is *endunamoō*, at the core of which is *dunamis*, the mighty, irresistible power, the inherent power that Jesus demonstrated in His life on earth. Paul told the Philippians, "I can do all things through Christ which strengtheneth me" (Phil. 4:13). And the same word is used to describe the valiant heroes of the Old Testament (Heb. 11:34). Saul increased the more in strength. He grew rapidly in the things of God.

The Jewish community was "confounded." The word is *sunchunō*. We find it used once already in the book of Acts. On the day of Pentecost, when the disciples came down from the upper room baptized, filled, and anointed with the Holy Spirit, the multitude came running together "and were confounded" (2:6). The same now happened in Damascus. The word means to pour together, trouble, confuse, or stir up. Saul burst upon the Jewish community in Damascus like a one-man Pentecost. It was to be a typical Pauline encounter with the unbelieving world.

When *we* preach, what happens? Little or nothing, all too often. What does the city know of our coming or going? Nothing! What difference does it make to the tavern keepers, to the dens of vice, to places where vileness parades itself brazenly and unashamed? What difference does it make to corruption and graft in City Hall? What difference does it make to the propagators of false religion? What stir do we cause in the halls of learning where godless humanism is taught with arrogance and pride? Too often it makes no difference.

But when Paul went into the city he could not be ignored. The whole town knew he was there. Riots broke out, Jews and pagans were infuriated, and he was an immediate storm center. Paul shook whole communities. Here at Damascus we have the first intimation of the stormy, but wonderfully successful, life of the great apostle.

The thing that caused the stir at Damascus was the fact that Saul was "proving that this was the Christ." The mantle of Stephen had fallen on Saul. No one was able to refute his arguments.

c. A NEW FIGHT (9:23–25)

(1) HOW THE CONSPIRACY WAS FORMED (9:23–24)

And after that many days were fulfilled, the Jews took counsel to kill him: But their laying wait was known of Saul. And they watched the gates day and night to kill him.

The confrontation continued for some considerable time. Then the Jews of the Diaspora followed the lead of the Jews in the homeland. They turned against the truth of God in Christ and rejected the Holy Spirit. Throughout the rest of the book of Acts that was to be the case. Blindness fell upon the whole Jewish people with the exception of a small minority of believers.

We do not know who was behind this first conspiracy to silence Saul by assassination. Maybe the initiative came from the ruler of the Damascus synagogue. Maybe it came from the Sanhedrin in Jerusalem, which must have viewed with considerable alarm what was happening in Damascus. Maybe it came from some of the hotheads and fanatics in the Jewish community. At any rate, it met with approval, for a careful watch was set at the city gates to make sure that Saul did not escape. He had to be silenced at all costs.

(2) HOW THE CONSPIRACY WAS FOILED (9:25)

Then the disciples took him by night, and let him down by the wall in a basket.

One of Saul's friends, it seems, had a house on the city wall. Saul went in through the door and out through the window. This is the first of the many hairbreadth escapes that were to mark his history. The basket in which he was lowered down the outside of the wall was a large woven container such as was used by the disciples in conserving the food left over after the feeding of the four thousand (Matt. 15:37). Thus ended Saul's first effort to evangelize his own people.

d. A NEW FELLOWSHIP (9:26–29)

(1) SAUL'S NEW BROTHER IN THE LORD (9:26–27)

(a) THE FEAR OF THE BRETHREN (9:26)

And when Saul was come to Jerusalem, he assayed to join himself to the disciples: but they were all afraid of him, and believed not that he was a disciple.

Paul's arrival in Jerusalem was not greeted with enthusiasm by the church. (We can imagine how the news was received by the Sanhedrin.) His new sympathy for the saints was extremely suspect. One and all the believers shunned him, naturally thinking he had come to spy on them.

What happened to Peter's spirit of discernment? Why did not John befriend him, take him home, introduce him to Mary, the Lord's mother? Where was Andrew? Of all the apostles, Andrew was the one always reaching out to bring outsiders to Jesus. What happened to Nathaniel, that "Israelite indeed, in whom [was] no guile"? (John 1:47). How disappointing that none of the apostles were willing to so much as investigate the testimony of Saul. Surely a few minutes' conversation with him would have enabled the Spirit of God in Saul to bear witness with the Spirit of God in them. "They were all afraid," the Holy Spirit says. They "believed not."

As we read these early chapters of the book of Acts, we have a feeling of disappointment in the disciples. Why did God have to raise up a Stephen and a Philip and now a Saul of Tarsus? There seems to have been an almost palpable reluctance on the part of the apostles to get on with the great mission of the church (Acts 1:8). Only belatedly do they seem to have stirred themselves. One of the deacons has to show them that the blood of the martyrs is the seed of the church. Another of the deacons has to blaze the trail to Samaria. The same deacon has to make the first contact with the Gentile world of the Ethiopian. Now another church member has to take the initiative in making a friendly overture to Saul.

(b) THE FRIENDSHIP OF BARNABAS (9:27)

But Barnabas took him, and brought him to the apostles, and declared unto them how he had seen the Lord in the way, and that he had spoken to him, and how he had preached boldly at Damascus in the name of Jesus.

We have already met Barnabas (4:36–37). He was a Cypriot Jew, of the tribe of Levi. The meaning of his name is variously rendered, one lovely derivation being Son of Consolation. What a consolation he must have been to Saul! Barnabas believed him. Nothing in this world can be more frustrating than to be an object of universal suspicion and mistrust, to be eyed by everyone, to be kept at arm's length. Saul was a social leper to everyone in Jerusalem. But Barnabas believed him. Barnabas came to visit him, talked to him, sensed the innate honesty of the man, perhaps quietly but prudently checked out his story, and befriended him. No tongue can tell what that must have meant to Saul.

Then Barnabas introduced Saul into the the highest church circles. He introduced him to Peter, James, and John, to Thomas, Matthew, and Bartholomew, Andrew, and the rest. What a meeting that must have been! To see Saul looking Simon Peter in the face, to see Simon, his suspicion melting, give Saul a big fisherman's bear hug! To see Saul and John greet one another with a holy kiss!

And how they must have talked once the barriers were finally down! To the end of his days Paul never forgot what he owed to Barnabas, the first man to trust him in Jerusalem.

May we not seek to play the part of a Barnabas to some new believer?

(2) SAUL'S NEW BOLDNESS IN THE LORD (9:28–29)

And he was with them coming in and going out at Jerusalem. And he spake boldly in the name of the Lord Jesus, and disputed against the Grecians; but they went about to slay him.

The mantle of Stephen had fallen on Saul. He kept company with the apostles, identified himself with the church, and plunged into debate with the

Hellenist Jews. If they had been unable to withstand Stephen, how must they have felt when confronted with Saul of Tarsus, one of the most formidable intellects of that day? Saul had all that Stephen had and more. He was a trained rabbi, a former student of the most respected doctor of Hebrew law in Jerusalem.

It did not take the Hellenist Jews in Jerusalem long to endorse the opinion of their compatriots in Damascus that Saul could not be permitted to live. He was far too dangerous to the survival of Judaism, far worse than Stephen. So they sought ways to have him killed.

Increasingly now Judaism was turning against Christ, the Holy Spirit, the church, and Christianity. Within a few decades judgment would fall. The Temple, now the rallying point of opposition to the gospel, would be burned to the ground, and the Jews would be scattered again, left to wander deeper and deeper into the maze of an ever-growing Talmud.

     e. A NEW FUTURE (9:30–31)

         (1) A PERIOD OF RETIREMENT FOR SAUL IN TARSUS (9:30)

Which when the brethren knew, they brought him down to Caesarea, and sent him forth to Tarsus.

Caesarea, a thoroughly Romanized city and the Roman capital of Palestine, was on the coast and was the home of Philip the evangelist.

From there Saul took ship for home. Probably the Jerusalem believers breathed a sigh of relief. Now they could settle back into a more peaceful life. A man like Saul in their midst threatened to stir up another round of persecution.

Meanwhile Saul arrived back in his native Tarsus in Cilicia, part of the territory ruled by the Roman legate in Syria. Tarsus was a thousand years old. It had a checkered history under the Assyrians, Persians, Greeks, and Romans, who had constituted it a free city in 64 B.C. It was a university town, along with Athens and Alexandria one of the three great centers of learning in the Roman world.

We can have little doubt that Saul of Tarsus threw himself into the evangelization of his hometown with his typical zeal as soon as he had the Holy Spirit's permission to do so.

         (2) A PERIOD OF REST FOR THE SAINTS IN PALESTINE (9:31)

Then had the churches rest throughout all Judea and Galilee and Samaria, and were edified; and walking in the fear of the Lord, and in the comfort of the Holy Ghost, were multiplied.

It is not only the blood of the martyrs that is the seed of the church. God can use times of rest and tranquility as well as times of rage and tribulation.

He brings His people into green pastures and beside the still waters from time to time. He makes even our enemies to be at peace with us.

A truce now seems to have been accepted in Palestine. Jews and Christians decided to leave each other alone. Judaism set its sails towards the sunset in its stubborn refusal to acknowledge Jesus as Messiah. The church dropped anchor for the time being before spreading its sails again in search of new worlds to win for Christ.

In this lull the believers grew in grace and increased in the knowledge of God. The Holy Spirit was evident in their gatherings everywhere throughout the Holy Land. Numbers continued to be saved. It was a welcome respite.

B. A MAN OF THE GENTILES IS SAVED (9:32–11:18)

1. PETER'S MOVEMENTS (9:32)

And it came to pass, as Peter passed throughout all quarters, he came down also to the saints which dwelt at Lydda.

The focus now swings back to Peter. The door of the church was about to be opened formally to the Gentiles. With so many thousands already saved, there must have been some sizeable congregations, but the church was still Jewish in character. The Samaritans were semi-Jewish. Peter's ministry must have been very much in demand. Everyone would want to hear from his own lips the wonderful story of Jesus. Invitations must have kept pouring into Jerusalem for Peter or John or one of the resident apostles to come to this gathering or that to tell again the things Jesus did and said.

Accordingly we now see Peter beginning to move out. His first move was to Lydda on the road to Joppa. It is likely Saul had passed through here shortly before on his way to the coast; that could have prompted Peter's move. One rather suspects that Saul might have asked some searching questions as to why all the apostles were concentrated in Jerusalem when there was a whole world waiting for the Word.

Probably the church at Lydda had been founded by disciples fleeing from Jerusalem at the time of Saul's fierce persecution. One can imagine how eagerly yet sorrowfully Saul would have inquired after the various scattered groups of believers—eagerly, to learn more how God had made even the wrath of man to praise Him; sorrowfully, because he himself had been the cause and instrument of that wrath.

So, Peter "came down also," the Bible says, "to the saints which dwelt at Lydda." It is worth noting that in Acts and the New Testament in general the names given to God's people are all universal—"saints," "brethren," "disci-

ples," "believers." The New Testament recognizes no sectarian or denomina-
tional names such as would divide God's people into groups. The church
universal is always kept in mind in the New Testament when God's people are
named.

2. PETER'S MIRACLES (9:33–43)

a. A MIRACLE OF RESTORATION (9:33– 35)

(1) THE NEEDY PERSON (9:33)

*And there he found a certain man named Eneas, which had kept his bed
eight years, and was sick of the palsy.*

Eight years is a long time to be sick in bed, day after day, week after
week, month after month, year after year, and no end in sight. The doctors
had long since given up the case of Aeneas as hopeless. There was not only the
pain and suffering, the sense of uselessness, of being a constant burden to
others; there was the nagging and unanswerable question, Why me? There
was also the loss of income, the accompanying poverty, the hardship and
strain that go along with a debilitating illness. That had been the lot in life
for Aeneas of Lydda. Truly he was a needy person.

(2) THE NECESSARY POWER (9:34)

*And Peter said unto him, Aeneas, Jesus Christ maketh thee whole: arise,
and make thy bed. And he arose immediately.*

Peter had the gift of healing, one of the validating gifts of the early
church. He instantly healed this man in the name of Jesus. That is how it was
with the gift of healing: Find the most difficult case. Seek him out. Heal him
instantly, beyond all shadow of doubt, permanently. There was no mass
meeting, no hysteria, no healing of psychosomatic illness as though it were
the real thing, no stage-managed effects, and no offerings—just a simple
exercise of a rare and temporary but awesome and convincing spiritual gift.

(3) THE NOTED PURPOSE (9:35)

And all that dwelt at Lydda and Saron saw him, and turned to the Lord.

Up and down the plains of Sharon the news flashed. People came to see,
and they went away saved. That was the purpose of the miracle. The healing
of the sick man was not an end in itself, but a means to another end—the
salvation of many. Had healing been intended to be an end in itself, Peter
would have healed all the sick people in town. That he did not do so shows
that the healing was selective and of far wider purpose than the mere relief of
physical suffering. And certainly the healing was not for the purpose of
promoting Peter and enriching his coffers.

The primary purpose of the healing was to open a door for the gospel, to
lead to the salvation of souls, and to spread abroad the name of the Lord
Jesus.

b. A MIRACLE OF RESURRECTION (9:36–43)

(1) THE DEEDS OF DORCAS (9:36)

Now there was at Joppa a certain disciple named Tabitha, which by interpretation is called Dorcas: this woman was full of good works and almsdeeds which she did.

Ten miles northwest of Lydda was the seaport of Joppa. Here, too, there was a local church. One of its members had achieved a lovely reputation of being "full of good works." Her name, Tabitha in the Hebrew (Dorcas in Greek), meant "gazelle." The gazelle is a graceful creature. Dorcas certainly lived up to her name. She was a gracious woman filled with love and compassion for the poor.

There is a tendency in evangelical circles to be suspicious of good works. We have reacted against the social gospel of good works so forcefully that we have sometimes gone to the other extreme. Good works are an essential part of Christianity. They do not earn salvation, but they evidence salvation. Jesus "went about doing good" (10:38). A truly saved person ought to have compassion for the sick, the poor, the oppressed, the weak. Dorcas did, and her compassion took on a practical character. Her zeal in doing what she could to alleviate suffering is noted by the Holy Spirit.

(2) THE DEATH OF DORCAS (9:37–39)

(a) WHERE SHE WAS LAID (9:37)

And it came to pass in those days, that she was sick, and died: whom when they had washed, they laid her in an upper chamber.

The Jews had great respect for the dead. Their remains were always treated with dignity and buried with solemn regard. Jacob, for instance, made his own funeral arrangements before his death, and his wish to be buried in Canaan was scrupulously observed by Joseph. Similarly, Joseph's dying demand that his bones be carried to the family sepulcher in Canaan was carefully obeyed by Moses centuries later. Indeed, Genesis is a book of funerals, setting a deep tradition, rooted in the promises of God, of respect for the mortal remains of the deceased.

So Dorcas died, and her body was tenderly washed and laid out in an upper chamber pending burial.

(b) WHY SHE WAS LAMENTED (9:38–39)

i. HOW PETER WAS SUMMONED TO HER FUNERAL (9:38)

And forasmuch as Lydda was nigh to Joppa, and the disciples had heard that Peter was there, they sent unto him two men, desiring . . . that he would not delay to come to them.

Why did they send for Peter? It would be natural, no doubt, to want the ministry of so notable an apostle at the funeral if possible. Surely Peter would have words of consolation and hope for the bereaved at such a time as this. Is that why they sent for him?

Had Dorcas, perhaps, expressed the hope that she might see so notable an ambassador of Christ when she heard he was in nearby Lydda? One would expect so. The visit of one who had spent three-and-one-half years with Jesus would be no small event. How eagerly a saint like Dorcas would look forward to some long conversations with a man like Peter.

Or, when she was sick and her case pronounced serious, had she heard of the healing of Aeneas? Had she expressed the hope that Peter might come and heal her?

Or was it that the believers at Joppa hoped for an even greater miracle? The delegation of two men seems to be a common formality in Acts. Peter's presence was to be urged in the most vital way, as the express wish of the church. The need for haste would be obvious, as a body could not be long kept unburied in that climate. Did the believers hope against hope that, even yet, Peter might be able to work a miracle?

In any case the delegation was dispatched and Peter's presence urgently requested.

ii. WHAT PETER WAS SHOWN AT HER FUNERAL (9:39)

Then Peter arose and went with them. When he was come, they brought him into the upper chamber: and all the widows stood by him weeping, and showing the coats and garments which Dorcas made, while she was with them.

These people seem to have been some of the recipients of Dorcas's goodness. We can easily picture them showing Peter the fruit of her labors, pointing out the quality of the material, displaying the neat stitches, the good workmanship, the loving embroidery. The death of Dorcas was deeply felt by all, as is the death of any truly good person.

Peter could not but have been deeply moved himself by the grief all around him, the sobs of the saints, the abundant evidence of the goodness of the departed Dorcas.

(3) THE DELIVERANCE OF DORCAS (9:40–43)

(a) THE SUPERNATURAL AWAKENING OF DORCAS (9:40–41)

But Peter put them all forth, and kneeled down, and prayed; and turning . . . to the body said, Tabitha, arise. And she opened her eyes: and when she saw Peter, she sat up. And he gave her his hand, and lifted her up; and when he had called the saints and widows, presented her alive.

Peter's actions were evidently modeled on what his Master said and did at the raising of Jairus's daughter (Mark 5:35–43; Matt. 9:23–25). On that occasion Jesus put all the mourners out of the room, took the child by the hand, and said, "Tabitha cumi" ("Little girl, I say unto thee arise"). Peter had the room completely cleared. We can see him on his knees, praying. What did he say? Would we not dearly love to know what one says in a prayer that has the power to raise the dead?

Then, still on his knees it would seem, Peter faced the body and addressed it by name. "Tabitha cumi," he said. To his joy, the eyelids of the corpse quivered, then the eyes opened. She looked at Peter, who extended his hand. Who can imagine the emotions that flooded his soul as he performed this, his greatest miracle. Who can imagine the emotions of the saints and widows when they saw their dear Dorcas alive!

(b) THE SPIRITUAL AWAKENING OF JOPPA (9:42–43)

And it was known throughout all Joppa; and many believed in the Lord. And it came to pass, that he tarried many days in Joppa with one Simon a tanner.

Again we see the selective and spiritual nature of miracles in the book of Acts. The purpose was never the aggrandizement and enrichment of the evangelist but always the conversion of people. The little seaport of Joppa, famous since the days of Jonah, rocked with the news. Many were saved. The sight of Dorcas resuming her interrupted mercy mission was an argument nobody could deny.

As for Peter, he found lodgings in Joppa. The needs of the believers in town and the continual stream of converts gave him plenty to do. His lodgings are of considerable interest. He stayed in the home of a tanner, a man occupied all day with the skins of dead animals. To touch a dead body of any kind rendered a Jew ceremonially unclean. A tanner, therefore, was socially despised, so the fact that Peter was willing to stay with one shows that his prejudices were weakening.

3. PETER'S MINISTRY (10:1–11:18)

    a. HOW THIS MINISTRY WAS COMMANDED (10:1–23)

        (1) THE HEAVENLY VISITOR WHO AROUSED CORNELIUS (10:1–8)

            (a) THE ACTIONS OF CORNELIUS TOWARDS GOD (10:1–2)

There was a certain man of Caesarea called Cornelius, a centurion of the band [cohort] called the Italian band. A devout man, and one that feared God with all his house, which gave much alms to the people, and prayed to God alway.

The first Gentile with whom Jesus had dealings in His public ministry was a Roman centurion whose faith He commended and in whose faith He saw the beginning of the flow of the great Gentile tide into the kingdom of God (Matt. 8:11; Luke 7:2).

A normal Roman cohort, consisting of 600 men, was the tenth part of a legion. Each company of 100 men was commanded by a centurion, a tough-minded, iron-disciplined, well-trained, brave-hearted man. The Italian cohort would have been a cohort levied in Italy.

Caesarea, on the coast of Palestine, was a largely Gentile city and the seat of the Roman power base in the country.

Cornelius was a "God-fearer," that is, he was one of the many Gentiles who were greatly attracted to the moral, ethical, and spiritual aspects of Judaism. Many of them attended the synagogue and were instructed in the Scriptures and even observed the Sabbath and, to some extent, the Jewish dietary laws. They drew the line, however, at becoming full proselytes by circumcision, baptism, and sacrifice.

The Holy Spirit underlines three things about this very fine person, Cornelius. He mentions *his faith*. He was "a devout man, and one that feared God." Cornelius lived up to the light that he had. When more light was given he responded to it instantly. He did not yet know Christ, but he feared God. If he did not yet know the Holy Spirit, the Holy Spirit certainly knew him and wrote him down as a devout, God-fearing man.

He mentions also *his family*. He "feared God with all his house." This veteran soldier, hardened in a rigorous school, brought his family and those dependent on him to like faith in the living God. Not for them the pagan gods of Greece and Rome! Their faith was directed to the true and living God of the Jews, the God of Abraham, Isaac, and Jacob.

Then, too, the Holy Spirit mentions *his fervor*. He "gave much alms to the people and prayed to God always." "Faith without works is dead" (James 2:26), says James. This man exhibited his faith Godward by his works manward. Cornelius was generous in his acts of charity towards the poor and needy. All that was in addition to a disciplined devotional life as manifested in his regular prayer to the living God of Israel.

(b) THE ACCEPTANCE OF CORNELIUS BY GOD (10:3–4)

He saw in a vision evidently about the ninth hour of the day an angel of God coming in to him, and saying unto him, Cornelius. And when he looked on him, he was afraid, and said, What is it, Lord? And he said unto him, Thy prayers and thine alms are come up for a memorial before God.

The ninth hour was three o'clock in the afternoon, the very hour Jesus had died, the time of the evening sacrifice, and the hour for public prayer in the Temple.

The appearance of the angel frightened this seasoned Roman veteran, but his alarm was immediately stilled. The angel knew his name and knew about his spiritual exercise. He told Cornelius that his prayers and alms had ascended to God like the fragrance of the Hebrew burnt offering.

(c) THE ADVICE TO CORNELIUS FROM GOD (10:5–8)

i. HOW PRECISELY IT WAS HERALDED (10:5–6)

And now send men to Joppa, and call for one Simon, whose surname is Peter: he lodgeth with one Simon a tanner, whose house is by the sea side: he shall tell thee what thou oughtest to do.

The Lord knew all about Peter. The herald angel was able to give Cornelius exact instructions for finding him. God never forgets a name, never loses an address, never makes a mistake, never has a moment's hesitation in knowing where we are or what we are doing. There is something immensely comforting in · that to God's saints. He who tracks the journeyings of a hundred billion stars in each of a hundred million galaxies, who knows the path, the history, and the destiny of every speck of dust in cosmic space, knows all about me! In all my comings and goings by land and sea and air, He knows exactly where to find me any time He wants me. He knows how to send people across my path and into my life to fulfill His own inscrutable purposes. Nothing is more interesting in the book of Acts than to see how God keeps track of men. Does He need a man to meet an Ethiopian traveling at high speed away from Jerusalem with a great longing in his soul? He knows where Philip lives. Does He need a man to find blind Saul of Tarsus on the street called Straight? He knows where Ananias lives. Does He need a man to give the gospel to a good but still unregenerate Roman centurion? He knows Peter's present, temporary address.

So the angel gave Peter's name and address to Cornelius. "Go and send for him," he said. "He will tell you what to do." God has not given the ministry of reconciliation to angels. The work of the gospel has been entrusted to men. World evangelism may be slower that way, but it is sweeter. The testimony of a believer has special weight. "I was once lost like you, but one day Jesus saved me." No angel can talk like that. If a man had a choice to go and hear one of God's saints preach or go and hear an angel preach, Cornelius could tell them what to do. "Go and hear the man," he would say. "I heard an angel, and he told me to send for Peter."

ii. HOW PROMPTLY IT WAS HEEDED (10:7–8)

And when the angel which spake unto Cornelius was departed, he called two of his household servants, and a devout soldier of them that waited on him continually; and when he had declared all these things unto them, he sent them to Joppa.

Two servants and a soldier were selected at once and briefed on their commission. The word used to describe the way Cornelius communicated his experience is an interesting one. He "declared" all these things, it says. The word is *exēgeomai*, from which we get our word "exegesis." It means to make known by expounding. It is the word used by John to describe the Lord's mission on earth: "No man hath seen God at any time; the only begotten Son, which is in the bosom of the Father, he hath declared (*exēgeomai*) him" (John 1:18). Cornelius evidently was very careful to make known to his messengers exactly what had happened and why Peter was needed. Cornelius would be familiar enough with Jewish sensibilities and prejudices against social contact, even with God-fearing Gentiles, to appreciate the need for making the extraordinary circumstances clear and plain.

The prompt action of Cornelius was in character both with the man and the solemn experience he had just had.

(2) THE HEAVENLY VISION THAT ARRESTED PETER (10:9–23)

(a) HOW PETER WAS PREPARED BY GOD (10:9–16)

i. A VERY HUMAN KIND OF DICHOTOMY (10:9–10)

On the morrow, as they went on their journey, and drew nigh unto the city, Peter went up upon the housetop to pray about the sixth hour: and he became very hungry, and would have eaten: but while they made ready, he fell into a trance.

The scene now moves from Caesarea to Joppa and from Cornelius to Peter. It was noon. Peter had retired to the flat roof of his host's house to enjoy the sea breeze and a few minutes peace and quiet in which to commune with his loved Lord in heaven. This time he was overcome by hunger (2 Cor. 4:7). It is a constant battle to keep the mind on prayer. The body and its clamorous demands intrudes itself on even so glorious and thrilling a privilege as communing directly with the Lord of glory.

It was lunch time. The fact that it was also prayer time made no difference. All Peter could think about was his need to eat. While waiting for food to be prepared, he manfully sought again to compose his thoughts to prayer.

It is interesting to observe how "all things work together" (Rom. 8:28). Peter was thinking about food. God used food as the basis for the vision that now fell upon him. Far from being put out by Peter's wandering thoughts He used them as the basis for the revelation now to be made to him.

ii. A VERY HEBREW KIND OF DIFFICULTY (10:11–16)

a. THE COMMAND (10:11–13)

And saw heaven opened, and a certain vessel descending unto him, as it had been a great sheet knit at the four corners, and let down to the earth: wherein were all manner of fourfooted beasts of the earth, and wild beasts, and creeping things, and fowls of the air. And there came a voice to him, Rise, Peter; kill, and eat.

What a veritable Noah's ark of animals! Clean and unclean, wholesome and abominable, all mixed together. The very sight must have astonished Peter.

The vision was accompanied by a voice, which commanded Peter to get up and satisfy his hunger from the assorted meats available to him in the sheet. That must have been the last thing Peter ever expected to see or hear in a vision. It seemed to him, with all his Jewish prejudices, more of a nightmare than a revelation from God. He recoiled in horror from the very thought, scandalized by the unholy mixture of animals set before him.

b. THE CONFLICT (10:14–15)

But Peter said, Not so, Lord; for I have never eaten any thing that is common or unclean. And the voice spake unto him again the second time, What God hath cleansed, that call not thou common.

A tremendous struggle took place in Peter's soul. His ingrained religious prejudice, reinforced by the clear commands of biblical ritual law, strengthened by years of rabbinical teaching and tradition, and enforced by lifelong practice, warred against the clear demand of the vision. Peter, as always, blurted out what was on his mind. "Not so, Lord."

A young believer, facing the choice of obeying the call of God to the mission field or of continuing in a rewarding and comfortable business position, once consulted a veteran missionary. He explained how clearly God had called and yet how hard it was to make the choice to go. The missionary opened his Bible at this passage and pointed out to the young person Peter's words, "Not so, Lord." "You cannot say that," the wise, older man explained. "It is either 'Not so' or it is 'Lord.' The two words put together are a contradiction in terms. Now then," he continued, "take my Bible and take this pencil. Sit down here and pray about it. Then cross out one of the expressions. Cross out the words 'not so' and leave the word 'Lord,' or cross out the word 'Lord' and leave the words 'not so.' You cannot have it both ways."

So Peter very soon discovered. He was bluntly told not to label "common" that which God had cleansed. Peter had to learn that the ritual law of the Old Testament was no longer binding and that some of his attitudes would have to change.

c. THE CONFIRMATION (10:16)

This was done thrice: and the vessel was received up again into heaven.

How Peter must have stared after that net in his vision as it went up to heaven! The threefold repetition of the words "What God hath cleansed, that call not thou common," however, still rang clearly in his soul. Evidently Calvary's cleansing power extended much further than Peter had ever dreamed.

Heaven was going to be occupied by a much broader spectrum of earth's population than his narrow Jewish views allowed. But for the moment Peter was not quite sure what the vision portended.

(b) HOW PETER WAS PROMPTED BY GOD (10:17–23)
i. HIS DOUBTS (10:17–20)
a. HIS SECRET PERPLEXITY (10:17a)

Now while Peter doubted in himself what this vision which he had seen should mean . . .

He was wide awake now. Above him the sun shone down and over yonder he could see the Great Sea (so much bigger than his little Sea of Galilee), its horizons stretching farther and farther away to the west and to the Gentile nations of the mighty Roman world. Down below could be heard the sounds of the tanner and his men busy at their dubious trade. And up from the kitchen wafted the provocative smell of food sizzling in the pan.

But Peter's mind was occupied with his vision. A sheet from heaven! All kinds of creatures, clean and unclean. Now all declared clean and destined for heaven! What could it mean? Surely it did not mean that animals of all kinds were to be taken to heaven! Surely it meant that some radical change had taken place in Levitical ritual law! But was that all it meant? So Peter "doubted in himself," or "was perplexed," as the phrases could be stated. How many times, in seeking to do the Lord's work, we have found ourselves in the very same place—perplexed!

b. HIS SUDDEN PERCEPTION (10:17b–20)

Behold, the men which were sent from Cornelius had made enquiry for Simon's house, and stood before the gate, and called, and asked whether Simon, which was surnamed Peter, were lodged there. While Peter thought on the vision, the Spirit said unto him, Behold, three men seek thee. Arise therefore, and get thee down, and go with them, doubting nothing: for I have sent them.

Here we have a grand illustration of all things working together. Three men were at the gate calling his name, and Peter was on the roof pondering the purpose of a thrice-repeated vision. Moreover, in case Peter should still have doubts when he discovered that the strangers calling for him were Gentiles, the Holy Spirit told him bluntly he was to go with them.

It is not often in life we see the Lord showing His hand so prominently in our decisions. But can we doubt that He is at work and actively involved in each one of them? It is worth reminding ourselves of that when we come to a puzzling crossroad in life, when a decision one way or another will affect our life for a very long time. The Holy Spirit is actively involved and will enable us to make the right decision if we will wait on Him.

It is not usually wise to make a decision so long as the perplexity lasts. "If you don't know what to do, don't do it," was the best advice I ever received at one time of crisis in my life. Just wait a little while, and the perplexity will be resolved, and a clear intimation of the mind of the Spirit will be given. Sometimes water run into a glass will be cloudy. If we set down the glass for a few moments the sediment will sink and the water become clear. It is so with our decisions. Waiting will often clarify the issues. Many of our mistakes come from acting out of impatience.

So Peter tarried on the rooftop until all of a sudden a pounding at the gate and the sound of his name being called coincided with a clear intimation from the Holy Spirit as to what course of action he should take.

ii. HIS DECISION (10:21–23)

a. HIS COURTESY (10:21–23a)

Then Peter went down to the men which were sent unto him from Cornelius; and said, Behold, I am he whom ye seek: what is the cause wherefore ye are come? And they said, Cornelius the centurion, a just [righteous] man, and one that feareth God, and of good report among all the nation of the Jews, was warned from God by an holy angel to send for thee into his house, and to hear words of thee. Then called he them in, and lodged them.

One can imagine the stir in the house of Simon the tanner when his wife went to the door and saw these strangers standing there, obviously Romans and one of them a soldier! The initial reaction was probably one of fright. Roman soldiers did not socially visit Jewish tanners.

Peter, however, had hurried downstairs (on the outside of the house in an oriental home) and put everyone's mind at rest. But he, too, must have had a moment's surprise when he discovered the nature of his visitors' mission. He had not been the only one to receive intimation from heaven. God was evidently at work. The Holy Spirit had already told him he was to go with these men "doubting nothing" (10:20). Perhaps the full scope of what his own vision meant was already dawning on him.

He had been pondering deeply over its significance. The number three connected with it clearly matched the number of Gentiles at the door. The vision, then, must have something to do with the Gentiles. The unclean animals in the sheet must also point towards the Gentiles. The animals were ceremonially unclean according to the Mosaic law, mostly on account of their feeding habits. Jews regarded Gentiles as unclean on much the same ground. Gentiles ate animals forbidden to Jews, they ate food offered to idols, and they even defiled the animals Jews could eat by eating them with the blood.

The unclean animals in the sheet, then, were the Gentiles, as the ceremonially clean animals represented the Jews. But both were in the sheet together. There was neither difference nor discrimination. And both were caught up together at last, into the clouds—all declared clean by God.

Light was dawning fast on Peter. The sheet must represent the church! Paul tells us that he had no absolute monopoly on church truth. It was revealed to God's holy apostles and New Testament prophets by the Spirit (Eph. 3:5). It was dawning on Peter that God was calling out both Jews and Gentiles (Eph. 2:11–22; Acts 15:7–11,14). The obvious inference to be drawn from the vision of the sheet was that, in the church, differences between Jew and Gentile no longer existed.

How much of that Peter grasped at the time is difficult to say. That he grasped it fully in due course is evident from his own words at a later date.

In the meantime, in response to the prompting of the Holy Spirit Peter hurried down to welcome his visitors as guests into the house. They all sat down together to enjoy the meal that was already being prepared. Peter's prejudices were disappearing fast.

Anyone who has been a guest in a stranger's home knows how these Romans must have felt at first, and anyone who has suddenly been called upon to entertain at table some total strangers knows how Simon Peter and Simon the tanner and his family must have felt. At first the conversation would have been stilted and formal, comments on the weather, on the state of each other's health, "And do you have a family, sir?" Peter might have asked the soldier. "You were once a fisherman?" the soldier might have commented in response to some remark made by Peter. Or turning to Simon the tanner he might have said, "And what's the leather market like in these parts, Mr. Simon?" or, "Do you export most of your goods?" Gradually the atmosphere would thaw, and soon all kinds of interesting information would be flowing back and forth across the table.

By the time the meal was over it was too late for Peter to start out with his new friends for Caesarea. So, in hearty good fellowship, overnight accommodation was found for the visitors and plans made for a prompt start on the morrow.

b. HIS CAUTION (10:23b)

And on the morrow Peter went away with them, and certain brethren from Joppa accompanied him.

It was quite a company that set out for the thirty-mile tramp to Caesarea the next day. There were the three Gentiles, there was Peter, and there were a half dozen believers from the Christian community in Joppa—ten men in all. Peter's native caution prompted him to take these witnesses along. He knew only too well that his fellowship with Gentiles was unprecedented and that he could expect to be called to account by the Jewish believers all up and down the country when he returned.

We can picture them, then, these ten men walking towards Caesarea, and we can well imagine the conversation. Peter would want to know more about this man Cornelius who had sent for him, and the Romans would eagerly fill in the details, eulogizing their beloved master in glowing terms. The Gentiles would pump Peter for information about Jesus. And how glowingly Peter would tell them the whole glorious story now preserved for us in the four gospels. The miles must have melted away until, at last, the skyline of the largely Roman city of Caesarea stood boldly on the horizon.

> b. HOW THIS MINISTRY WAS CONFIRMED (10:24–48)
>> (1) THE MEETING THAT WAS CONVENED FOR PETER BY CORNELIUS (10:24–33)
>>> (a) THE GATHERING (10:24)

And the morrow after they entered into Caesarea. And Cornelius waited for them, and had called together his kinsmen and near friends.

Caesarea! The very name evoked thoughts of a far-flung Gentile world, of an imperial Caesar, of a world that was anathema to the Jew, a world with which his exiles and wanderings had made him familiar, a world whose commerce and profits he loved but whose customs and people he loathed.

Herod the Great, with his passion for building, had transformed Caesarea from a comfortless landing place on the bleak Palestinian coast into a splendid city of palaces, amusement, and commerce. Its boast was its harbor and its sweeping breakwater that flung a protecting arm into the sea, behind which the ships of the world could nestle in safety. The city contained a theater and an amphitheater so that the Roman masters of Palestine could enjoy their debased pleasures regardless of the violation such buildings caused to Jewish sensibilities. Herod had built the place in twelve years and dedicated it to Augustus. A decade or so later, Vespasian would be declared emperor by his troops at Caesarea and would make it into a colony. For the Roman occupation force, Caesarea was the one civilized place in an otherwise inhospitable land; for the Jew, it was the symbol of the detested power of Rome.

As Peter entered the city, he was entering a world far removed from the little Galilean village in which he had grown up.

In the meantime Cornelius himself had been busy. He had rounded up his family and friends, and an eager and expectant company were waiting for the arrival of the mysterious Simon Peter who was known in heaven and introduced by an angel.

Presently the lookout reported to the centurion, "They're coming, sir. I can see our three men, and there are about half a dozen more. They look like Jews." Cornelius came out to greet his guests.

(b) THE GREETING (10:25–27)

i. HOW PETER WAS WORSHIPED (10:25–26)

And as Peter was coming in, Cornelius met him, and fell down at his feet, and worshipped him, but Peter took him up, saying, Stand up; I myself also am a man.

Cornelius was overawed, and Peter was astonished. To Cornelius, the very sight of Simon Peter, whose authority in the faith had been made known to him by an angel of God, was the climax of days of anticipation. He did something he would have done to no other man, certainly to no Jew, to no one save Caesar: he went down on his knees. More, he worshiped. He was overcome by the thought that here, in the flesh, was the answer to his lifelong search after God. As for Peter, he was embarrassed. All Jew, he could not conceive a man's giving worship to another man or receiving worship from another man. With a gesture of good fellowship he raised the Roman to his feet. "I am only a man," he said.

ii. HOW PETER WAS WELCOMED (10:27)

And as he talked with him, he went in and found many that were come together.

Cornelius must have been a man of considerable influence and charm. He had many friends. The place was packed with people all eager to meet the man who had been heralded by an angel. Peter felt every eye turn upon him as he entered. They for their part looked with keen interest at the new arrival.

(c) THE GUIDANCE (10:28–33)

i. HOW GOD OVERRULED PETER'S NATIONAL INTOLERANCE (10:28–29)

And he said unto them, Ye know how that it is an unlawful thing for a man that is a Jew to keep company, or come unto one of another nation; but God hath shewed me that I should not call any man common or unclean. Therefore came I unto you without gainsaying, as soon as I was sent for: I ask therefore for what intent ye have sent for me?

In the silence that followed his entry, Peter spoke. He did not elaborate on his former religious scruples. Every Gentile knew the way Jews avoided social contact with Gentiles. It was that Jewish exclusiveness that generated much of the ill will felt by Gentiles towards Jews. Cornelius no doubt attributed Peter's presence in his home to the invitation sent him because of the angel's visit. That was not enough for Peter. "*God* hath showed *me*," he said. Somebody else's guidance is not good enough for us. If God wants me to be a missionary to some foreign land, surely He will speak to me about it personally. In a sentence or two, Peter set his Gentle audience at rest by deftly disposing of the age-old racial barrier between Gentile and Jew.

ii. HOW GOD OVERRULED CORNELIUS'S NATURAL IGNORANCE (10:30–33)

a. HIS EXEMPLARY CONDUCT (10:30a)

And Cornelius said, Four days ago I was fasting until this hour; and at the ninth hour I prayed in my house . . .

What a man this Cornelius was! As Gentiles we should say a sincere, "Thank you, dear Cornelius," for the hospitality of his home, the gates of which have become the portals of heaven to the Gentile world. We can see this sincere man standing there before the fisherman from Galilee explaining what he was doing when the guidance came—fasting and praying. What un-Roman and unsoldierly things to be doing! His comrades in the legion would be looking over the day's sports offerings at the arena, noting which entertainers were in town and placing their bets on their favorites in the various events. Cornelius was praying. While they were recovering with headaches and groans from last night's escapades, Cornelius was fasting with his heart uplifted to God.

b. HIS EXCITING CONFIRMATION (10:30b–32)

And, behold, a man stood before me in bright clothing, and said, Cornelius, thy prayer is heard, and thine alms are had in remembrance in the sight of God. Send therefore to Joppa, and call hither Simon, whose surname is Peter; he is lodged in the house of one Simon a tanner by the sea side: who, when he cometh, shall speak unto thee.

This story, of course, Peter had heard before from the servants of Cornelius. Now he heard it from Cornelius himself. The Holy Spirit goes over and over all the events in this section of Acts. Peter's vision was detailed for us and then told all over again by Peter himself later. The visit of the angel to Cornelius was detailed for us, and then the story was told again by Cornelius himself. The Holy Spirit wants to impress upon us the importance of these events. A monumental change was about to take place. The middle wall of partition between Jew and Gentile (Eph. 2:14) was to be broken down, and Gentiles were to become members of the church in full equality with Jews. That Gentiles could be saved was no mystery, for many an Old Testament Scripture spoke of that. But that there should be *no difference* was something new. In a few short years Jews would become a permanent and ever smaller minority in the church. That the Holy Spirit knew. He repeats the details for us so as to underline its importance.

The "man . . . in bright clothing" is called "an angel of God" by the Holy Spirit (10:3); by Cornelius's own messengers he was called "an holy angel"

(10:22), and Peter, in retelling the story later, referred to him as "an angel" (11:13). From this and other accounts of angelic appearances we learn that they may look like men but have something about them that makes it evident they belong to a brighter, better world than this. They often inspire fear, even in God's choicest saints, but they always treat God's people with politeness and deference. They show no curiosity about us and allow no familiarity with them. They are a different order of creation than ours. When their world intrudes on ours they confine themselves scrupulously to the commission entrusted to them, then vanish.

As we have seen, this angel told Cornelius to send for Peter, who would tell him what he needed to know. Had it been possible for someone to say to this angel, "You've just come from heaven, you've been gazing on the Lord in glory. You've seen the nailprints in His hands. You know that He is seated at God's right hand as Prince and Savior, as Lord and Christ, as High Priest and King—why don't *you* tell him?" he would have said, "That's not my job."

One other interesting thing about the testimony of Cornelius is the amount of acceptance he already had in heaven. Both his prayers and his alms had "come up for a memorial before God" (10:4). A person's works are never accepted by God as the basis of his salvation, but they are accepted as an evidence of his faith. The prayers and alms of Cornelius could not have secured him salvation; the blood of Christ alone could do that. But they were accepted as a token of his faith, and as evidence that when he had more light he would instantly respond to it. How Cornelius responded to the light he already had was a clear indication as to how he would respond when more light was given. In the meantime God accepted his alms and prayers as evidence of his willingness to believe all that God might say to him.

c. HIS EXPECTANT CONDITION (10:33)

Immediately therefore I sent to thee; and thou hast well done that thou art come. Now therefore are we all here present before God, to hear all things that are commanded thee of God.

Thus Cornelius turned the meeting over to Peter. On what would be said in the next five minutes hinged the fate of the world and the course of history for two thousand years. The moment was pregnant with suspense. Never has a meeting been so charged with excitement and expectation.

We must remember that Cornelius knew little or nothing about Peter, and the rest of the guests even less. He came from a corner of the Roman world known only in official circles as troublesome, narrow, bigoted, and fanatical about religion, one that would probably need another Roman thrashing before it could be taught its place. Cornelius and his guests might have had some contact with the urban, sophisticated, traveled, successful Hellenist

Jew, but with fisherfolk from Galilee, probably none. The story of Jesus had circulated to some extent in Caesarea (we must remember that Philip the evangelist lived there), but the official synagogue attitude would be colored by the propaganda of the Sanhedrin. So what would this man Peter say?

Suppose he had said to Cornelius, "My dear friend, you are what we Jews call a God-fearer. You have come a long way. There's one step more—*be circumcised!* Become a full Jew!" Doubtless some were dreading to hear words like that. One can almost hear the sigh of relief when it became evident Peter was about to say no such thing.

(2) THE MESSAGE THAT WAS CONVEYED BY PETER TO CORNELIUS (10:34–43)

(a) WHAT PETER PERCEIVED (10:34–35)

Then Peter opened his mouth, and said, Of a truth I perceive that God is no respecter of persons: but in every nation he that feareth him, and worketh righteousness, is accepted with him.

That God was no respecter of persons was a revelation to Peter. He had always thought that a Jew, just because he was a Jew, occupied a "most favored nation" status with God. Indeed, God had entered into a covenant relationship with Abraham and his seed, the children of Israel. Basic to the agreement was that Israel become a holy nation. Moreover, the Abrahamic covenant and the New Covenant contain unconditional promises made exclusively to the Hebrew people, promises God yet intends to make good to Israel. Yet the individual Jew was a man like anyone else, needing a personal relationship with God.

Peter suddenly saw that a righteous, God-fearing Gentile was just as acceptable to God as a righteous, God-fearing Jew. There was no difference. This was the climax of the revelation that began with the vision of the sheet and that paved the way for the total breakdown of the middle wall of partition between Jew and Gentile.

(b) WHAT PETER PROCLAIMED (10:36–43)

i. HE TALKED ABOUT THE LIVING WORD (10:36–38)

a. THE POINT OF THE MESSAGE (10:36)

The word which God sent unto the children of Israel, preaching peace by Jesus Christ: (he is Lord of all:)

Peter's sermon seems to be a summary of the apostolic preaching and a précis of Mark's gospel (often thought to be a reflection of Peter's preaching). Peter seems to assume that his listeners, living as they did in Palestine, had some general knowledge of the story of Jesus.

He reminded his Gentile listeners that "the Word" was originally sent by God to the children of Israel. For thousands of years God had spoken through the prophets exclusively to Israel. His last word had been sent to Israel. It was a word of peace. It had been brought down to earth by Jesus Christ, the One who was Lord of all. In other words, the Lord Jesus was God. In Jesus the Word had been made flesh. God had translated Deity into humanity. The Lord Jesus had come to bring men God's great offer of peace.

Peter began, then, by directing his listeners to Christ. That was the main point of the message—not Judaism, but Jesus.

b. THE PREACHING OF THE MESSAGE (10:37)

That word, I say, ye know, which was published throughout all Judea, and began from Galilee, after the baptism which John preached.

As Paul would later say to King Agrippa, "This thing was not done in a corner" (26:26). John the Baptist had caused a nationwide stir with his preaching. Thousands had flocked to hear him and had been baptized in the Jordan. His arrest by Herod and the circumstances of his murder were well known. The supreme burden of John's preaching had been that another was coming, One so far greater than he that he was not fit to untie His shoes.

The Messiah was formally announced to the nation by John, and then for three-and-one-half years He tramped the length and breadth of the land. He preached the Word of God in a particularly memorable and undiluted form. He spoke with authority and not as the scribes. He set forth principles for holy living in the Sermon on the Mount. He told stories that put truth in a vivid, unforgettable way. He tore aside the veil of the future in the Olivet Discourse, fearlessly denounced the establishment for rejecting Him, and boldly claimed to be the Son of God.

c. THE PROOF OF THE MESSAGE (10:38)

How God anointed Jesus of Nazareth with the Holy Ghost and with power: who went about doing good, and healing all that were oppressed of the devil; for God was with him.

It was not only what Jesus had declared that had proved Him to be a Man apart, anointed by the Holy Spirit, uniquely walking with God. It was what He had done. "He went about doing good," said Peter, summing up his impression of the astonishing three-and-one-half years he had spent with Jesus. What an epitaph! And in His wake had been the mighty miracles that had demonstrated His deity—a ceaseless flow of genuine, documented, fully authenticated miracles, performed under all conditions on all kinds of cases, setting people free from the oppression of the devil.

The fame of these things had reached the four corners of the land, and, although Jesus never visited Caesarea, the nationwide stir He caused must have raised ripples even there.

So Peter talked about the living Word, the Word that, as John put it, "was made flesh, and dwelt among us" so that people "beheld his glory, the glory as of the only begotten of the Father, full of grace and truth" (John 1:14). How Peter's Gentile audience must have listened!

ii. HE TALKED ABOUT THE LIVING WITNESSES (10:39–42)

a. THEY WITNESSED THE REALITY OF CHRIST (10:39a)

And we are witnesses of all things which he did both in the land of the Jews, and in Jerusalem.

Our faith does not rest on fable but on fact. It is fully authenticated by the united witness of eleven men who spent crucial years in the company of the Son of God. They went where He went, lived where He lived, fared out of a common bag. They saw all He did, they heard all He said. They were witnesses of His conduct, conversation, and character day and night, week after week, month after month, for three-and-one-half years. They are entirely credible witnesses, chosen with the same care that our courts would use in paneling a jury. Indeed, they were intended to be a kind of jury, chosen from various classes of men, men of different backgrounds and levels of education and age.

John was young and impressionable. Peter was a hard-working fisherman. Simon Zelotes was from the fiery ranks of the Zealots, whose political aspirations aimed at the emancipation of the country from Rome. Nathanael and Thomas were inclined to be skeptics. Matthew had been a hard-bitten businessman in the pay of Rome, considered by most a traitor to his country. Andrew had an attractive, approachable disposition. Philip was somewhat calculating. James was another businessman.

"We are witnesses of all these things," Peter assured Cornelius. He, along with the others, had witnessed the reality of Christ. All the wonderful stories told about Him in the gospels were true. His sayings as recorded in the gospels were genuine. All three dozen miracles later recorded in the gospels and the countless others batched together in summary statements are true. He did change water into wine; Peter drank some of it. He did walk upon the waves; Peter had done the same at His command. He had raised Jarius's daughter from the dead; Peter had been there. He had cleansed lepers and cast out even the most ferocious demons; Peter had witnessed those things. He had been transfigured; Peter had seen it. It was all true.

There is something solidly reassuring in Peter's statement: "We are witnesses." If Peter had been telling lies, a whole generation still living was able to rise up and say so, but Peter was telling the sober truth. The life and miracles of Jesus of Nazareth "both in the land of the Jews, and in Jerusalem" was such public knowledge and so well authenticated by public opinion that

His words needed no verification. Almost everybody knew the general outline of the story to be true. Peter and the other ten were special witnesses, however, because they had been with Him all the time.

>   *b.* THEY WITNESSED THE REJECTION OF CHRIST (10:39*b*)

Whom they slew and hanged on a tree.

Thus Peter indicted the Jewish people for the crucifixion of Christ. But the Romans were involved, too. It was well known that the Jews killed people by stoning; hanging on a tree was a Roman form of execution. Thus tacitly, while blaming the Jews, Peter brought in the Gentiles for their share of guilt in the murder of an innocent man, and no ordinary man, but the Son of Man, the Son of the living God. It was Pontius Pilate, after all, who signed the death warrant after saying again and again that he could find no fault in Jesus. However, Peter puts the weight of the blame on the Jews.

The chosen witnesses had seen the death of Christ. Peter had been present at one of the mock trials. John had been present almost to the very end and left the scene of the crime only when the dying Savior entrusted the care of His mother to him. That Jesus of Nazareth had died on a Roman cross cursed by the Jews was a historical fact.

>   *c.* THEY WITNESSED THE RESURRECTION OF CHRIST (10:40 42)
>   *1.* THE CHOSEN FEW (10:40–41)

Him God raised up the third day, and shewed him openly; not to all the people, but unto witnesses chosen before of God, even to us, who did eat and drink with him after he rose from the dead.

Peter now came to the greatest fact of all—the resurrection. This was the keynote of all apostolic preaching, and it is what sets Christianity apart from all other religions. For we do not preach a religion with all the attendant rituals and rules; we preach a risen, living Christ. Christianity does not say, "Come and keep these commandments"; or, "Observe these ordinances"; or, "Revere these relics"; or, "Perform these penances." Christianity says, "Come and meet the Man!"

The resurrection of Christ, like everything else about Him, was public knowledge in the country. The empty tomb was a fact. So was the impotence of the religious leaders of Israel and the Roman authorities to explain it.

The resurrection appearances of Christ were not made to everyone, but they were numerous enough and diverse enough to convince any open-minded person. On one occasion He appeared to a group of more than five hundred people, most of whom were still alive and bearing testimony in Peter's day. Any incident accredited by so many witnesses would need no further documentation in a court of law.

The specially chosen witnesses had ample proof that Jesus was truly alive from the dead. The most notable, as Peter implied, was the fact that this resurrected Man actually sat down and ate and drank with them. It was no ghost they saw but a living, tangible, audible, visible Man. The same Jesus they had known and loved before the crucifixion was alive from the dead and as real as ever.

2. THE CHALLENGING FACT (10:42)

And he commanded us to preach unto the people, and to testify that it is he which was ordained of God to be the Judge of quick and dead.

The murder and subsequent resurrection of Christ put the human race in a fearful predicament. God had sent His only begotten Son into the world. He had attested His deity in a thousand ways. He had lived a sinless life, a life overflowing in love and good works. And men had murdered Him, Jew and Gentile alike. Now He was back, alive from the dead, proof of human guilt written into the nail prints in His hands, and ordained to be man's Judge.

Well might men tremble. The challenging fact was that guilty men cannot hope to escape judgment. Man does not have the last word—He does. God is certainly not going to let men get away with the murder and rejection of His Son forever.

iii. HE TALKED ABOUT THE LIVING WAY (10:43)

To him give all the prophets witness, that through his name whosoever believeth in him shall receive remission of sins.

There has been, however, a postponement of judgment; grace has stepped in. God is giving men a chance to change their minds, to sue for mercy, to come to the living Savior and receive remission of sins from Him instead of well-deserved vengeance. The vital thing is to believe in Him—not just to give mental assent to the logic of a sermon but to wholeheartedly trust the living Christ of God.

Such was Peter's message. He had brought his listeners face to face with a decision. Now they had to do something about this wonderful person, Jesus of Nazareth.

(3) THE MYSTERY THAT WAS CONSUMMATED IN PETER AND CORNELIUS (10:44–48)

(a) THE OUTPOURED SPIRIT (10:44)

While Peter yet spake these words, the Holy Ghost fell on all them which heard the word.

Before Peter could finish speaking it happened! There was no need for a formal conclusion to his message, no need for a pressing invitation to believe and receive Christ. The Gentiles, drinking in the gospel word by word like a dry and thirsty land drinking in the rain, believed already, every word of it. Their hearts, long prepared by the Holy Spirit, were completely receptive.

Suddenly, the moment Peter got to the words "whosoever believeth in him shall receive remission of sins," the moment their eager hearts drank in that blessed truth—down the Holy Spirit came! Had He not been there in that room all the time, energizing Peter, enlightening the Gentiles?

What happened in Cornelius's home was just what had happened to the original small group of Jewish believers in the upper room, and the parallel was so obvious that Peter noted it and mentioned it later (11:15; 15:8).

But there were differences, too. When the Holy Spirit came upon the 3,000 on the day of Pentecost there was a demand that the convicted Jews repent, be baptized for the remission of sins, and thus receive the Holy Spirit. There was none of that here. The Gentiles were not nationally guilty of murdering a Messiah as were the Jews.

With this descent of the Holy Spirit on the Gentiles the mystery of the church was completed. The "middle wall of partition" between Jew and Gentile was broken down; from now on, in the church, the Lord Jesus made "in himself of twain one new man" (Eph. 2:14–15). The Gentiles were "no more strangers and foreigners, but fellow citizens with the saints, and of the household of God" (2:19).

Later Paul would develop the theology of that mystery, glorying in his ministry to the Gentiles and telling them of "the mystery of Christ, which in other ages was not made known unto the sons of men, as it is now revealed unto his holy apostles and prophets by the Spirit; that the Gentiles should be fellow heirs, and of the same body, and partakers of his promise in Christ by the gospel" (Eph. 3:1–6).

(b) THE OUTWARD SIGN (10:45–47)

And they of the circumcision which believed were astonished, as many as came with Peter, because that on the Gentiles also was poured out the gift of the Holy Ghost. For they heard them speak with tongues, and magnify God. Then answered Peter, Can any man forbid water, that these should not be baptized, which have received the Holy Ghost as well as we?

The gift of the Holy Spirit was manifested in the home of Cornelius in the same way the gift of the Holy Spirit had been manifested in the upper room. The Gentiles spoke with tongues.

This sign gift was necessary. Peter and the other Jews would probably have never received the Gentiles as "'fellow heirs and of the same body" (Eph. 3:6) apart from this sign. That, of course, is in keeping with the basic purpose of the gift of tongues, which was to bear witness against the unbelief of the Jewish people. On the first occasion of its use it testified against the unbelieving Jews at large. This time it testified against unbelieving Jews in the church who, without this sign, would never have believed that in the church Gentiles were no different from Jews.

The half dozen men who came with Peter were astonished, but Peter accepted the situation at face value at once. He realized that these Gentiles were now Christians. They needed to be baptized in order to publicly identify themselves with Christ and His church and as the first public step of obedience to the Lord. However, before acting on his conviction, he challenged the Jews who were with him. Was there any reason why these Gentiles should not be baptized? The Jews could think of none. Like Peter, they were convinced. The sign gift of tongues swept away any hesitation they might have had. The Holy Spirit had spoken. Who were they to argue?

(c) THE OUTRIGHT STAND (10:48)

And he commanded them to be baptized in the name of the Lord. Then prayed they him to tarry certain days.

Peter now set the truth of Christian baptism before the new believers and commanded them to submit to this ordinance of the church commanded as by the Lord Himself. He did not order them to be circumcised; he told them to be baptized. Circumcision would have identified them with Judaism and would have made them proselytes of a dead religion. Baptism identified them with Christ and His church and proclaimed them members of the mystical Body of Christ. The one would have linked them with the old covenant; the other linked them with the new. If Peter had commanded them to be circumcised, it would have made Christianity a Jewish sect.

Later, Peter himself must have been astonished at his own action, and he would undoubtedly give much thought to it. But it would have to await the coming of Paul and the crisis in the church at Antioch before Peter would fully understand the significance of what he had done in commanding baptism.

The new believers at Caesarea requested Peter to remain with them. Follow-up instruction for the new converts followed. Peter doubtless told them all the story of Jesus, showed them the relevance of the Old Testament Scriptures, and described the birth and development of the church from the beginning. Perhaps, too, he introduced Philip the evangelist to the new congregation before finally taking his leave.

c. HOW THIS MINISTRY WAS CRITICIZED (11:1–18)
(1) THE ACCUSATION (11:1–17)
(a) HOW THE ACCUSATION WAS MADE (11:1–3)
i. HOW THE GREAT NEWS WAS RECEIVED (11:1)

And the apostles and brethren that were in Judea heard that the Gentiles also had received the word of God.

How they heard we are not told. Palestine was a little country. The distance from Jerusalem to Caesarea was less than fifty miles. Between the Roman seat of government in Caesarea and the principal Jewish city of

Jerusalem there must have been continual coming and going. Besides, the Jews had a highly efficient "grapevine." Also, Peter could have spent longer than he originally intended at Caesarea, or he may have visited other places before returning to Jerusalem. The fact that only his return is mentioned in the next verse might mean that the six men from Joppa returned home at once or, perhaps, preceded him to Jerusalem. We can be sure they would have talked freely about what had happened.

In any case the news arrived in Judea before Peter did, and it had sufficient time to be digested and to turn sour in some Jewish minds. Stephen and the Hellenists had caused plenty of trouble, but so far the apostles had remained free from any taint of Gentile leanings. If the apostles, however, were now going to start fellowshiping with Gentiles, then more trouble could be expected. In any case the Hebrews in the Christian community, always suspicious of the Hellenists in their midst, took instant alarm. There was no way they could ever accept a Gentile into fellowship apart from circumcision.

ii. HOW THE GREAT NEWS WAS RESENTED (11:2–3)

When Peter was come up to Jerusalem, they that were of the circumcision, contended with him, saying, Thou wentest in to men uncircumcised, and didst eat with them.

In their eyes, no more serious charge could be leveled against a fellow Jew. Peter had broken the religious taboo: he had ceremonially defiled himself, and he deserved to be excommunicated. The other apostles seem to have been embarrassed by all this. Certainly, so far as the record goes, they made no attempt to defend him. We want to cry out: "Come on, Andrew! Don't you have a good word for your own brother? John! Why remain silent when your fellow apostle and partner is attacked?"

(b) HOW THE ACCUSATION WAS MET (11:4–17)

i. PETER RECOUNTS THE STORY OF DIVINE CONSTRAINT (11:4–12)

a. THE VISION (11:4–10)

1. ITS REVOLUTIONARY NATURE (11:4–9)

But Peter rehearsed the matter from the beginning, and expounded it by order unto them, saying, I was in the city of Joppa praying: and in a trance I saw a vision . . . a great sheet, let down from heaven . . . it came even unto me . . . fourfooted beasts of the earth, and wild beasts, and creeping things . . . I heard a voice saying unto me, Arise, Peter; slay and eat. But I said, Not so, Lord . . . But the voice answered me again from heaven, What God hath cleansed, that call not thou common.

Thus Peter's Jewish critics were silenced. With Peter's first statement they recognized that Peter was a man of prayer. He had not acted in a spirit of self-will; he had been praying. That was where the thing began—with a man of God on his knees talking to his Lord.

Then, too, mention of the vision would direct their thoughts at once to the dietary laws of Leviticus 11. They knew those laws by heart, as Peter did. The sheet descending from and ascending to heaven filled with creatures ceremonially unclean gripped them. Nor did the fact that the thing was done three times escape them. A threefold testimony was crucial in Israel to establishing the truth of a matter. That God had pronounced the creatures clean and thus put an end to Peter's religious scruples was remarkable and wholly unexpected. That such diverse creatures should be received finally and emphatically into heaven was astonishing.

The revolutionary nature of the vision must have impressed Peter's listeners almost as much as it had impressed him. Evidently the vision heralded some drastic changes in the Levitical law, upon which they had cut their eyeteeth and by which they had lived since infancy. The dietary laws controlled every facet of their everyday lives; for the Hellenists, the Jews of the Dispersion, those laws protected them from assimilation into the great Gentile world in which their lot was cast. Burdensome the laws might have been, but they were tremendously effective in keeping a Jew a Jew. Was all that now to be changed? And on the strength of one man's vision?

2. ITS REPETITIVE NATURE (11:10)

And this was done three times: and all were drawn up again into heaven.

"If one prevail against him, who shall withstand him; and a threefold cord is not easily broken" (Eccl. 4:12), was the word of God. So Peter tried to impress the repetitive nature of the vision on his listeners—"Three times." Even the dullest scholar in the school of God could hardly miss the point of a lesson that was gone over three times by the teacher. "Precept upon precept; line upon line . . . here a little, and there a little," was the Holy Spirit's way of teaching the dull hearts of Israel (Isa. 28:10). "Three times," Peter said. "God had to drill this thing into me. I couldn't see it. Then I wouldn't see it. Now I can see it clearly."

b. THE VISITORS (11:11)

And behold, immediately there were three men already come unto the house where I was, sent from Caesarea unto me.

"You will note again, brethren," Peter might have said, "the significant number three—the three connected with the vision, the three connected with the visitors. And as soon as they mentioned Caesarea I could see the drift of the vision. I was being directed towards the Gentile world, which, like yourselves, I had always considered unclean."

c. THE VOICE (11:12)

And the spirit bade me go with them, nothing doubting. Moreover these six brethren accompanied me, and we entered into the man's house.

How thankful Peter must have been for his foresight in taking those witnesses with him! From now on it would not be his word alone but the corroborating testimony of six witnesses, twice the number demanded by the Mosaic law.

The urging of the Holy Spirit had endorsed the message of the vision. If the exclusive members of the Jerusalem church were going to argue with what followed, let them beware, for the Holy Spirit was in this business. Peter had not made this move lightly. The Holy Spirit had directed him implicitly and explicitly.

It is a great thing when contemplating some course of action to be sure that we have the mind of the Spirit. That is true of all of life's decisions but particularly so when contemplating some major change of direction or some wholly new course of action. The Holy Spirit does not lack for means to impress His will upon us, but usually we are in too big a hurry. Peter himself, by nature, was a very impetuous man. In this whole incident, however, the Holy Spirit impresses upon us how Peter's natural impulses were kept under the restraint of the Holy Spirit. If Peter had been left to himself he would either have stubbornly refused to go or else would have blundered by himself into a situation that would have permanently impaired his usefulness as the apostle to the circumcision. Where the Holy Spirit leads, all is done decently and in order.

ii. PETER RECOUNTS THE STORY OF DEFINITE CONVERSION (11:13–17)

a. HOW CORNELIUS RECEIVED THE GUIDANCE OF GOD (11:13–14)

"And he shewed us how he had seen an angel in his house, which stood and said unto him, Send men to Joppa, and call for Simon, whose surname is Peter; who shall tell thee words, whereby thou and all thy house shall be saved."

Peter now directed his critics to the other side of the story. He told them what had happened to Cornelius and how it was that these three men came to be knocking at his door.

One can picture the scene vividly enough. We can see Cornelius taking Peter by the arm and pointing out to him the exact spot. "It was right here he stood, Simon, right where I'm standing now. It was an angel. I've never seen anything like it. I've never been so scared in my life, and I could tell you some stories, believe me, of dangerous situations I've been in as a soldier."

So with a quick thumbnail sketch Peter carried his Jewish audience across the miles to the home of a devout Gentile God-fearer in the Roman garrison town of Caesarea. He recounted for them the fact that God had been just as much at work preparing the soul of the centurion as He had been at work preparing his own heart for this new move.

    b. HOW CORNELIUS RECEIVED THE GIFT OF GOD (11:15–17)

    1. IT WAS AN IDENTICAL GIFT (11:15–16)

And as I began to speak, the Holy Ghost fell on them, as on us at the beginning. Then remembered I the word of the Lord, how that he said, John indeed baptized with water; but ye shall be baptized with the Holy Ghost.

What had happened in that Gentile home was the same as had happened in the upper room. Jesus had said to His disciples on His last walk with them to Olivet: "Ye shall be baptized with the Holy Ghost not many days hence" (1:5). He had been preparing them for the impending fulfillment of the prophecy of John the Baptist regarding the baptism of the Spirit.

Ten days later the Jewish church had been born, and people had been baptized, with accompanying signs, into the church, the mystical Body of Christ. Peter now uses the Lord's own expression "baptized with the Holy Ghost" to explain what had happened in the house of Cornelius. Gentiles had now been added to the church, the mystical Body. They had been added by the Holy Spirit. He had given similar signs; the two experiences were identical.

    2. IT WAS AN IDENTIFYING GIFT (11:17)

Forasmuch then as God gave them the like gift as he did unto us, who believed on the Lord Jesus Christ; what was I, that I could withstand God?

Peter now put the ball in their court. Now was the time for them to speak or forever hold their peace. He had no intention of withstanding (hindering) God. What about them?

The men of the circumcision in the Jerusalem church had been effectively checkmated by the Holy Spirit. They must have looked at each other, looked hard at Peter, and looked at Peter's witnesses, solid citizens of the kingdom, standing by, nodding their heads. They must have looked at the Hellenists beaming at Peter's story. It was a large and bitter pill to swallow. Two thousand years of growing Jewish prejudice against Gentiles had to be gulped down. But it was evident, even to the narrowest, most exclusive, and insular of them, that there was nothing they could possibly say against Peter. His story was evidently an account of God's clear leading, and his earnestness was unmistakable. The conclusions he had reached were incontrovertible. Cornelius and the Gentiles had been accepted by God as equal heirs of the grace of God, first-class citizens in the kingdom, fellow members of the Body of Christ.

    (2) THE ACCEPTANCE (11:18)

When they heard these things, they held their peace, and glorified God, saying, Then hath God also to the Gentiles granted repentance unto life.

The expression "held their peace" is *hēsuchazō*. We find the word used, significantly enough, in Luke's account of the burial of Jesus. When Joseph of Arimathaea and the women followers of Jesus had put Jesus' body in the tomb we read, "And they returned, and prepared spices and ointments; and rested [*hēsuchazō*] the sabbath day according to the commandment" (Luke 23:56).

Those of the circumcision did what those women did. They stopped working. They had to. What else could they do? A Sabbath rest on the issue came over the church. With those of the circumcision it was a somewhat reluctant and grudging cessation of active opposition, just as those devout women had grudgingly ceased ministering to the mortal remains of Jesus.

The same word is used by Luke in another connection. When the enemies of Jesus brought Him, on the Sabbath day, a certain man who had dropsy, they watched Him like hawks. Would He violate the Sabbath? Jesus was not intimidated. "Is it lawful to heal on the sabbath day?" He said to the lawyers present. Luke says, "And they held their peace [*hēsuchazō*]" (Luke 14:3–4). It was the grudging silence of those who were cornered and who decided it was best to say nothing.

The acquiescence of those zealous for the old Jewish traditions and privileges seems to have been less than enthusiastic. Henceforth they would look to the austere James (the Lord's brother) to champion their exclusive views.

The rest were more generous. They glorified God. They rejoiced that Gentiles, too, were now to be admitted to the fellowship of the church and to the ranks of those who had passed from death unto life.

The principle of evangelizing Gentiles was now established.

C. A MULTITUDE OF THE GENTILES SAVED (11:19–12:25)

    1. THE PLANTING OF THE CHURCH AT ANTIOCH (11:19–30)
      a. TWO NEW MOVES (11:19–26)
        (1) A MOVE TO REACH HEBREW PEOPLE IN FOREIGN LANDS (11:19)
          (a) THE REASON FOR THE MOVE (11:19a)

Now they which were scattered abroad upon the persecution that arose about Stephen travelled as far as Phenice, and Cyprus, and Antioch . . .

The door having been opened to the Gentiles, the Holy Spirit moves us at once into predominantly Gentile lands. Phenice was old Philistine country, which ran for about forty miles along the seacoast, varying between ten and twenty miles wide. It was the great thoroughfare between Phoenicia and Syria in the north and Egypt and Arabia in the south. Philip the evangelist had been that way.

Cyprus, soon to figure more prominently in the story of the church, was an island off the coast of Syria that was annexed by Rome to the province of Cilicia. It was one of the chief seats of the worship of Venus.

Antioch, three hundred miles north of Jerusalem, was situated about fifteen miles from the mouth of the Orontes, where the mountains of Lebanon running northward abruptly meet the Taurus mountains running eastward. In the immediate vicinity was Daphne, the cult of Artemis, and the celebrated sanctuary of Apollo, where the most licentious forms of worship imaginable were carried on. The city, founded by Seleucus Nicator in 300 B.C., was the capital of the Seleucid Empire. Pompey had made it a free city, and it was incorporated into the Roman Empire in 64 B.C. It had a population of some 200,000 people, making it the third largest city in the Empire.

These were the places where the Christians went to escape the growing hostility in Jerusalem. They were "scattered abroad," says the Holy Spirit. Satan overreached himself. By scattering the burning coals of Christian witness he made it possible for fresh fires of testimony to spring up elsewhere.

(b) THE RESULT OF THE MOVE (11:19*b*)

Preaching the word to none but unto the Jews only.

The door had been formally opened to the Gentiles, but the scattered Jewish refugees contented themselves with spreading the good news of the gospel among such of their own people as they found in various places. "To the Jew first" was still the basic program. However, Jews of the Dispersion in faraway places were being brought under the sound of the gospel.

(2) A MOVE TO REACH HEATHEN PEOPLE IN FOREIGN LANDS (11:20–21)

(a) THE DARING VENTURE (11:20)

And some of them were men of Cyprus and Cyrene, which, when they were come to Antioch, spake unto the Grecians, preaching the Lord Jesus.

Cypriot and Cyrenian Jews took the first daring step. There in that pagan, utterly immoral city of Antioch, these inspired Jewish Christians crossed the great divide. Peter had unlocked the door in Caesarea; they pushed it open wide.

We can easily picture these men talking together about the things of God and of the salvation they enjoyed in Christ. They would talk, too, about the church and the way it was now reaching out to Jewish communities in various places. Then one of them might have said: "How I wish we could share this good news with the Gentiles. I was coming back to Antioch the other day and had to go past Daphne. Oh, the debauchery! All in the name of religion! My heart burned to tell those poor, deluded people about Christ." There was a moment of silence, perhaps, then someone might have said: "Well, why not? Why not tell the Gentiles? I heard the apostle John say that

'God so loved the *world*, that he gave his only begotten Son, that *whosoever* believeth in him should not perish, but have everlasting life' (John 3:16). Doesn't *that* include the Gentiles?"

Another may have added: "I heard Peter once say that just before the Lord ascended into heaven He said we were to be witnesses in Jerusalem and Judaea and Samaria and to the *uttermost parts of the world*. Surely that includes Gentiles."

Another might have remarked: "I heard something interesting the other day. I was talking to a brother here on business from Jerusalem. He said that Peter had taken the gospel to a Roman centurion in Caesarea. Apparently he visited the man's home, and the Holy Spirit fell on the Gentiles in the centurion's house in just the same way He fell upon the Jews in the upper room on the day of Pentecost. My friend said it caused quite a stir in Jerusalem. If Peter can go to the Gentiles, why can't we?"

So these farsighted Cypriot and Cyrenian Jewish Christians took the first major step in Gentile world evangelism. They began to preach the Lord Jesus to the hungry, waiting Gentiles in one of the most wicked cities of the world.

(b) THE DIVINE VINDICATION (11:21)

And the hand of the Lord was with them: and a great number believed, and turned unto the Lord.

There was instant revival! The message was like water to a thirsty man, like bread to the starving. The Gentiles, worn out and wearied with their pagan superstitions, heartsick over the deadness of their gods and the debaucheries of their priests, instantly recognized the truth. The name of the Lord Jesus wrought an instant response in their souls. The hand of the Lord was with His people in proclaiming the saving, sovereign Name to the Gentiles. Soon Jews would be a permanent minority in the church as ever increasing numbers of Gentiles turned gratefully to Christ.

b. TWO NEW MEN (11:22–30)

(1) THE MAN CHOSEN BY THE BRETHREN IN THE MOTHER CHURCH AT JERUSALEM (11:22–24)

(a) HE WAS A SENT MAN (11:22)

Then tidings of these things came unto the ears of the church which was in Jerusalem: and they sent forth Barnabas, that he should go as far as Antioch.

The news of what was happening at Antioch caused a considerable stir in Jerusalem. Though Peter had officially opened the door of the church to the Gentiles it never occurred to anyone, apparently not even Peter, to take the next logical step and begin evangelizing the Gentile population of Jerusalem and Judea. There was the Roman garrison and the Roman diplomatic corps with its staff. There were business people and visitors such as those Greeks who, in the days of Christ's ministry, came to the disciple Philip with the request, "Sir, we would see Jesus" (John 12:20–21).

When the news of what was happening at Antioch reached Jerusalem, instead of seeing it as a logical extension of Peter's ministry in Caesarea and as a challenge to do the same in the homeland, the Jerusalem church decided the thing needed investigation. What an opportunity Jerusalem missed—to be the first church to begin Gentile world evangelism! But the idea was too new, and it challenged too many ingrained traditions. "We've never done it before" was the attitude, and "We're not at all sure we agree with what's going on." Barnabas was selected to go and see what was happening in Antioch. We have met Barnabas before (4:36–37), and we shall hear more of him. He was a generous, godly, warmhearted man—just the man for this job. A better man could not have been chosen, and as a Cypriot his sympathies would naturally be broader than those of native-born Palestinian Jewish believers.

(b) HE WAS A SENSIBLE MAN (11:23)

Who, when he came, and had seen the grace of God, was glad, and exhorted them all, that with purpose of heart they would cleave unto the Lord.

That is the kind of man Barnabas was—not a bit critical or jealous of someone else's success, but thrilled and delighted. To see all those Gentiles responding to the gospel, to hear them talking about Jesus, to listen to their testimonies—Barnabas rejoiced.

Barnabas would have been one of those in the Jerusalem church who had "glorified God" at Peter's news. He would have been one of those who said, "Then hath God also to the Gentiles granted repentance unto life" (11:18). It did his heart good now to see just what was happening at Antioch and to assess for himself this great step forward for mankind.

However, he was a practical man, too, and he could see the danger in people making too light a decision for Christ. The old way into the fold by means of circumcision was too hard. This new and living way by simple faith in Jesus the Lord was not too easy, but it might seem so to some. There was the danger of a false profession of faith. Barnabas warned them to make their calling and election sure. The case of Simon Magus was a warning to all, so "he exorted them all, that with purpose of heart they would cleave unto the Lord." Salvation is a matter of the heart, not the head.

The word translated "purpose" here is *prothesis*. It suggests "a setting forth" and comes from a root meaning to place before or to exhibit. The word is used, interestingly enough, for the showbread (Matt. 12:4; Mark 2:26; Heb. 9:2), which was exhibited on the table in the Tabernacle. Once a week the priests were required to take twelve loaves of bread, one for each of the tribes of Israel, and put them on the table before God, each in its proper place. At the end of the week the bread was replaced, and the loaves that were removed were ceremonially eaten by the priests. In all that there was deliberate, planned purpose.

So then, when Barnabas urged Gentile converts that "with purpose of heart" they should "cleave unto the Lord," he was encouraging them to be deliberate and purposeful about their decisions for Christ.

The expression *cleave unto* literally means "abide with." The word is used of Paul's stay at Corinth: "And Paul after this *tarried* there yet a good while" (Acts 18:18).

So although Barnabas was delighted with what was happening, he was a sensible man, and was not carried away by the excitement of a revival. He added a note of encouragement and exhortation.

     (c) HE WAS A SPIRITUAL MAN (11:24)

For he was a good man, and full of the Holy Ghost and of faith: and much people was added unto the Lord.

What more could be said about a man? He was "a good man." That says something about his *character.* He was like Jesus, who "went about doing good" (10:38). He was the kind of man, Paul says, that people would die for (Rom. 5:7). He was "full of the Holy Ghost." That says something about his *Christianity.* A person "filled with the Spirit" will be one whose life overflows with "psalms and hymns and spiritual songs," a person Christlike in character, conduct, and conversation (Eph. 5:18–21). He was "full . . . of faith." That says something about his *commitment.* Barnabas was a great believer. He took God at His word and trusted the Lord Jesus implicitly.

This was the man who exhorted the new Gentile converts to make a life commitment to Christ. They could take it from him. We can all take exhortation from a man whose whole life exhibits the principles he expounds.

     (2) THE MAN CHOSEN BY BARNABAS FOR THE MISSION CHURCH AT ANTIOCH (11:25–30)

         (a) HOW HE WENT FOR SAUL (11:25)

Then departed Barnabas to Tarsus, for to seek Saul.

The thing was too big for him—Barnabas soon realized that. What was happening at Antioch was much larger than anything Barnabas had anticipated, and it was only the beginning. The whole vast Gentile world loomed before his mind's eye: the great Roman world reaching from the Euphrates to the Atlantic Ocean and from Britannia to the cataracts of the Nile; the exotic lands beyond the Euphrates, Parthia, India, the fabled lands beyond that. Millions upon millions of Gentiles—all waiting for the gospel of Jesus Christ.

Whom could he get to come and exploit such an inexhaustible mine? Peter? No! Peter was a good man, but no man for a job like that. John? Andrew? No, they were just fishermen—anointed apostles, but fishermen. Philip the evangelist? A good man with a sizeable family and settled down in Caesarea—and needed there. What a pity Stephen was dead! Stephen would have been an ideal man. Saul? Saul. Why, of course! Saul of Tarsus! The very man—bold as a lion, brilliant, burdened for souls, a Jew by birth, a Greek by culture, a Roman by citizenship. The very man! Saul of Tarsus!

So Barnabas packed his bags and instead of heading south to make his report to the apostles he headed north to find the one man in all the world with the zeal, the breadth of vision, the education, the natural talents, and the spiritual anointing big enough to become an apostle to the Gentiles.

He had to look for him. The word *anazēteō* literally means to seek up and down. Luke used the word once before in a fascinating connection. When Mary and Joseph missed the young Jesus from their company and returned to Jerusalem to search for Him, Luke says that they "sought Him [*anazēteō*—they searched up and down] among their kinsfolk and acquaintance. And when they found him not, they turned back to Jerusalem, seeking [*anazēteō*—searching all the way as they went] him" (Luke 2:44–45). Thus it was that Barnabas went off to Tarsus in search of Saul. Finding Saul was probably no easy task.

It has been suggested that Saul had been disinherited for his faith in Christ (cf. Phil. 3:8). It has also been inferred that it was during these years that he suffered some of the hardships he describes to the Corinthians (2 Cor. 11:23). Perhaps he had already begun reaching out to Gentiles on his own, for he had already been commissioned by God for the task (Acts 22:21). Perhaps Barnabas had heard word of Saul's activities among the Gentiles in Cilicia. In any case, he initiated a diligent search for Saul, convinced that his friend was the one man who could do justice to the open door of evangelism now beckoning in Antioch.

(b) HOW HE WORKED WITH SAUL (11:26–30)

i. THEIR FAITHFULNESS (11:26a)

And when he had found him, he brought him unto Antioch. And it came to pass, that a whole year they assembled themselves with the church, and taught much people.

It would have been immediately apparent that Saul was the man. Some years had passed since Barnabas had said farewell to him, but he had evidently grown in grace and increased in the knowledge of God. He had become a giant. The magnificent teaching that forms the backbone of his epistles was already formulated in his mind. He would expound to these new converts at Antioch and to this growing church the mystery of Christ's cross as it would be taught in Romans, the mystery of Christ's church as it would be taught in Ephesians, and the mystery of Christ's coming as it would be taught in Thessalonians. There would be correction at any hint of doctrinal departure from the truth, and there would be reproof of any display of moral departure. Saul would declare the whole counsel of God. Barnabas, an apt and admiring pupil, would soon not only be marveling at the depth and discernment in Saul's teaching but would be echoing what he heard. This went on for a year.

ii. THEIR FRUITFULNESS (11:26b)

And the disciples were called Christians first in Antioch.

Christian was at first a nickname, and perhaps a derogatory one, but a singularly appropriate one. Some have suggested the name was derived from the Greek word *chrastos* ("useful"), the name of a slave, a common enough name at that time. More likely the name derived from *christos*, the Greek form of the title *Messiah*, the One about whom disciples were always talking. The Jews could not have given the name to the disciples of Jesus, for *christos* was a sacred word among them, and they repudiated the claim that Jesus was the Messiah. However it was derived, the name *Christian* is a singularly lovely and appropriate name for believers in the Lord Jesus. The Holy Spirit adopts it and uses it (1 Pet. 4:16). The word for "called" is *chrēmatizō* and is generally used of a divine communication. For instance, aged Simeon haunted the Temple because "it was revealed [*chrēmatizō*] unto him by the Holy Ghost, that he should not see death, before he had seen the Lord's Christ" (Luke 2:26). So although the name may have been given in mockery, it was a wonderful name, and its real origin was divine.

The name stuck and became a badge of honor. It is the name by which the Lord's people are known to this day. The name identifies us with Christ and Him with us. What manner of people ought we to be in all godliness of character, conduct, and conversation who, by the name we bear, advertize to the world that we are His!

iii. THEIR FELLOWSHIP (11:27–30)

a. HELP FROM JERUSALEM (11:27–28)

And in these days came prophets from Jerusalem unto Antioch. And there stood up one of them named Agabus, and signified by the spirit that there should be great dearth throughout all the world: which came to pass in the days of Claudius Caesar.

The church at Jerusalem could no longer ignore what was happening at Antioch. Men with the gift of prophecy arrived in Antioch to help in the ministry of the Word.

The New Testament gift of prophecy was unique to the early church. Like the gift of tongues, it was expressed by direct inspiration of the Spirit of God. It was a transitional gift of great value until the New Testament had been written and put into circulation, after which it ceased to be relevant. Unlike the gift of tongues, which was a judgment sign on the nation of Israel, prophecy was delivered in the speaker's own language. For the most part, like their Old Testament counterparts, New Testament prophets were "forth-tellers" rather than foretellers. Their function was to communicate to local congregations truth revealed by the Spirit and relevant to present needs.

However, as we learn from the incident recorded here, the ministry of the prophet was not confined to specially illuminated preaching. Sometimes they did foretell the future. One of the prophets ministering in Antioch was Agabus. He announced the coming of a widespread famine. Luke appends the note that the prophecy was fulfilled in the days of the emperor Claudius, the fourth Roman emperor (A.D. 41–54), whose reign was indeed marked by several severe famines in various parts of the empire. This advance warning would have enabled the believers to take prudent measures for the future.

b. HELP FOR JERUSALEM (11:29–30)

Then the disciples, every man according to his ability, determined to send relief unto the brethren which dwelt in Judea: which also they did, and sent it to the elders by the hands of Barnabas and Saul.

The famine hit Judaea severely. In Antioch the Christians were deeply concerned, and each one made a contribution to a relief fund according to his ability. This is the first time a church is said to have taken up a collection to help another church. It is worth noting the way money flows in Acts. It does not flow, as we would expect, from the parent church to assist in evangelizing the far-flung foreign fields. On the contrary, the money flows the other way—from the mission field towards the homeland! That certainly runs contrary to our ideas. There were no "rice Christians" on the mission fields of the early church, eager to cash in on material benefits provided from churches in the homeland. That does not say that the missionaries were not financially supported from the home churches. Perhaps they were. What is significant is that the book of Acts does not say so. Money flowed the other way. Paul was apt to go to work when necessary, to supply his own needs and those of others. (18:3), although the foreign church at Philippi did help support him (Phi. 4:15). That he received financial help from other churches he told the Corinthians (2. Cor. 11:9). It is strange that no mention of financial support is made concerning the Antioch church, and the Jerusalem church had little or no interest in Paul's missionary activities.

As the funds accumulated, Saul and Barnabas were chosen to take the money to Jerusalem. There it was given to the elders (*presbuteroi*). This is the first time we meet with elders in the Christian church. The Jerusalem elders were a group distinct from the apostles. James, the Lord's brother, might have been one of them.

This visit to Jerusalem seems to be the one mentioned by Paul in Galatians 2, at which time he took advantage of being in the city to make sure the apostles, particularly Peter and John, along with James the Lord's brother, recognized his own unique apostleship. Not, of course, that he needed their endorsement, but it was good policy to have facts out in the open and well understood.

2. THE PERSECUTION OF THE CHURCH AT JERUSALEM (*12:1–23*)

    a. HOW IT WAS ORGANIZED (12:1–4)

        (1) THE DEATH OF JAMES (12:1–2)

            (a) THE MURDERER (12:1)

Now about that time Herod the king stretched forth his hands to vex [maltreat] certain of the church.

This was Herod Agrippa I, a grandson of Herod the Great and the Hasmoneon princess Mariamne. His father, Artistobulus, was murdered by Herod the Great, as was later his grandmother Mariamne. Upon the death of his father, Agrippa was sent to Rome by his mother to get him out of his murderous grandfather's way. At Rome, Agrippa grew up on intimate terms with members of the imperial families, particularly with Gaius, grand-nephew of Tiberius. When Gaius became the Emperor Caligula in A.D. 37 he bestowed on his friend Agrippa tetrarchies in southern Syria, gave him the title of king, and later added to his domain Galilee and Perea, formerly ruled by Agrippa's uncle Antipas. Caligula was murdered in A.D. 41, and Claudius became emperor; he added Judaea to Agrippa's realm.

Herod Agrippa I zealously courted his Jewish subjects. He espoused the law and coveted popularity with the people. He possessed considerable personal charm, and he was more acceptable to the Jews than most of the masters imposed upon them by Rome because of his Hasmoneon descent. Like the other Herods, however, he was an Idumean and a descendant of Esau.

Luke calls him Herod the king. He was the only Herod to have royalty bestowed upon him and to govern all of Palestine since the death of his grandfather, Herod the Great.

Herod saw a cheap way to curry favor with his Jewish subjects by persecuting the church. To him, Christian believers, the very aristocracy of heaven, were defenseless nobodies and therefore safe targets for attack. Herod reckoned without God.

(b) THE MARTYR (12:2)

And he killed James the brother of John with the sword.

James and John, the sons of Zebedee, were among the first of the Lord's disciples. James was the first of the apostles to suffer martyrdom. His execution took place some time between the prophecy of Agabus and the arrival of Barnabus and Saul in Jerusalem. James thus drank of that cup and participated in that baptism of which the Lord had spoken when the mother of these two young men sought preferential treatment for them in the kingdom (Matt. 20:20–22). James was the first and John the last of the apostolic band to head for home as martyrs to the faith.

(2) THE DETENTION OF PETER (12:3–4)

(a) WHY HE WAS IMPRISONED (12:3*a*)

And because he saw it pleased the Jews, he proceeded further to take Peter also.

This is a commentary on the Jews as much as on Herod. The Jews were now well embarked on that course of Christ-rejection that was to bring their nation to shipwreck in less than three decades. As for Herod, he trimmed his sails to catch the favorable breeze and set out to further damage the Body of Christ. Accordingly he arrested Peter, the acknowledged leader of the apostles.

The Jews took vindictive satisfaction in that. Not only had Peter defied the Sanhedrin, snapping his fingers at its authority and its command that he refrain from preaching Christ, but Peter was the one who had scorned age-old taboos against socializing with Gentiles. Worse, he had offered Jewish fellowship to Gentiles without the time-honored requirement that Gentiles be circumcised and become proselytes of the Jewish faith.

(b) WHEN HE WAS IMPRISONED (12:3*b*)

Then were the days of unleavened bread.

The feast of unleavened bread was closely associated with the annual feast of Passover. The Jews were required to scour their houses to make sure no corrupting leaven remained. Thus, while the Jews were ridding their houses of leaven in accordance with their ritual law, their hearts were fermenting with the hidden leaven of malice and wickedness.

The feast of unleavened bread lasted a week, from Nisan 14 (Passover Eve) to the 21st. The whole period began with the keeping of the Passover. Herod's intention was to keep Peter imprisoned during that period and then bring him out for execution. It must have been a trying week for Peter, who was essentially a man of action, to be cooped up behind bars counting down the days to his death.

(c) WHERE HE WAS IMPRISONED (12:4)

And when he had apprehended him, he put him in prison, and delivered him to four quarternions of soldiers to keep him; intending after Easter to bring him forth to the people.

Peter was kept in the maximum security ward, probably in the fortress of Antonia on the northwest corner of the Temple area. As we learn from the story, he was guarded by sixteen soldiers, two chains, keepers, an iron gate, and two wards. Herod took no chances of his prisoner escaping. Peter had plenty of sympathizers in the city, and the king saw to it that any attempt to rescue the popular apostle would fail. Herod's plan was to execute Peter "after Easter," that is, after the Passover.

b. HOW IT WAS OBSTRUCTED (12:5–19)

(1) HUMAN INTERCESSION (12:5)

Peter therefore was kept in prison: but prayer was made without ceasing of the church unto God for him.

But! That "but" spelled Herod's doom. The "buts" of the Bible are remarkable and well worth noting. They usually denote a change.

As the iron gates of Herod's prison clanged shut, the gates of heaven swung open wide. The church sank to its knees, and a ceaseless volume of prayer ascended to the throne of grace. Luke says that prayer was made "without ceasing." The word is *ektenēs*, meaning intense prayer. The only other time that word is used in the New Testament is by Peter himself (1 Pet. 4:8). The comparative word *ektenesteron* is also found elsewhere once in the New Testament. Luke in reporting the intensity of the Lord's prayer in Gethsemane says that "being in an agony he prayed *more earnestly* [more intensely]: and his sweat was as it were great drops of blood falling down to the ground" (Luke 22:44).

That kind of praying bombarded the throne of God during the week Peter lay in prison. It was the kind of prayer that makes iron gates yield.

(2) HEAVEN'S INTERVENTION (12:6–17)

(a) PETER'S RESTFULNESS (12:6)

And when Herod would have brought him forth, the same night Peter was sleeping between two soldiers, bound with two chains: and the keepers before the door kept the prison.

The order for execution had been signed. The date was set. Peter was to die tomorrow.

What was he doing that last night? Was he shaking, white with fear, prepared perhaps to deny his Lord with oaths and curses as he had eleven years before? Indeed no! Was he pacing the floor of his cell then, fiercely resolving to die like a man, confessing his sins to the Lord and seeking absolution in the precious blood of Christ? Was he summing up his reserves of courage as he asked God to enable him to face death as a Christian with a smile and a word of forgiveness on his lips for his murderers? Not a bit of it!

He was asleep. He ate his supper, commended himself to the Lord, said goodnight to the two soldiers chained to him—and went to sleep. He was not only conqueror, he was more than conqueror. "O death, where is thy sting? O grave, where is thy victory?" (1. Cor. 15:55).

(b) PETER'S RESCUER (12:7–10)
i. THE ANGEL'S DESCENT (12:7a)
And, behold, the angel of the Lord came upon him, and a light shined in the prison.

Luke uses an interesting word for prison. It is *oikēma*, a word that occurs only here in the New Testament. It literally means dwelling. The Lord's continuing presence in that prison had converted Peter's cell into a home. Peter had quietly made himself at home in those uncongenial surroundings. If it was the Lord's will for him to be committed to prison, he would be contented in prison.

And that was how the Lord's angel found him—restful and relaxed as though he were at home in bed and the armed guard his honored guests. How the angel would tell *that* story when he arrived back in glory! It is generally inferred that the angel was Peter's guardian angel. Jacob had an angel who protected him from Laban (Gen. 48:16). Daniel had an angel who protected him from the lions (Dan. 6:27). Little children have their angels who report to God's throne any mistreatment they receive (Matt. 18:10). Paul had an angel who strengthened him when on board the sinking ship (Acts 27:23). The Holy Spirit tells us that angels are "ministering spirits, sent forth to minister for them who shall be heirs of salvation" (Heb. 1:14).

ii. THE ANGEL'S DEMAND (12:7b–9)
And he smote Peter on the side, and raised him up, saying, Arise up quickly. And his chains fell off from his hands. And the angel said unto him, Gird thyself, and bind on thy sandals. And so he did. And he saith unto him, Cast thy garment about thee, and follow me. And he went out, and followed him; and wist not that it was true which was done by the angel; but thought he saw a vision.

Peter, naturally enough, thought he was still asleep and having a particularly delightful but impossible dream. We do not know why the angel demanded haste. He certainly could not have been afraid of the guards. Indeed, all his dealings with Peter seem to have been somewhat brusque. He gave him a blow on the side to wake him up, then curtly ordered him to quickly get up, put on his coat, and follow him.

Throughout the Scripture, angels sent to men seem in a hurry to discharge their duties and vanish again from sight. They never linger long, nor do they unduly fraternize with men. Perhaps the sin of "the sons of God" (fallen angels) in the days of Noah (Gen. 6:2) remains fresh in the minds of those sinless shining ones. Perhaps, too, they wish to avoid the embarrassment of man's tendency to worship them (Rev. 22:8–9).

In any case, the angel went about his work in a businesslike way. Light filled the cell. Peter's chains fell off, the door opened. Peter did as he was told, leaving the guards behind to face the shock of their discovery in the morning.

iii. THE ANGEL'S DEEDS (12:10a)

When they were past the first and the second ward, they came unto the iron gate that leadeth unto the city; which opened to them of his own accord: and they went out, and passed on through one street.

Down the corridors they went, past the cells, through two security wards to the main gate of the prison itself, the angel clearing the way and Peter following in a daze. At last they stood before the barred and bolted main gate, which swung open before them. Silently the bolts slid back, the lock turned itself, and the great steel gate swung upon its hinges. Peter walked out. Still following the angel, Peter walked the length of a street with the cool night air fanning his cheeks, making him glad the angel had told him to take his coat. If it were not all a particularly vivid dream he would have thought it was real.

iv. THE ANGEL'S DEPARTURE (12:10b)

. . . and forthwith the angel departed from him.

The angel's work was done. There was no farewell, no word of instruction as to what he should do or where he should go. Apart from telling him to get up, get dressed, and get going, the angel had said nothing at all. He had one commission from the throne—to set Peter free—and he kept well within the limits of his mandate. He was not sent to tell Peter all about heaven—he would find that out for himself one day. He was not sent to tell Peter how to proceed with the ministry entrusted to him—that was the Holy Spirit's work. He was not authorized to tell Peter what to do next—he left that to Peter's common sense. He was simply sent to set Peter free in answer to the prayers of an importunate church. When that was done he disappeared.

(c) PETER'S REASONING (12:11–17)

i. WHAT HE DECIDED (12:11–12)

And when Peter was come to himself, he said, Now I know of a surety, that the Lord hath sent his angel, and hath delivered me out of the hand of Herod, and from all the expectation of the people of the Jews. And when he had considered the thing, he came to the house of Mary the mother of John, whose surname was Mark; where many were gathered together praying.

In other words, Peter's deliverance was God's deliberate answer to Herod's defiance and to the Jews' malicious delight. The word used by Luke to describe the "expectation" of the Jews is *prosdokia*. It means "eager looking" and is found in only one other place in the New Testament. Luke uses it to describe the watchfulness of people in the coming apocalyptic age as they see, with growing apprehension, end-time events approaching. "Men's hearts failing them for fear, and for *looking after* [*prosdokia*] those things which are coming on the earth" (Luke 21:26). The same kind of anticipation marked the Jews who were eagerly looking for Peter's execution. They devoured the news and watched things with the closest attention, just as people will when end-time events become commonplace. Incidentally, the Jews of Jerusalem were particularly glad to be able to push the odium of Peter's murder onto Herod, just as they had been delighted to palm off responsibility for the death of Christ onto Pilate.

Peter suddenly realized that his release from prison was no dream but a reality. God had checkmated Herod and the Jews! Peter took an understandable and natural satisfaction in that. He stood there alone on the dark street, considering his situation. The obvious thing to do was make contact with some of the Christians in town.

One of the principal gathering centers in Jerusalem at that time was the house of Mary the mother of John Mark, who was later to become famous as the author of the gospel that bears his name. Mary was the sister of Barnabas. As Barnabas had put his property at the disposal of the church, so his sister put her house. Peter seems to have had a measure of intimacy with the family, for he affectionately calls Mark "my son" (1 Pet. 5:13). It was to that house Peter decided to go and report his release before going into hiding from Herod's police.

ii. WHAT HE DISCOVERED (12:13–15)

And as Peter knocked at the door of the gate, a damsel came to harken, named Rhoda. And when she knew Peter's voice, she opened not the gate for gladness, but ran in, and told how Peter stood before the gate. And they said unto her, Thou art mad. But she constantly affirmed that it was even so. Then said they, It is his angel.

The Holy Spirit records this incident with a touch of humor. A large prayer meeting had been convened in Mary's house. Many of the Lord's people were there, spending the night praying for Peter's last-minute release from prison. When their prayers were answered they refused to believe it.

"Come on, Rosie," they said, "you're mad!" When she insisted, they said, "You're hearing things. It's his angel." Luke says of Rhoda that she "constantly affirmed," literally "kept on affirming," that Peter was at the gate. In the only other place in the New Testament where this expression occurs, it is used of Peter as well. Luke records that an hour after Peter denied the maid's assertion "This man was also with him" and the affirmation of a man, "Thou art also of them," another man "confidently affirmed," saying, "Of a truth this fellow also was with him" (Luke 22:56–59). The expression is the same.

So Rhoda kept insisting Peter was at the gate, and everyone kept telling her that was impossible, though why nobody thought to go and see, or why Rhoda didn't go back and unlock the gate, or why it should not occur to anyone that God had answered their prayer, is hard to say. The news simply seemed too good to be true.

iii. WHAT HE DID (12:16–17)

But Peter continued knocking: and when they had opened the door, and saw him, they were astonished. But he, beckoning unto them with the hand to hold their peace, declared unto them how the Lord had brought him out of the prison. And he said, Go shew these things unto James, and to the brethren. And he departed, and went into another place.

Peter had enough sense to keep knocking. Presently his knocks were heard, the door was opened, and there he was, much to the astonishment of the crowd. The hubbub was so great that Peter had great difficulty in making himself heard. Finally his gestures for silence were heeded, and the excited chatter died away. Peter hurriedly told of his escape and urged that the news be conveyed to James the Lord's brother, and the others. Then he went underground.

At this time James seems to have assumed the leadership of the Jerusalem church. He maintained good relations with the Jewish community by his rigid and dutiful attendance at the Temple services. He was the acknowledged leader of the legalists in the church, though he seems to have been somewhat more tolerant than most of them. When Saul and Barnabas arrived in Jerusalem he was one of the three "pillars" of the church there, even Peter and John being named after him (Gal. 2:9). He was martyred in A.D. 61 by the high priest Annas. There were those who said that the destruction of Jerusalem nine years later resulted from the fact that James was no longer there to pray for the peace of the city.

(3) HEROD'S INDIGNATION (12:18–19)

(a) THE EXCITEMENT OF THE GUARD (12:18)

Now as soon as it was day, there was no small stir among the soldiers, what was become of Peter.

The soldiers were in serious trouble. Peter was gone; and what was worse, they did not know how he had freed himself from the chain, how he had escaped through two wards of the prison, or how he had passed the iron door that led to the street. We can well imagine that a hasty but thorough search was made of the entire prison to make sure Peter was not hiding somewhere. We can imagine, too, the frightened tones of the soldiers as they compared notes. They could remember falling asleep, perhaps, but nothing after that. Peter had been spirited away. It was impossible, but it had happened.

The expression "no small stir" occurs again in Luke's account of Paul's impact on Ephesus, which resulted in a city-wide riot (19:23).

(b) THE EXAMINATION OF THE GUARD (12:19a)

And when Herod had sought for him, and found him not, he examined the keepers . . .

News of Peter's disappearance was reported to Herod, who summoned the guards and listened grimly to their story. It had all the marks of an inside job to him. A man simply does not vanish from a maximum security ward into thin air and leave no trace of his departure. The most diligent search failed to give a clue to Peter's whereabouts. Spies and informers might be planted in the Christian community in vain. Nobody, not even Peter's best friends, knew where he was. Herod's plans to ingratiate himself with the Jews at Peter's expense had exploded in his face, and his fury knew no bounds.

(c) THE EXECUTION OF THE GUARD (12:19b)

. . . and commanded that they should be put to death. And he went down from Judea to Caesarea, and there abode.

According to the code of Justinian, a guard who allowed a prisoner to escape was liable to the same penalty the prisoner would have suffered. Whether or not Herod was influenced by that is uncertain. He was furious enough at having lost face with the Jews to order the execution of those he deemed responsible for Peter's escape. Some have sought to soften the statement "put to death." The word literally means "led away," but it is almost certain they were led to execution. The same word is used by Matthew to describe what happened to Jesus: "And after that they had mocked him, they took the robe off from him, and put his own raiment on him, and *led him away* to crucify him" (Matt. 27:31).

As for Herod, disgusted at the whole business, he turned his back on Jerusalem, Judea, and the Jews, and went to the city of Caesarea "and there abode." The word for "abode" is *diatribō*, literally "to rub away." Herod thus tried to erase from his mind the memory of his humiliation by spending time in the more pagan and Roman environment of the seaside resort.

c. HOW IT WAS OVERTHROWN (12:20–23)
(1) HEROD'S PROGRESS (12:20)

And Herod was highly displeased with them of Tyre and Sidon: but they came with one accord to him, and, having made Blastus the king's chamberlain their friend, desired peace; because their country was nourished by the king's country.

After all, Caesarea was the Roman seat and the center of the local administration, and Herod was a man to be feared. In some way not clarified, the two ancient Phoenician cities were dependent for food supplies on Caesarea. After his humiliation in Jerusalem, Herod no doubt was only too eager to find someone to bully. The authorities in Tyre and Sidon sought suitable means to approach the king, and they secured the cooperation of the king's personal valet. Such a person, with direct access to the king, constantly in attendance upon him and able to judge his moods and take advantage of them, was always a man to be cultivated. In the grimy politics of the East, the greased palm often did more to secure a desired result than nobler means.

Herod, then, venting his ill will on Tyre and Sidon, proceeded headlong to his doom. He had dared to murder James, one of the Lord's closest friends. He would have murdered all the apostles had he been able. Thwarted, his pride and presumption broke out in another direction, petty persecution of two unfortunate cities. The senseless man was hurrying recklessly on to that line God draws in the sand for everyone, beyond which we go at our peril.

(2) HEROD'S PRIDE (12:21)

And upon a set day Herod, arrayed in royal apparel, sat upon his throne, and made an oration unto them.

At Caesarea, Agrippa assembled his deputies and other dignitaries and prepared to celebrate the games and to offer vows for the safety, honor, and prosperity of the emperor Claudius. The date was probably August 1, the emperor's birthday. Josephus supplements the biblical account. On the second day, early in the morning of the celebration, the king arrayed himself in a garment woven with silver threads. When the sun's rays fell upon that robe it glittered and shone with a resplendence that dazzled the crowds packed into the theatre.

The awe that fell upon the people gave Herod an opportunity to make a speech (the word used for "oration" suggests a political speech), which he did with seeming great success, riding the crest of a wave of superstitious awe and veneration.

(3) HEROD'S PRESUMPTION (12:22–23)
(a) THE INVISIBLE WATCHER (12:22–23a)

And the people gave a shout, saying, It is the voice of a god, and not of a man. And immediately the angel of the Lord smote him, because he gave not God the glory.

Was this "angel of the Lord" the angel who released Peter? Perhaps it was. In God's administration of the universe He is pleased to use agents. There are watchers in the unseen world, angelic beings who carry out the orders of God's throne. Just as Satan has his angelic princes, unseen powers, rulers of this world's darkness, and wicked spirits in high places, so God has His own angelic administrators who rush to do His bidding.

Evidently Herod was being watched, as we are all being watched. He could not see the watcher, but this powerful being, sent from heaven to put a check on this man's presumption and pride, could see him. He was allowed to place his order with his tailors for that dazzling suit of silver. He was allowed to admire himself in the mirror and to congratulate himself on what a dashing, royal figure he cut. He was allowed to parade up and down his bedroom before his valet, calling for an adjustment here, a minor alteration there. He was allowed to wear that robe to the theater. He was allowed to sit upon his throne in conscious pride. He was allowed to stand so that the rays of God's sun might flash upon the silver threads, throwing out an aura of their own. He was allowed to open his mouth to speak and hear the multitude cry, "It is the voice of a god, and not of a man."

Then the watcher smote. Herod had gone too far. He had exhausted the patience of God. He had crossed the hidden boundary between God's mercy and His wrath. Well may we all beware.

(b) THE INVINCIBLE WORM (12:23b)

. . . and he was eaten of worms, and gave up the ghost.

Five days later he was dead. Even as he stood there, bathing himself in the adoration of the flattering crowds, the worm struck him. Wracked with severe abdominal pains, he was hurried back to his palace. The physicians were summoned, but no human skill could save him now. The worms were already at work. The word, in the plural, occurs only here in the New Testament. Its counterpart is used by Mark in recording the Lord's description of hell "where their worm dieth not, and the fire is not quenched" (Mark 9:44, 46, 48).

Day after day for five days Herod Agrippa I, who thought he was a god, who martyred an apostle of the Lamb, who hoped to destroy the leadership of the church, who paid his tithes to the Temple but who knew not God, writhed upon his bed. Then he died and went out to meet eternal sorrows. No doubt, like the rich fool of the Lord's story (Luke 16) he had a splendid funeral.

3. THE PROGRESS OF THE CHURCH AT LARGE (12:24–25)

a. MULTIPLICATION (12:24)

But the word of God grew and multiplied.

Here we have another of those significant "buts." Stephen may be martyred, but at once the precious seed of the kingdom, stored in the Jerusalem granary, is thrown to the four winds of heaven to settle in distant parts and to spring up everywhere in abundant harvest. Herod may murder James, but again the blood of the martyr becomes the seed of the church, and the word of God grows and multiplies. Satan does his worst, but that only makes evident that God is at work, doing His infinite, glorious best.

The Holy Spirit sets down this progress report here in evident contrast with the ignominous death of Herod. The *worms* are set in contrast with the *Word.* Both are God's instruments. Herod might want to destroy the church, but the Word of God, inspired, infallible, inerrant, invincible, marched gloriously on. The armed might of government may be mobilized against it, but the Word of God knows no boundaries to its empire, no barriers to its progress.

b. MOTIVATION (12:25)

And Barnabas and Saul returned from Jerusalem, when they had fulfilled their ministry, and took with them John, whose surname was Mark.

Mark was a nephew of Barnabas (Col. 4:10). It would be likely enough that while they were in Jerusalem, Barnabas and Saul would make their home with Mary, Mark's mother. It is not hard to see what an impact these two dynamic men would have on the impressionable Mark. What a story they would tell of mission work among the Gentiles. What plans and dreams they would discuss, perhaps within the hearing of Mark. Saul would tell of his desire to evangelize the vast Gentile world. He would recount some of his experiences since he became a Christian. Barnabas would spread the warmth of his loving personality over it all. How attractive and personable he was! And how dynamic and daring Saul of Tarsus!

By the time the two began packing their bags to return to the mission field, Mark was asking Uncle Barnabas if he could come along.

So the two veterans said "good-bye" to Jerusalem and took with them the eager young man who, little did any of them know it, would one day write a gospel especially for the Roman world.